The Lazy South

DAVID BERTELSON

New York   OXFORD UNIVERSITY PRESS   1967

For my mother and father

Preface

In the late 1940's in an article entitled "Are Southerners
Really Lazy?" * H. C. Brearley speculated upon explanations
for the association of laziness with the South, which goes
back to early colonial times. He listed poverty, ill-health and
poor food, the degradation of work because of slavery, the
type of agriculture followed in much of the South, and
finally the Southerners' belief in simply enjoying themselves.
A warm climate may have a psychological effect, he argued,
but there is no evidence that it reduces efficiency. While all
of these reasons are valid, they leave many questions un-
answered. Why should Southerners emphasize enjoying themselves? Why should a region of great natural potential
contain so many underfed and unhealthy people? It is no
answer to turn to slavery without explaining why it was so
widespread in the South. Nor is it an answer then to point
to staple crops. One must still explain why staples dominated
the Southern economy.

Brearley concluded that in recent years "many of the
situations that have fostered the South's reputation for laziness have shown significant improvement," and he foresaw
the day when " 'these lazy Southerners' will be recognized as
an inaccurate stereotype that has gone with the music and

* *The American Scholar*, XVIII, 1948–49.

the magnolias of the South that almost never was." In spite of evidence that this stereotype is and perhaps has always been in many respects inaccurate, it has persisted for centuries and still persists. It carries with it the assumption that laziness is intimately bound up with what is uniquely Southern and therefore with what distinguishes the South from the rest of the nation. Whether the South will cease to be Southern because of changes in the outward conditions of life is debatable, but regardless of what may happen in the future the problem of explaining laziness remains. To get at what lies behind poverty, slavery, staple crops, and stressing personal enjoyment one must consider historically the meaning of work in the South.

The conception of this essay is taken from Max Weber and Ernst Troeltsch. In their studies of the social implications of Christian thought both have pointed to a direct connection between the ideas which particular groups have of work and the larger assumptions upon which they believe their societies are built. To understand the meaning of labor is to understand many things about what men have thought of their societies: what is the social function of work? why do people work? what is the relationship of the individual to his society? what holds a society together? how does the society deal with those whose labor is considered unacceptable? Because the groups of people who laid the foundations of American civilization had literally to create societies in the wilderness, what work and its social context meant to them determined in large measure what kinds of societies theirs would become.

In tracing the consequences of these attitudes for the South and indirectly for the rest of the country, I must confess that I have been less preoccupied with similarities than with differences—which doubtless reflects the influence of the times in which I am writing. Thus W. J. Cash speaks most meaningfully to me, and my debt to him is obviously great. My approach necessitates many comparisons with the North; otherwise it may seem as though I am describing as uniquely

Southern attitudes and reactions which might be assumed to have been common to all Americans.

Because I employ quotations extensively to present rather than to embellish my arguments, I have modernized spelling, capitalization, and punctuation (and in a very few instances the form of a word) to facilitate reading. Moreover, this seemed desirable simply from the standpoint of consistency. It has not always been possible to cite original texts, nor has it seemed desirable where modern reprints are more readily accessible. Every editor seems to have his own criteria about what to change and what to leave as it was originally written, and so for my purposes it seemed best to reduce everything to a single standard. In using modernized texts printed in England I have changed spellings where necessary to conform to American usage.

I should like to thank George Fredrickson and Ted Marmor for reading and criticizing an earlier version of this work and for sharing with me many of their insights during the course of my research and writing. Sheldon Meyer of Oxford University Press has offered many helpful suggestions in guiding me through the stage of final revisions. I am also indebted to William R. Taylor and Louis Hartz, in whose seminars I first began to work out my ideas on the South. I started the doctoral dissertation, of which this book is a revision, under the late Perry Miller. In pointing out this association I have in a sense been guilty of the sin of pride, which would only be further indulged in attempting to elaborate my debt to him as a scholar and a teacher. After his death Donald Fleming generously consented to direct my efforts. I am deeply grateful to him for his thorough criticisms of organization and style, his suggestions as to content, and his patience (despite shortcomings which have persisted) in insisting that I express my ideas lucidly and concisely. Finally, I especially wish to thank Alan Heimert, specifically for his many valuable suggestions concerning my research, more generally for his lectures on colonial literature, his seminar in which I wrote the first version of my dissertation, and his own work on the Great Awakening and the Revolution which has greatly influenced my understanding of these events, and lastly for the countless ways in which he has helped me during the course of many years to appreciate the complexities of the study of American civilization.

Berkeley, California   D.B.
August 1966

Contents

THE LAZY SOUTH

That common strumpet idleness

Prologue

If Sir Thomas More's *Utopia* is taken as the first delineation by an Englishman of the impact of the New World, idleness must be acknowledged as among the most ancient social problems men have looked to America to resolve. To More, England under Henry VIII seemed an abyss of idleness, a land filled with idle gentlemen and their servants and with husbandmen forced by enclosures to lead lives of idleness.[1] By contrast, there is no idleness in Utopia. Those of a religious inclination abhor it because of their conviction that happiness after death is the result of "busy labors and good exercises." [2] The most elaborate precautions, supplemented by strict punishments and even bondage, are taken to insure that no one has liberty to "loiter" or any "cloak or pretense to idleness." Virtually the only function of the "Syphogrants" is to see that everyone works diligently at his appointed tasks.[3]

In spite of its importance, however, work is thought of largely in negative terms, for in contrast to intellectual activities it is onerous.[4] Ironically, the imperative that everyone must work implies the possibility of what would now be called overproduction. To obviate this danger the work day is only six hours, and often this number is reduced by proclamation.[5] Production is further restricted by the nature of the soil, which is not very fertile. Nevertheless, the Utopians are

3

so diligent that their land surpasses all others in its abundance of grain and livestock, and so limitations upon productivity would seem to be a necessary accompaniment to governmental coercion in the incessant war against idleness. Moreover, if the government's coercive powers were weak, it is doubtful that the problem of idleness would have been solved. Precisely because it is cursed with neither excessive abundance nor an ineffective government, Utopia is utopia—a land whose inhabitants are, "when need requireth, able to abide and suffer much bodily labor. Else they be not greatly desirous and fond of it, but in the exercise and study of the mind they be never weary." [6]

To see More's ideas on labor and idleness as basically a restatement of medieval notions helps to explain the tension between the requirement that everyone must work and the fact that work is neither personally satisfying nor continuously necessary for subsistence. His great fear of idleness is not found in the utopian speculations of Plato, for whom emancipation from toil is precisely what distinguishes the elite.[7] In medieval Christian thought, according to Ernst Troeltsch, work is necessary for both positive and negative reasons. As a means of subsistence and thus of preserving Christian society it is a good thing. More important, it promotes love since commercial profits help to support churches and monasteries. Negatively considered, among fallen men work is a means of self-discipline and an exhortation to humility. It is wholly an earthly activity, and however necessary it may now be, it is part of a process of salvation which aims beyond nature to supernature and the motionless beatitude of Paradise. It is also intimately related to the Thomistic conception of the organic state, the cornerstone of which is social order and stability. From this notion arises the idea of a cosmos of callings, meaning the individual's fixed place in the social framework, his passive acceptance of the inequalities fixed by God.[8]

The actual spirit of the doctrine of work, however, applies only to peasants and workers in the towns—not to the ruling aristocracy, nor to scholars and men of the Church.[9] It would seem reasonable to argue that the persistence of this distinction owed something to the fact that in the final analysis ease was considered an ultimate good. Also a corporate view of society justified ease in some areas, provided necessary work was performed in others.[10] As long as social conditions remained stable, few questioned the double meaning of labor, as applying positively only to the lower orders and negatively to all sinful descendants of Adam. It was only when a person's place in the social structure was disturbed—when he ceased to fulfill a recognized and presumably useful social role—that he really appeared idle. Then the belief that idle hands are the workshop of the devil became increasingly a source of concern. In the *Utopia* Thomas More was unable to resolve this dilemma. He questioned a great many social roles without adequately defining new ones. Hence he could only emphasize labor as manual activity aimed largely at the avoidance of idleness. Unfortunately, his vision of America failed to correct the conditions in English society which he so much lamented, and "that common strumpet idleness,/ The very root of all viciousness,"[11] remained one of the nation's most formidable adversaries.

Because labor was considered meaningful only in terms of its relationship to a clearly defined social order, concern for the disruption of the visible organization of society accompanied anxiety over idleness. "The towns go down, the land decays," a ballad writer in 1520 lamented. Enclosure was returning England to a pre-civilized state, and from this outward change proceeded such miseries as "great dearth and much idleness."[12] In a sense to blame men for being idle was irrelevant. They were simply adhering to their innate inclination "to follow pleasure, quietness, and ease."[13] Commentators were reasonably consistent in concerning themselves less with accusations than with devising social means to prevent idleness. Besides outlining useful activities for the idle nobility, they sought to deal with idleness among the lower orders by stressing the need for stimulating faltering trades and restoring husbandmen to the land. This was obviously an effort to recapture the past. It was assumed that most men would willingly return to their traditional tasks if society only made this possible. Partly because this policy was impossible to effect systematically, partly because it seemed not to work with the more incorrigible types, critics insisted that it be supplemented by the coercive powers of the state. There were good laws to deal with England's multitudes of unemployed wanderers, Sir Thomas Elyot maintained, and he considered it vain pity not to make use of them.[14]

The persistent association of disorder with idleness was based on the assumption that in a state of inactivity men are most subject to temptation and sin. Concern over idleness, therefore, represented both the expectation that society ought to benefit by the labor of all its members and an anxiety about potential violence. Without social organization critics did not expect anyone to engage in useful labor, and without the power to coerce they saw no possibility of eliminating idleness and hence violence. Because they regarded the structure of society as moulding the individual, their concern was to contain and control human nature, not to change it. Here More's Utopian vision is typical. As J. H. Hexter observes, what makes Utopians better is their laws and their rearing. "The sound social, political, and economic regimen under which they live is the cause of the civic virtue of the Utopians, not the other way about; their institutions are not the creation but the creator of their good qualities." [15] Throughout the sixteenth century many social critics and most formulators of public policy continued to stress the regulatory powers of organized society as the answer to the problem of idleness.[16] Because they represent a clearly definable intellectual position, for purposes of easy identification they may be called coercionists.

On first consideration it would seem that the English Puritans accepted the same general premises. References in their writings to social order and the importance of a hierarchical arrangement of society, as well as condemnations of idleness, are commonplace. Yet one can also find elements of a wholly different attitude toward work. William Perkins noted that as soon as Adam was created God assigned him a personal calling, which was to cultivate the Garden.[17] This notion that labor was required of man even before the Fall constituted a fundamental rejection of the belief that work is a consequence of sin. It became a means of fulfillment rather than of punishment. The concept of a personal calling avoided entirely the ambiguities of the coercionist belief that although men must work, rest and not labor is the highest good to be imagined.[18] Moreover, the distinction between manual labor and other activities was obliterated. To the Puritans all legitimate callings were equally worthy. As Perkins insisted, God looks at the heart of the worker, not at the kind of work he does.[19]

Perkins's statement further illustrates the relationship between the dignity of labor and man's responsibility to fulfill his calling. Work was not a requirement imposed by the laws and institutions of society. It was a personal demand made upon every practicing Christian, who, as Joseph Hall noted, follows his calling in willing obedience to God.[20] The personal injunction to work implied a certain relation to and concern for society, but the chain of command ran from God to man to society, not from God through society to man. As Perkins put it: "A vocation or calling is a certain kind of life ordained and imposed on man by God for the common good." [21] Puritans believed passionately in commonwealth and in social obligation, but it was an obligation enforced by God's directive rather than society's ordinance.

Ultimately this emphasis upon personal responsibility rested upon the notion of freedom by grace through faith. A "Supplication" to Henry VIII in 1544 noted that despite good laws conscientiously administered sin still flourished, for while laws may temporarily restrain it only faith can abolish it. Puritanism, by rejecting the efficacy of proceeding from the social structure to the individual, in effect maintained that while men still had to obey laws, they were to do so willingly. Hence the "Supplication" insisted that faith would create and nourish true obedience and all other virtues in men's hearts.[22] In time this emphasis manifested itself in the theory of the Social Covenant, which Perry Miller describes as one of several expressions of the movement in European thought to change social relationships from status to contract.[23] But what is important here is that the Puritans' stress upon personal responsibility profoundly altered the way they thought about the make-up of society long before they discarded medieval notions of hierarchy and stability. Social unity was conceptualized less in terms of the binding power of formal institutions than in terms of individuals' attitudes and loyalties toward one another and toward the stated ends of the society. Thus Perkins argued that because God had decreed the existence of human society, He had established the bond of love to link men together.[24]

Obviously if attitudes and beliefs were meaningful in binding society together and perfecting it, they were also related to social ills. Only the assumption that what men think and feel is socially relevant would justify the constant appeals for moral reformation. Because idleness was a sin, its remedy too was repentance. The jeremiad, the great tool for effecting this, precisely epitomizes the difference between Puritans and coercionists. The latter had little expectation that idleness could ever be dealt with by persuasion. Puritans did not reject the efficacy of law nor the utility of constraint, but they regarded these as punishments to be meted out when exhortation had failed rather than as unremitting aspects of social policy. William Holbrook blamed the great amount of idleness in London both upon men who would not work and upon magistrates who would not enforce the laws. His reasoning was simple. If men "will not of conscience fall to this course, let them be constrained by law." [25]

Max Weber has demonstrated the efficacy of the Puritan notion of calling, in inducing men to labor willingly. Here it is only necessary to underscore the fact that the inducement was a personal willingness, a compulsion from within, which did not depend upon legal requirements nor upon a fixed definition of one's status. Nor did this inducement really depend upon the end-product of labor, the material reward which would result from diligent application. Puritans were constantly worried lest riches in any way become an inducement. Perry Miller has shown how the conception of a National Covenant developed as an answer to the otherwise inevitable connection between wealth and the decay of true religion. "They are not caught in an irresistible succession of poverty and wealth; their outward state is a sign of their inward health and will vary only as their spirit alters." Miller has also noted how the conception of a National Covenant came very close to Arminianism.[26] Here prosperity was seen as an effect rather than a sign of moral worthiness, but still the reward was not the inducement to action. Idleness, carnal temptations, and distraction from the pursuit of a righteous life were the unwholesome fruits of a concentration upon the enjoyment of wealth.[27]

There was a way of looking at the covenant relationship, however, which substantially modified the emphasis upon inner necessity in favor of external inducements. If this relationship with God implied a blessing on His part, this blessing could be viewed as a claim upon men to live up to their part of the compact. The logic of the jeremiad would also apply to this line of reasoning. God has blessed a hard-hearted people, and unless they repent He will withdraw His blessings. The most elaborate statement of this position is found in the sermons of Edwin Sandys, Archbishop of York and father of Sir Edwin Sandys of the Virginia Company. Lest God's majesty should simply awe men rather than prompt them to obedience, the Archbishop noted, "with rough commandments He joineth oftentimes sweet allurements; . . . not enticing men with fair and sweet words only, but pouring His benefits also plentifully upon them." [28] Such earthly blessings, he observed in another sermon, are given to test whether or not men will obey God's law.[29] If material blessings are a part of God's covenant relationship to man and if God provides them as allurements, this obviously implied that the desire for wealth is not necessarily reprehensible. Although excessive greed might be a sin, if God offers enticements it is not wrong to respond to them. From this point of view, material opportunities could be regarded as a new solution to the problem of idleness.

One of the most complete early statements of the argument from economic motivation, *A Discourse of the Common Weal of This Realm of England,* was probably written in 1549. The main speaker remarks that all men acknowledge the truth of the old Latin saying that "profit or advancement nourisheth every faculty." He goes on to argue significantly that coercion and legal penalties apply only to some things which should be done in a commonwealth, whereas others are to be effected "by allurement and rewards rather." No law can make men industrious in either physical or mental labors, but they can be "provoked, encouraged, and allured" into activity if the industrious are rewarded for their efforts and allowed to benefit materially from them.[30] In a different way Puritanism had embodied a protest against the failure of coercion—an assertion that labor is not necessarily onerous and need not be exacted from men by compulsion.

The solution to the problem of idleness, consequently, lay in the conjunction of opportunity and a willingness to respond to it. In 1580 Robert Hitchcock brought out a pamphlet promoting the fishing trade in which he discussed "that loathsome monster idleness (the mother and breeder of vagabonds)" and the failure of all the laws of the realm to deal with it. God, however, had provided a remedy, and once exposed to the sweet allurements which the fishing trade offered, "the lusty vagabonds and idle persons (the roots, buds, and seeds of idleness) shall at all hands and in all places be set on work and labor willingly, and thereby prove good subjects and profitable members of this commonweal."[31] If God's blessings were properly regarded, therefore, idleness would be utterly banished and the nation benefited by enticements that dovetailed with men's natures and drew them to activity without violating their freedom. The proponents of this position may for convenience be called attractionists because of their conviction that the attraction of material advantage entices men to work. This coinage seems more appropriate here than R. H. Tawney's term "economic individualism," [32] which detracts from the social emphasis of men like Hitchcock.

Attractionists resembled Puritans in their stress upon a covenant relationship with God and their postulation of a remedy for idleness other than coercion, yet they also had much in common with coercionists. If men must be allured out of idleness, this would seem to indicate that the state of ease has a hidden but most powerful appeal. While praising rest as a just means of refreshment after labor, Archbishop Sandys warned that because Christ hated the slothful above all others, men must not allow "the sweetness of rest" to induce them into thinking labor unnecessary.[33] Nevertheless, in spite of affinities with coercionist and Puritan views, the idea of allurement had its own unique content. In both the other approaches natural wealth and opportunities could not figure as positive sources of motivation. To coercionists they were a definite threat because they carried with them the danger of eliminating the compulsion to work.[34] To Puritans natural advantages, while the result of God's action, were not a precondition of man's obedience.

For Thomas More, America had not been associated with the inspiration of material opportunity, but with the perfection of the instruments of social order and coercion. Whether idleness could actually be cured by sending people to the New World would depend upon the unlikely possibility that social institutions could be made more effective there than in England. But this was not the point of the *Utopia*. More was concerned with reforming and strengthening institutions at home, and the expectation of greater success in a land initially devoid of all law and government would be more fantastic than utopian. The Puritans might eventually regard America as a fit though neutral place for a godly commonwealth, but for the attractionist the possibilities of the New World could conceivably be immense if it could be established that it was a land of vast opportunity. America then would be indeed a source of inspiration and vision, and its promise would lie precisely in the fact that it would not be More's Utopia.

From the time of the first Spanish and Portuguese expeditions in search of gold and treasure, material gain had driven men from Europe to the farthest corners of the earth, and early descriptions of these distant lands are filled with references to various forms of natural wealth.[35] There is no suggestion, however, in any of these writings that this wealth had been placed there by divine agency specifically to allure men across the waters. Instead glory and service to God were invoked as motivations for Englishmen to embark upon the enterprise of exploration and colonization. When Robert Thorne sought in 1527 to induce Henry VIII to take part in the new discoveries, he noted that it was only natural for monarchs to wish to extend their dominions. Moreover, the reputation of the nation was at stake, for Englishmen would be justly considered cowardly unless they proved themselves more courageous than the Spanish and Portuguese.[36] While he referred to the countries at the end of the Northwest Passage as "the richest lands and islands of the world," he saw wealth not as a special providence of God for enticing men to act but strictly as a function of geography. Just as lead, tin, and iron were the metals of a northerly country like England, so gold, silver, and copper were appropriate to lands nearer the equator.[37]

A half-century later, however, men were speaking about colonizing America specifically in terms of a divine scheme in which the role of allurement was crucial. Sir George Peckham called the attention of his countrymen to "the manifold benefits, commodities, and pleasures heretofore unknown," which had been revealed "by God's especial blessing." Hitherto Englishmen had slumbered in ignorance like "dormice," but now they must further the glory of God and "become industrious instruments" to themselves.[38] In his "Discourse on Western Planting" the younger Richard Hakluyt argued that once initial success had been achieved in the colonies, Englishmen from all walks of life would support the enterprise because of the realization "that the same tendeth to the ample vent of our clothes, to the purchasing of rich commodities, to the planting of younger brethren, to the employment of our idle people, and to so many noble ends." [39] The allurements of America were magnificently certified as evidence of God's wisdom and great goodness, for here at last was the answer to the problem of idleness in England. Surely no man would be content to remain idle at home or abroad once he recognized that, in the New World, God had heaped opportunity upon opportunity.

Many observers considered the enterprise of colonization a means of stimulating the English economy. Raw materials and new markets would revive depressed trades and thus induce the idle at home to return to work.[40] Beyond these benefits there was the expectation that great numbers of the idle would find employment in the colonies. Peckham foresaw the possibility that "our idle women (which the realm may well spare)" would be employed in processing a variety of products "to be found in those countries most plentifully." His long list of activities for the men further revealed how intimately the natural resources of the New World were connected with the alleviation of the problem of idleness.[41] The assumption upon which all this speculation rested was that the chance of gain would be alone sufficient to induce people to work. Opportunity, moreover, would help to wipe out the social dangers that idleness allegedly bred. Hakluyt noted that because the idle at home had nothing to do, they were a potential source of political upheaval, whereas in America there were countless tasks to keep them busy. He also saw in colonization a remedy for religious dissension, for clergymen would be too busy converting the savages to devote themselves to the disputes over fine points of doctrine that idleness permitted them to do in England. Finally, he saw in plantations an appealing solution to the problem of idle and therefore potentially rebellious soldiers.[42]

The constant references to the richness of the land were generally accompanied by an insistence that this wealth must be worked for in order to be realized. The whole argument for colonization as a cure for idleness would be meaningless if richness implied effortless ease, and so Sir Richard Grenville predicted that the land in America, "being once by our industry manured, will prove most fertile." [43] Because allurement by definition functioned so as to stimulate activity and thus banish idleness, presumably the harder the work stimulated the more effectively idleness would be routed. Yet conceivably if things were too difficult, people might not be enticed at all. They were therefore both admonished to work for the opportunities God had placed in America and assured that really very little effort was required. In his ode, "To the Virginian Voyage," Michael Drayton noted that success would entice brave young Englishmen "To get the pearl and gold" and retain control over "Virginia,/ Earth's only paradise." Here nature had provided all manner of bounties

And the fruitful'st soil,
Without your toil,
Three harvests more,
All greater than your wish.[44]

In his references to Virginia as "Earth's only paradise" and to the Golden Age, evidenced among the carefree savages in a country without severe winters to plague them, Drayton was obviously influenced by the Virgilian ideal of a Golden Age of ease and plenty, which had been revived during the Renaissance.[45] This ideal had also influenced a description by Captain Arthur Barlowe of one of the islands near Virginia, which was inhabited by gentle natives, who "lived after the manner of the Golden Age. The earth bringeth forth all things in abundance, as in the first creation, without toil or labor." Hakluyt omitted this last sentence in the 1600 edition of the *Principal Navigations*.[46] While these attractionist proponents of colonization were not the only men drawn to the idea of the Golden Age, doubtlessly they found in it an appeal which can only be explained if deep within themselves they were still attracted by the notion that rest is superior to labor. If America were really to be a cure for idleness, they had constantly to remind themselves of Archbishop Sandys's injunction to "beware that the sweetness of rest do not cause thee to think that labor is unnecessary." [47] Perhaps this is why Hakluyt excised Barlowe's ominous suggestion that Virginia might be a land of effortless abundance.

In the decades ahead God would offer the immigrants to this chosen land an abundance of material blessings to allure them into forsaking their former idle ways and devoting their lives to labor. If they would prove themselves diligent workers in the vineyard by serving their God busily, great would be their reward—on earth.

All for a smoky witch

1

Despite the failure of Sir Walter Raleigh's Roanoke colony, faith in the allurements of the New World persisted. Thus men were confident about the prospects of Virginia because these rested upon the conjunction of personal opportunity with the glory of God and the honor of the realm. In 1609 Alderman Robert Johnson told the members of the Virginia Company in London that the first planters in Jamestown had been "so ravished with the admirable sweetness of the stream and with the pleasant land trending along on either side, that their joy exceeded and with great admiration they praised God." The inference which he wished to draw was that "if bare nature be so amiable in its naked kind, what may we hope when art and nature shall join and strive together to give best content to man and beast?" [1] God had done His part by providing a land of great wealth and beauty to assure the love and activity of Englishmen. Now things were up to them, as they were reminded in 1610: "God in this place is ever concurring with His gracious influence if man strangle not his blessings with careless negligence." [2]

Outposts designed to transship valuable raw materials back to the mother country could logically have produced the profits sought by adventurers who had invested in the Virginia Company. Still, in looking to colonies as a cure for idleness men seem to have had in mind something closer to busy, industrious, and fairly elaborate commercial societies.³ Johnson expressed such social expectations when he noted that the colony would need a large labor force, which, happily, England was able to furnish, "our land abounding with swarms of idle persons, which, having no means of labor to relieve their misery, do likewise swarm in lewd and naughty practices." He soon insisted, however, that he did "not mean that none but such unsound members and such poor as want their bread are fittest for this employment; for we intend to have of every trade and profession, both honest, wise, and painful men, whereof our land and city is able to spare." ⁴ He was not clear as to how distinct the idle and the industrious would remain from each other. Presumably the allurements which God had provided would sweetly draw the idle into laborious and co-operative activity in "this earthly paradise." ⁵

Earlier George Percy had described "fair meadows and goodly tall trees with such fresh waters running through the woods" that he "was almost ravished at the first sight thereof." Yet in the midst of this paradise his "men were destroyed with cruel diseases, as swellings, fluxes, burning fevers, and by wars; and some departed suddenly, but for the most part they died of mere famine." ⁶ What concerned those who sought explanations for such occurrences was how, in the words of a writer in 1610, "plenty and famine, a temperate climate and distempered bodies, felicities and miseries can be reconciled together." ⁷ While many in England were only too eager to conclude that all talk of the fruitfulness of Virginia was merely propaganda, promoters of colonization at home and in America emphatically denied that the disasters could in any way be attributed to the country itself. In 1610 the governor and council in Virginia asked the Company in London to "let no rumor of the poverty of the country" discourage men from coming, "as if in the womb thereof there lay not those elemental seeds which could produce as many goodly births of plenty and increase" as in any land similarly situated.⁸

Still, the problem remained of explaining disease, confusion, and even rebelliousness. In a sermon preached in Virginia in 1613, Alexander Whitaker traced the colony's failures to the moral shortcomings of both the adventurers and the planters, many of whom had "not been reconciled to God nor approved of Him. Some of our adventurers of London have been most miserable covetous men, sold over to usury, extortion, and oppression. Many of the men sent hither have been murderers, thieves, adulterers, idle persons, and what not besides, all which persons God hateth even from His very soul." The explanation for what had happened was obvious, for "how then could their alms or anything else which they do be pleasing unto God?" [9] Whitaker was examining conditions in terms of the society's covenant responsibility, and his call for repentance proceeded logically from his analysis. If colonization had not really cured, among other sins, the sin of idleness, repentance would be necessary or the enterprise would never flourish.

Whitaker was perhaps extreme in tracing Virginia's troubles exclusively to the moral shortcomings of those involved. In a sermon delivered in England in 1610 William Crashaw noted that "money may win and profit may allure men to assist" the undertaking, "but prayer alone can prevail with God to bless it." [10] In practice, however, Crashaw looked more to effective leadership than to moral exhortation. He dealt with the argument that it was foolish to send the idle to Virginia; for such "loose, lewd, licentious, riotous, and disordered men, they that cannot be kept in compass at home, how can they be ordered there?" In part his reply was "that as long as we have wise, courageous, and discreet governors, together with the preaching of God's word, we much care not what the generality is of them that go in person." His reasoning was that even the most disorderly men are often reformed "and prove good and worthy instruments and members of a commonwealth" if they are removed "from the licentiousness and too much liberty of the states where they have lived into a more bare and barren soil, as every country is at first, and to a harder course of life wanting pleasures and subject to some pinching miseries and to a strict form of government and severe discipline." [11]

Like Crashaw, many of the attractionists involved in the affairs of the colony either in England or America increasingly supported authority and even coercion as the best way to deal with idleness in Virginia. In a truly remarkable reversal of earlier assumptions, America, which had once promised freedom from coercion, was now being praised for its coercive possibilities. Crashaw's position differed from a strictly coercionist approach in that he viewed the New World as a special place where those in authority would be able to deal more effectively with the problem of idleness than they could in England. Moreover, he did not reject the efficacy of allurement. "We will not deny," he admitted, "but as we are men, we may be induced in the beginning with hope of great profit, of winning a goodly country for Englishmen to live in (which now by multitudes are thrust out at home), and of living a more free and pleasant and contented life." Some of the more corrupt planters "may dream of greater ease and licentiousness," but for Christians "the principal and predominant ends are of a far more high and excellent nature." [12] He was apparently not opposed to economic motivations if they were properly limited and controlled, but he had nothing good to say about "many of the vulgar and viler sort, who went thither only for ease and idleness, for profit and pleasure and some such carnal causes." [13] Still, the idea that profit and pleasure were so closely linked to ease and idleness was an ominous suggestion, which, if pushed to its logical conclusion, could invalidate the whole attractionist argument.

The hard facts of the situation in Virginia were putting many of the presuppositions of the promoters of colonization to the test. In a sermon preached in 1609 Robert Gray had rebuked those who would give up if the plantation proved unprofitable. To him this betrayed a "brutish" lack of concern for the future because "posterity and the age yet ensuing have not the least part in our life and labors." [14] One might question how God was enticing planters and adventurers when there might not be any rewards in their own lifetimes. Gray was nevertheless convinced that if artisans and tradesmen were properly encouraged by those in authority to be diligent and honest in their callings, "the country itself will make them rich." Those, however, without "professed arts and trades must painfully employ themselves in some labor or other, to the furthering of this plantation. A drone will in short space devour more honey than the bee can gather in a long time, and therefore the magistrate must correct with all sharpness of discipline those unthrifty and unprofitable drones which live idly." [15]

The use of force in Virginia had been authorized all along; the president and council had power "to punish all manner of excess through drunkenness or otherwise and all idle, loitering, and vagrant persons which shall be found within their several limits and precincts." [16] Nevertheless, those in charge seem to have been genuinely surprised by the confusion which developed in the colony, and like the ministers they vacillated between moral explanations in the tradition of the jeremiad and support of authoritarian policies. In his description of conditions in the colony in 1608 Captain John Smith told how Virginia had been nearly destroyed because of dissension among its leaders, "through which disorder God (being angry with us) plagued us with such famine and sickness that the living were scarce able to bury the dead." Because of sickness and discontent among the leaders the others were "in such despair as they would rather starve and rot with idleness than be persuaded to do anything for their own relief without constraint." [17] In practice Smith moved increasingly toward an authoritarian policy, and his *Map of Virginia* (1612) included a speech in which he had rebuked his men for expecting to be supported "in idleness and sloth." Though all were not guilty, "the greater part must be more industrious or starve," for "he that will not work shall not eat, except by sickness he be disabled." Smith made a gesture in the direction of enticement by posting a notice board "as a public memorial of every man's deserts to encourage the good and with shame to spur on the rest to amendment. By this many became very industrious, yet more by severe punishment performed their business." [18]

Smith's opponents were not reticent about attacking his policies as tyrannical arrogance. George Percy described him as "an ambitious, unworthy, and vainglorious fellow, attempting to take all men's authorities from them." [19] Edward Maria Wingfield noted that he had begged Smith to be "more sparing of law until we had more wit or wealth." For "laws were good spies in a populous, peaceable, and plentiful country, where they did make the good men better and stayed the bad from being worse; yet we were so poor as they did but rob us of time that might be better employed in service in the colony." In fact, he went on to observe, "were this whipping, lawing, beating, and hanging in Virginia known in England, I fear it would drive many well affected minds from this honorable action of Virginia." [20] Wingfield was merely reiterating an old attractionist axiom that a policy of force makes bad economic sense.

In 1610 the Company laid the cause of the distress of the first colonists to "the misgovernment of the commanders" and "the idleness and bestial sloth of the common sort, who were active in nothing but adhering to factions and parts even to their own ruin, like men almost desperate of all supply so conscious and guilty they were to themselves of their own demerit and laziness." [21] The disposition to regard the problem in moral terms was evidenced not only in the way in which the men were blamed, but in the very use of the word laziness, with its strong volitional and moral connotations. Nevertheless, as a matter of policy it had been decided that persuasion was not enough and that force was necessary to root idleness out of Virginia. The series of reorganizations beginning in 1609 can be interpreted as moving steadily in the direction of an authoritarian rather than a moral solution to the problems of the colony. These opposing tendencies within the attractionist position were becoming increasingly difficult to balance, as Wingfield's argument with Smith foretold.

When Lord De La Warr arrived as governor in 1610, he spoke to the people, "laying just blame upon them for their haughty vanities and sluggish idleness, earnestly entreating them to amend those desperate follies lest he should be compelled to draw the sword of justice and to cut off such delinquents." His remarks were effective, and one "might shortly behold the idle and resty diseases of a divided multitude, by the unity and authority of this government, to be substantially cured." [22] In accordance with instructions from the Company Sir Thomas Gates, lieutenant governor of the colony, drew up a series of laws and orders. These were enlarged in 1611, mainly with respect to martial affairs, by De La Warr's successor, Sir Thomas Dale, and codified in 1612 by William Strachey, the first secretary of the colony. Known as Dale's Laws, the code clearly represented a consolidation of the policy of authoritarianism and is chiefly remembered for its strictness.[23]

In his preface to the Laws, Strachey argued that how to govern and how to obey are "the end indeed of sociable mankind's creation," for "without order and government . . . what society may possibly subsist or commutative goodness be practiced?" His expectation was that the "laws being published, every common eye may take survey of their duties and carrying away the tenor of the same, meditate and bethink how safe, quiet, and comely it is to be honest, just, and civil." In this way social order would be established through wise laws "with their due penalties, according unto which we might live in the colony justly one with another and perform the general service for which we first came thither." [24] Evidently Governor Dale was satisfied with the effectiveness of his policy, for upon his return to England in 1616 he informed his superiors "of the good estate of that colony and how by the blessing of God and good government there is great plenty and increase of corn, cattle, goats, swine, and such other provisions." [25] Without denying the superintending power of God, he had presumably demonstrated the efficacy of authority in promoting industry and establishing an orderly commonwealth.

Besides tightening laws and controls in an attempt to put down early outbreaks of idleness, the Company published a broadside which declared that "former experience hath too dearly taught how much and many ways it hurteth to suffer parents to disburden themselves of lascivious sons, masters of bad servants and wives of ill husbands, and so to clog the business with such an idle crew as did thrust themselves in the last voyage, that will rather starve for hunger than lay their hands to labor." It was therefore resolved "that no such unnecessary person shall now be accepted, but only such sufficient and good artificers" as were enumerated in a list which followed.[26] This was a denial of the reforming value of colonization, even if the policy seemed in the best interest of Virginia. Not surprisingly, however, emigration did not particularly appeal to many settled tradesmen, and this left the idle, who were by definition available for colonization. While the leaders of the Company made every effort to recruit established tradesmen, stark reality prevented them from abandoning the policy of augmenting the colony's labor supply from the ranks of the idle. In 1620 Sir Edwin Sandys, discussing the possibility of recruiting laborers from among the poor children of London, lamented that many "declare their unwillingness to go to Virginia of whom the city is especially desirous to be disburdened, and in Virginia under severe masters they may be brought to goodness." He was not opposed to constraint in taking the children away, provided he could secure official permission to do so.[27]

Although the leaders of the Virginia Company wanted their undertaking to be profitable, one cannot explain many of their expectations or their restrictive actions unless one concedes that they also wanted to establish a commonwealth in America. The repeated attempts to attract laborers of all sorts exemplified this desire. The problems implicit in such a goal were recognized in 1612 by a person who argued that nothing is "so difficult as to establish a commonwealth so far remote from men and means and where men's minds are so untoward as neither do well themselves nor suffer others."²⁸ The quasi-military organization of society under Dale's Laws may be seen, therefore, as an attempt to establish by force some kind of orderly social arrangement.²⁹ In 1621 the governor was instructed to "cause our people to apply themselves to an industrious course of life in following their businesses, each in the several degree and profession," and to insure "that no man be suffered to live idly, the example whereof might prove pernicious to the rest." He was also told not to allow tradesmen from England "to forsake their former occupations for planting tobacco or such useless commodities."³⁰

The repeated criticisms of tobacco production, which began less than a decade after the colony was founded, contained an element of irony, for this endeavor perfectly exemplified the idea of the allurement of profit. Returns were immediately forthcoming because the planter did not need to await the lengthy development of complex social and economic structures. In fact only the exploitation of easily accessible raw materials or the production of readily marketable staple crops really fufilled the requirements of the doctrine of allurement. Virginia tobacco sold in the early years for a very high price, and it was even planted by eager colonists within fortified areas and in the streets of Jamestown. Artisans who still pursued their trades usually rented or purchased land and devoted part of their time to tobacco production.³¹ Doubtless some of the Company's opposition to tobacco was due to King James's violent antipathy to it, but even more important the attempts to promote diversification were part of an effort to create a real society in Virginia. In 1625 tobacco and sassafras were criticized for being "matters of present profit, but no ways foundations of a future state."³²

Arguments against tobacco production, nevertheless, did not completely repudiate the doctrine of allurement. A broadside published in 1620 warned that the exclusive concern for "the planting of tobacco and the neglect of other more solid commodities have not only redounded to the great disgrace of the country and detriment of the colony, but doth also in point of profit greatly deceive them which have trusted to it." [33] When John Bonoeil, at the request of the king, published a book in 1622 to promote silk culture and other products, he brought out all the ammunition of allurement to induce Virginians to give up tobacco. Nature speaks: "Friends of my best beloved nation, view me well and tell me if you are not come into another land of promise, into another paradise?" She has abundantly provided mulberries and vines, and the colonists are entreated to take advantage of them because "they are rich and beautiful. How haps it then that I and they are slighted so much by you? And that which worst is, all for a smoky witch!" [34] The futility of such entreaties is self-evident. To use the desire for gain as an appeal to individuals who were profiting abundantly from tobacco was both useless and inconsistent, unless a careful distinction was made (and it was not) between personal aggrandizement and general social goals.

Partly because of tobacco production, towns failed really to develop in Virginia. Thus by European standards the colony lacked one of the most visible signs of a recognizable society. The Company's repeated efforts yielded little in the way of tangible results. When the Virginia Council wrote to London of the 1622 Indian massacre, it lamented that the plantation "could not but be subject to much damages to be so dispersedly and promiscuously planted." The Company, upon receipt of this news, referred also to the planters' mode of settlement, "which error by so hard a chastisement we hope from henceforward they will be willing of themselves to amend; if not your authority must restrain them." Hence "for their better civil government (which mutual society doth most conduce unto) we think it fit that the houses and buildings be so contrived together as may make, if not handsome towns, yet compact and orderly villages." [35] Officials in the colony had asked for permission to bring all the remaining planters together so as to provide a better defense against the

Indians, but the Company insisted that territory formerly held must be resettled "lest the best fire that maintains the action here alive be put out." [36] Once again its leaders were unable to pursue a policy aimed exclusively at fashioning a recognizable social order in Virginia.

The Company's leaders would undoubtedly have denied that there were contradictions in its policy. In assuming control in 1618, Sir Edwin Sandys and his associates had been concerned about the venture as a public service and dedicated to the proposition that the exclusive devotion to tobacco must be checked. On the other hand, the policy of martial law that had existed under Sir Thomas Smith was totally abandoned.[37] The legislative reforms of 1619 were designed mainly to enhance the attractiveness of Virginia to prospective settlers and were in fact inducements to insure the willing cooperation of the colonists. Since the doctrine of allurement was supposed to involve the free play of economic opportunity within the context of an industrious society, it might be argued that it was not inconsistent to permit freedom and promote social development. Moreover, Sandys and his associates were convinced that an orderly society was necessary to provide an atmosphere of confidence. Women were thus sent over to make wives for the planters because of the belief that "the plantation can never flourish till families be planted and the respect of wives and children fix the people on the soil." [38] In defending its charter in 1623 the Company argued "that the people, who in former times were discontent and mutinous by reason of their inassurance of all things through want of order and justice, live now amongst themselves in great peace and tranquility, each knowing his own and what he is mutually to receive and perform." [39] Perhaps the Company tried too hard to fulfill the requirements of the doctrine of allurement without quite realizing that its permissiveness and its appeals to personal ambition often worked at cross purposes with its social aims.

Possibly one might say that there were fewer contradictions in policy under the administration of Sir Thomas Smith, at least after the Company had firmly decided upon an authoritarian emphasis. In the controversy which preceded the dissolution of the Company in 1625 the Sandys faction was accused of having "allured" many people to the colony on "false pretenses."[40] Yet the Smith faction cannot be described as entirely single-minded. Smith had initiated several reforms before Sandys gained control, and he did not protest at the time against the reforms Sandys made. Moreover, during the dissolution controversy each side contended with the other in defending the permissiveness of its policies. Alderman Johnson, a Smith adherent, petitioned the king that "in former times the government was so mild and moderate as a multitude of adventurers were brought in, but now there was much oppression and injury offered both to adventurers and planters."[41] He later condemned Sandys's policy of setting valuations on commodities, "for the merchant knows what to give and the planter loves his liberty and esteems this set price a bondage."[42]

The dissolution of the Virginia Company represented a failure for those attractionists who had moved in the direction of authoritarian policies. Though the Sandys faction was somewhat less committed to this position than the Smith faction, it had still endeavored to fashion an orderly society in Virginia—and failed, most conspicuously with regard to towns and tobacco production. While it is not strictly accurate to use any one person or even persons to typify this position, the statements of two of its more vocal advocates may help to illustrate that there was some inner logic in their alternate stress upon freedom and control. In 1612 Alderman Johnson noted that Dale's Laws had been established in part "for peace and love among themselves and enforcing the idle to pains and honest labors." He was obviously defending the suppression of idleness considered as a social vice, yet he was also concerned lest unwise coercion act as a brake upon individual pursuit of wealth. He advised the leaders to permit the common sort to "live as free Englishmen under the government of just and equal laws," and not to discourage them "in growing religious nor in gathering riches, two especial bonds (whether severed or conjoined) to keep them in obedience." [43] Long after his Virginia experience, Captain John Smith admitted that he was "not so simple to think that ever any other motive than wealth will ever erect there a commonwealth or draw company from their ease and humors at home to stay in New England to effect my purposes." [44] Later he wrote that in a new colony "some are more proper for one thing than another and therein best to be employed, and nothing breeds more confusion than misplacing and misemploying men in their undertakings." [45]

Like all attractionists these men believed in the potency of economic enticements, but they sought to distinguish between economic freedom and general social freedom. Hence profit may freely allure men to colonization, but an orderly government of the wise and good is to control, regulate, and channel economic activities. Government does not necessarily coerce men into working, but it does define what work is socially acceptable. They are free to profit along approved lines, but they must not mistake this freedom for the right to do what they please in all areas of life. The problem was how to create such an effective instrument in the wilderness, especially when those who professed to believe in strong government were in practice not sure how far its determining powers ought to extend. In an old and established society like England a confusion between economic freedom and general social freedom was much less likely to develop than in a new colony. Moreover, among men who had looked to colonization as an alternative to the use of force at home, coercion did as much to confuse as to clarify their policies and procedures.

The bankruptcy of the attractionist program by the early 1620's lay in the fact that its proponents had no answer to two key objections except force. The first objection may be expressed in the words of Samuel Purchas, who admitted that a "prodigious prodigal here is not easily metamorphosed in a Virginian passage to a thrifty planter." [46] Attractionists had initially denied this, yet almost twenty years of experience had not vindicated their assertions. In Richard Eburne's *A Plain Pathway to Plantations* (1624) the merchant, who expresses the author's position, deals with the familiar problem of "idleness the mother of many mischiefs, which is to be cured and may be rooted out of the land by this means, yea by this only and by none other, viz. by plantation." [47] When his foil, the farmer, counters that sending away the idle "is but the removing of evil from one place to another," the former concedes that with "such removal made, our land (which is the point in question) shall be cleared and cured." [48] Besides, in America "if any continue their former lewd and disordered courses, being but a few, so many of their wonted companions being severed and gone from them, there is hope that a little severity of the laws . . . will and may bring them also to a better course." [49] Experience had, however, demonstrated that this tactic was simpler to describe than to carry out.

The second objection lay in the motivation for emigration. In the words of Richard Whitbourne, "it is an hard matter to persuade people to adventure into strange countries, especially to remain there, though the conditions thereof be never so beneficial and advantageous for them." [50] Attractionists had adhered to the conviction that all men are motivated by the desire for profit and advancement, but bitter experience had demonstrated (though it had not convinced them) that, in the words of Max Weber, "a man does not 'by nature' wish to earn more and more money, but simply to live as he is accustomed to live and to earn as much as is necessary for that purpose." [51] Eburne could not help pleading: "Look upon the misery and want wherein you do, and abiding in England, you cannot but live. Look upon the plenty and felicity wherein going hence you may live. Prefer not poverty before riches nor your perpetual evil and wretchedness before perpetual good and happiness." [52] The merchant would prefer voluntary emigration, but if inducements "suffice not, as I believe also that they will not," then "it might be good that strict order were taken to take up all such vagrant persons" and ship them off. Even though many incorrigible ones might be included, it is his hope "that necessity, occasion, and opportunity may make many of them to leave loitering there." [53] Eburne's willingness to resort to force was an admission that the allurements of the New World had failed to attract the idle multitudes of England. The alternative was to expel them, but the meager hopes he held out for them in America could not disguise the fact that what had once been a vision of busy activity on both sides of the Atlantic had become simply a call for "dumping" the nation's idle.

Numerous Englishmen relegated to this category were sent to Virginia against their wills or else induced to emigrate by glowing descriptions, which had the opposite effect from what attractionists intended. For many whose lives had been totally disrupted by social and economic changes they could neither understand nor control—men and women who had never known anything but hunger and struggle—the talk of great plenty and opportunity designed to entice them to industrious labor seemed instead to promise at last a land of ease and plenty, of freedom from misery and pain—in short, a paradise. Instead "they end their day most miserably, some of them at their last, cursing them most bitterly that sent them over and persuading them of the plenty aforesaid which they should find. For all this plenty the poor tenants would think themselves happy if they had but butter and cheese upon festival days." [54] Richard Frethorne complained angrily to his parents in England that he and his associates were not allowed to hunt for game, "but must work hard both early and late for a mess of water gruel and a mouthful of bread and beef." To the extent, therefore, that allurement worked at all for these downtrodden people, it only brought false hopes and disappointment. Yet Frethorne's letter also contains the suggestion that "there is nothing to be gotten here but sickness and death, except that one had money to lay out in some things for profit." [55]

Virginia had been founded upon the premise that profit is the spring of action. Attractionists who had tried in vain to establish an elaborate society able to control men's activities and coerce the idle into industry could only conclude that the future of the colony would be dark indeed. Disorder and consequently more idleness must be expected now that positive direction within the society had collapsed. Yet Frethorne for one did not want to give up, especially when profit seemed the only avenue of survival. If Virginia offered economic opportunities, then the doctrine of allurement ought not to be considered false. Let the lazy stay home, the foolish weep over tobacco and the absence of towns, the misguided call for authority and coercion. America could still be a land of promise to those who had not lost faith in it.

2

In 1619 John Pory triumphantly wrote home that "all our riches for the present do consist in tobacco, wherein one man by his own labor hath in one year raised to himself to the value of two hundred pounds sterling, and another by the means of six servants hath cleared at one crop a thousand pounds English." What Pory wanted to emphasize was that "these be true yet indeed rare examples, yet possible to be done by others." [1] From the perspective of the individual planter the question was only what opportunities the country afforded him—how much wealth the ambitious might personally amass. Peter Arundle assured a friend in England in 1622 "that any laborious honest man may in a short time become rich in this country." The acquisition of personal wealth was assumed to lead to increasing "the Church of God by propagating the gospel" and augmenting "the greatness and glory" of king and country.[2] Perhaps all that had been said about the possibilities of America was true after all.

Evocations of the beauty and richness of the land might make receptive persons disposed to become "Americans" almost immediately. They came expecting to be "ravished" by the beauties of nature, and they were. The works of Captain John Smith are usually classified as American literature precisely because they reflect the inspiration of the American landscape. In his own words, "heaven and earth never agreed better to frame a place for man's habitation being of our constitutions, were it fully manured and inhabited by industrious people. Here are mountains, hills, plains, valleys, rivers and brooks all running most pleasantly into a fair bay compassed but for the mouth with fruitful and delightsome land." [3] In 1613 Sir Thomas Dale wrote that "the more I range the country the more I admire it." Though he had seen "the best countries in Europe," he insisted that "this country will be equivalent unto them if it be inhabited with good people." [4] Both of these men qualified their response by insisting upon industry from those who settled the land. Both turned to authoritarian means of promoting it because they felt idleness threatened the development of the colony.

There were other men, equally responsive to the beauties of the landscape, who did not consider an elaborate institutional framework and its restraints so necessary to promote industry or further the ends of society. In his description of Virginia, published in 1615, Ralph Hamor protested that he knew of "no one country yielding without art or industry so many fruits." [5] He celebrated the new policy of permitting individual landholding, a policy which would in time contribute greatly to the dispersed character of settlement in Virginia. "Every day by the providence and blessing of God and their own industry" colonists were now enjoying plenty. Even the most honest man formerly "would not take so much faithful and true pains in a week as now he will do in a day." [6] Interestingly enough, Hamor defended Dale's Laws on the grounds that "if the law should not have restrained by execution," he did not see "how the utter subversion and ruin of the colony should have been prevented." But by the period of his description things were "much mitigated, for more deserved death in those days than do now the least punishment." [7]

Although Hamor was prepared to acknowledge the necessity of law for the initial imposition of order upon the colony, thereafter he would look mainly to economic motivations to consolidate these gains. "As for profit it shall come abundantly," he insisted, "if we can with the husbandman but freely cast our corn into the ground and with patience wait for a blessing. And of victuals there is now no complaint at all." What had happened previously was "by the mere lazy negligence of our own people." [8] Hamor was therefore more inclined to blame individuals for what had occurred than to castigate the government for weakness. This individualistic and moralistic emphasis was carried even farther. He held the individual solely responsible for his success in the new land. Anyone who could not supply himself with a year's apparel was a spendthrift so unfit for the country that he ought not to come. Anyone more poorly clothed after a year in Virginia than when he arrived was "a worse husband than the former," for "the valuable commodity of tobacco of such esteem in England (if there were nothing else), which every man may plant and with the least part of his labor tend and care, will return him both clothes and other necessaries." [9]

In 1616 John Rolf described "tobacco (though an es-teemed weed)" as "very commodious." There it "thriveth so well that no doubt but after a little more trial and expense in the curing thereof, it will compare with the best in the West Indies." [10] He pointed out that the small population of Vir-ginia, "united, ordered and governed," lived "happily, every-one partaking of the other's labor" in possession of a land which could support many more people. Since at the same time "too many poor farmers in England work all the year, rising early and going to bed late, live penuriously, and much ado to pay their landlord's rent, besides a daily carking and caring to feed themselves and families, what happiness might they enjoy in Virginia, were men sensible of these things!" Unlike Eburne, who was preoccupied with "dumping" all of the poor as a matter of social expediency, Rolf was interested in what America offered each man. Here "they may have ground for nothing, more than they can manure," and so be able to "reap more fruits and profits with half the labor, void of many cares and vexations." [11] To the individual Virginia would thus be a new beginning, an opportunity for freedom and prosperity in the midst of "a peculiar people, marked and chosen by the finger of God to possess it, for undoubtedly He is with us." [12]

If one substitutes the freedom through grace for the freedom of allurement, Rolf's vision might very well be the vision of the first American Puritans. The distinction, however, is crucial to an understanding of the social differences which from the beginning distinguished Virginia from New England. The men who finally triumphed in the southern colony conceived of economic freedom, the allurements held out by God to each individual, as the foundation upon which the good society rested. For the Puritan the freedom to perform one's calling was only one aspect of "soul freedom." Some of the consequences of this distinction can best be brought out by comparing two works on colonization, one on Virginia and the other on New England.

The first, a sermon entitled *Virginia*, was delivered in London by William Symonds in 1609. Having taken as the warrant for colonization both Abraham's calling to go into another land and the general law of replenishing the earth, he explained that if God had enticed Abraham "by arguments taken from the opportunity and sweetness of the place, how should it be known whether he went by the power of the promise of God or by some carnal inducement?" Yet almost immediately he went on to state that after the children of Israel had received notice of the fruitfulness of Canaan, "sure if such motives as these could not make them ready to run to the place, it appeared that they had neither the fear of God that would not be persuaded by Him nor the wits of reasonable men that will not respect their own benefit." [13] Turning to the case of Virginia, he eloquently insisted that it is "a land more like the Garden of Eden, which the Lord planted, than any part else of all the earth." That God promises to enrich a man obedient to his calling is an "example of that sweet sanction of the law, when the Lord doth allure men to keep it by the abundance of His blessings." [14] For Symonds, economic opportunity for the most part moved people to immigrate to

America. From God's perspective this may have been a religious response, but for the colonist it was mainly an opportunistic one.

The second work, by the Rev. John White, *The Planter's Plea* for the colonization of New England, was published in 1630. Its author too considered God's command to replenish the earth the warrant for colonies. To fail to obey God's will is to neglect and despise His blessings.[15] These blessings in some sense make action imperative, but they do not or ought not to allure. White dealt specifically with this point in answering the objection that "there is nothing to be expected in New England but competency to live on at the best, and that must be purchased with hard labor, whereas divers other parts of the West Indies offer a richer soil which easily allures inhabitants by the tender of a better condition than they live in at present." In refutation he listed several reasons why "there is more cause to fear wealth than poverty in that soil." In fact, even the heathens knew "the overflowing of riches to be enemy to labor, sobriety, justice, love, and magnanimity, and the nurse of pride, wantonness, and contention." [16] This fear of a rich land is worth noting. Natural wealth ought not to constitute a danger to a people living up to their covenant obligations, but perhaps it was best not to be tempted by too great abundance.

At the same time a certain concern for economic opportunities did figure in White's thinking. Many in England lived "without employment, either wholly or in the greatest part," including "not only such as delight in idleness, but even folk willing to labor, who either live without exercise in their callings or are fain to thrust into other men's, to the evident prejudice of both." Coercion was not the answer, he maintained, for "good government though it do reform many, yet it cannot reform all the evils of this kind because it will be a great difficulty to find out profitable employments for all that will want." [17] The purpose of colonies then was to provide a place where men might freely exercise their callings. Because the environment was not seen as motivating men to labor, there was no expectation that emigration would change them. Rather, "men nourished up in idleness, unconstant, and affecting novelties, unwilling, stubborn, inclined to faction, covetous, luxurious, prodigal, and generally men habituated to any gross evil are not fit members of a colony." By contrast, those "chosen out for this employment ought to be willing, constant, industrious, obedient, frugal, lovers of the common good, or at least such as may be easily wrought to this temper." [18] Hence *The Planter's Plea* eloquently reflected a vision of social unity based upon personal responsibility.

Because of their emphasis upon individual social responsibility, Puritan writers were greatly concerned about personal motivations for migration—how each man was to know whether God would have him go to America. There is really no counterpart to this concern in the colonization literature of Virginia. White argued that "nothing can bear out the hazards and inconveniences of such toilsome and difficult undertakings as is the planting of colonies but a willing mind." Consequently, a person must weigh his "engagement unto his present condition in which he is settled" against the "tender and offer of the new service unto which he is called." "In both it must be first granted that callings are employments in which we serve one another through love." One decides for oneself by talking with godly friends, by weighing opportunities, and "by and consideration of the inclination of the heart proposing a right end and scope after frequent and earnest prayer." [19] White was thus speaking of colonists personally motivated by their belief in God's desire for them to go and willingly dedicated to performing their callings for the general good, not isolated individuals who may have been lured by opportunity.

If spokesmen for Virginia were vague about personal responsibility to society, they were equally vague about a sense of community among the colonists. They simply assumed that social unity would develop through the operation of the doctrine of allurement. By contrast the various Puritan groups of New England thought of themselves as small societies before they ever established their communities. Before coming to America, John Robinson and William Brewster wrote Sir Edwin Sandys that the Pilgrims were, "for the body of them, industrious and frugal, we think we may safely say, as any company of people in the world." Almost as a corollary they went on: "We are knit together as a body in a most strict and sacred bond and covenant of the Lord, of the violation whereof we make great conscience, and by virtue whereof we do hold ourselves straitly tied to all care of each other's good and of the whole, by every one and so mutually." [20] The language of the Mayflower Compact well reflects this sense of community based on individual consent. Here, it says, we "solemnly and mutually in the presence of God and one another covenant and combine ourselves together into a civil body politic for our better ordering and preservation." [21] Similar attitudes were reflected in the statements of the groups making up the larger Puritan colony and of those who moved to Connecticut.

Doubtless a significant number of the inhabitants of New England were as concerned with personal advancement and as impatient with social restrictions as their fellow colonists in Virginia. But they were not the spokesmen of their societies. Hence the Puritan communities were not heterogeneous aggregations whose social unity would hopefully grow from the pursuit of opportunity. Still, the initial task of establishing a functioning society in the wilderness must have seemed especially formidable to those charged with the burdens of leadership, and the doctrinaire inclination of some to dispense with authority only strengthened their determination to maintain control. At the beginning of the Puritan experiment John Winthrop noted that it was important for his people to avoid the "great and fundamental errors" of previous colonies, one of which was that "they did not establish a right form of government." [22] Control and order became increasingly important for Winthrop, and it was to protect the formal institutions of his society that he did battle with Roger Williams and Anne Hutchinson. Like Virginia, New England in its early years was the scene of a confrontation between two different groups, one stressing authority and order, the other personal responsibility and freedom. The curious difference is that the advocates of authoritarian social policy won as completely in Massachusetts as their counterparts failed in Virginia. Hutchinson and Williams were driven out, and apologists for the colony celebrated the purity of institutional forms at the time of the Puritan Revolution in England. In Virginia it was men of Rolf's temper (though he had died) who remained to celebrate the virtues of personal freedom and endless economic opportunity.

The different results can at least partly be explained by the fact that Winthrop would never have succeeded unless there had been a strong sense of community among the people. Although the Puritans conceived of social unity primarily in terms of individual attitudes and loyalties, they assumed that this unity would quickly manifest itself in such outward symbols as churches, towns, and civil government. When men like Winthrop found these symbols in danger and emphasized the importance of strict authority to prevent the community from flying apart, it was difficult to resist their arguments. Time would qualify Winthrop's achievement as settlement in Massachusetts Bay became more dispersed and the pursuit of opportunity increased social fragmentation. Indeed the very emphasis upon outward order evidenced a certain weakening of the sense of community, but beneath the external changes something of this sense persisted. As Sumner Chilton Powell has observed, the term "town" had not meant the same thing to all of the first settlers because they came from different kinds of towns in England, but it had meant "a life of uncertainty, balanced by a faith in social order and stability." [23] Because this faith was not wholly lost, towns were not abandoned as the basis of settlement although there were changes in patterns of organization. Thus New England remained different from Virginia, and towns continued in part to symbolize the difference.

The effect of the Puritan notions of society was eventually

felt not only in New England but even in New York and New Jersey, where little bands of saints established towns and villages. Daniel Denton wrote of New York, shortly after it had passed to the English in 1664, that the way land was procured was "for a company of people to join together, either enough to make a town or a lesser number. These go with the consent of the governor and view a tract of land, there being choice enough; and finding a place convenient for a town, they return to the governor" for admission to the colony and a patent "for themselves and associates." [24] At about the same time in New Jersey, a group of agents from several New Haven colony towns agreed to form the town of Newark, "according to fundamentals mutually agreed upon," desiring "to be of one heart and consent [that] through God's blessing with one hand they may endeavor the carrying on of spiritual concernments as also civil and town affairs according to God and a godly government." [25]

Perry Miller has noted the rapidity with which Virginia passed through "the cycle of exploration, religious dedication, disillusionment, and then reconciliation to a world in which making a living was the ultimate reality" in contrast to "a slow and almost imperceptible evolution, such as that through which the Massachusetts Zion was subtly transformed into a mercantile society." [26] Essentially what was true of Massachusetts was also true of Pennsylvania, the other important center of influence in the northern colonies. As Edwin Bronner has shown in a recent study, Penn conceived of Pennsylvania as a "holy experiment," a "community populated by virtuous people who were motivated by an all-pervasive love of God." [27] While the Quaker community never had the power of the Puritan community in Massachusetts, it was still "one of the strongest forces working for the success of the 'holy experiment' in the entire colony." [28] Like the Puritans, Penn conceived of society in terms of the individuals composing it. "Governments, like clocks," he wrote, "go from the motion men give them; and as governments are made and moved by men, so by them they are ruined too." [29] In 1685 he reported that he had been success-ful in preventing one kind of ruin. Settlement was in the form of townships or villages, but "many that had right to more land were at first covetous to have their whole quantity with-out regard to this way of settlement, though by such wilder-ness vacancies they had ruined the country and then our in-terest of course." Penn frustrated this tendency, which would have turned Pennsylvania into another Virginia, because he had in mind "society, assistance, busy commerce, instruction of youth, government of people's manners, conveniency of religious assembling, encouraging of mechanics, distinct and beaten roads." [30] As a result the colony was to have the out-ward form which the age expected.

In other respects as well during these early years Penn en-countered more disunity and controversy than he had antici-pated. He was, however, far more reluctant to adopt an au-thoritarian policy than the leaders of Massachusetts and Vir-ginia had been. For a period the Council was so weak that there was little visible evidence of government. In August 1685 Penn gave orders to punish vice and admitted that he had been perhaps too lenient. He appointed as lieutenant gov-ernor in 1689 a Puritan named John Blackwell, who soon re-signed because of local opposition to him. Penn was unhappy with Blackwell's recommendations for strict control and was only too willing to embrace a softer policy after his resigna-tion.[31] Despite all the confusion and the criticisms of the colony in the next decade, "Penn found it comparatively sim-ple to restore law and order in 1700, which indicated that firm foundations had been laid for a durable, responsible political existence during the first two decades." [32] Pennsylvania was not the scene of so complete a triumph of authoritarian poli-cies as Massachusetts under Winthrop, but in contrast to Virginia the sense of community was strong enough to pre-vent fragmentation. Secularization of the initial religious vi-sion took place slowly and in an environment characterized by the symbols of social unity, which in Virginia remained ex-pectations rather than realities. Thus Penn could still feel himself justified in saying that "we are an approved experiment what sobriety and industry can do in a wilderness against heats, colds, wants, and dangers." [33]

In marked contrast to the general pattern of settlement which was to predominate in the northern colonies, the seacoast from Massachusetts Bay north was the scene of early colonizing efforts similar to Virginia. The projects of Sir Ferdinando Gorges were the most important, but there were others—all aimed at the creation of society through exploitation of natural resources. These undertakings are notable mainly for their singular lack of success. One such effort was the colony of a Master Weston near Plymouth. Thomas Morton of Merrymount fame described many of Weston's servants as "lazy persons that would use no endeavor to take the benefit of the country." [34] Richard Whitbourne deplored the absence of effective government and the consequent outbreak of idleness in the fishing colonies of Newfoundland. When he arrived, he found "that divers idle persons which were hired for those voyages, when they come thither, notwithstanding that they were still in health, would not work and were so lazy and idle that their work was to little purpose." [35]

While Virginia in many respects had more in common with these colonies than with Massachusetts, because of tobacco it did not fail, even though it struggled along for years with a very small population. The efforts of the Sandys faction to change the colony met with little success but no great resentment since its policies were more permissive than those of Sir Thomas Smith. What Virginians feared was that Smith might be restored to power. As Wesley Frank Craven has argued, colonists in the early years would probably have welcomed a revival of the Company under Sandys if it would have helped their urgent needs. After the immediate crisis, however, experience soon showed that the agencies of royal rule were less vigorous than those of the Company. Thereafter all efforts to re-establish any kind of proprietary rule over them were strenuously opposed on the grounds of the inconsistency of Company rule with freedom and opportunity.[36] In 1631 it was argued that the "colony hath prospered much more since the dissolution of the Company than ever it did before." [37] Again in 1642 the Assembly protested that "the old corporation cannot with any possibility be again introduced without the absolute ruin and dissolution of the colony." Indeed, it was further noted, "by the admission of a company the freedom of our trade (the blood and life of a commonwealth) will be monopolized." [38] These fears were unnecessary, however. The Company was dead.

The triumph of authority and order in the northern colonies may also be seen as the triumph (at least temporarily) of Old World customs over New World experience. This would make the defeat of these forces in Virginia a victory for American ways. Struck with the beauty and promise of their country, Virginians had striven to vindicate the American experience as something special—a new beginning, an adventure in opportunity and freedom, a chance for each individual to achieve something on his own. If Virginia was more of a frontier than New England and Pennsylvania, with their numerous towns and villages, this too would seem to make it more American. Whether early Virginia was truly characteristic of the promise of American life is a matter of debate, but men of the seventeenth century agreed that the colony was indeed different from anything one might have expected. The question in the years after the dissolution of the Virginia Company was whether this distinctiveness was permanent and whether the other colonies in what was to become the South would resemble Virginia or the more acceptable northern models. Supporters of this latter way of life still hoped that Virginia could be changed. If not, at least it could be used as an example of what to avoid in the newer settlements.

3

Theoretically, Maryland as a proprietary colony represented the exact opposite of all that Virginia had become. At the heart of the proprietary scheme was the manor, which usually coincided with a single town.[1] Cecilius Calvert, Lord Baltimore, endeavored to prevent the kind of scattered settlement that had taken place in Virginia by directing those in charge to "cause all the planters to build their houses in as decent and uniform a manner as their abilities and the place will afford, and near adjoining one to another." The phrase, "as their abilities and the place will afford," however, is the real key to Baltimore's attitude. In the same instructions he stated that he wanted to help all his countrymen "that they may reap the fruits of their charges and labors according to the hopefulness of the thing with as much freedom, comfort, and encouragement as they can desire." [2] However feudal in theory Maryland was, Baltimore was an eminently practical man. He did not attempt anything on a communal basis as the Virginia Company had at first, but left settlement up to individual adventurers. In this respect the colony "was established from the beginning on the basis of individual initiative and freedom of enterprise." [3] Baltimore's permissiveness meant that he would not really oppose the natural tendency of his colonists to follow the lead the Virginians had given—especially when

47

allowing free play to personal ambition meant large revenues for him from tobacco duties. Without any real opposition economic individualism easily established itself. As Craven observes of the Chesapeake colonies, "the most noticeable feature of their life is the absence of a common purpose and goal except such as was dictated principally by the requirements of individual interests." [4]

How anomalous the situation in these two colonies seemed to men of the age can be seen in the repeated attempts by English officialdom and other interested persons to promote changes that would create at least the visible symbols of "civility"—towns, people of all classes, commerce and varied agricultural pursuits. In 1626 Governor Yeardley of Virginia was instructed that all new planters "be not suffered to sit down straggling but enjoined to live by those already planted or in sufficient number by themselves." [5] When Governor Berkeley came to the colony in 1642, his instructions contained the same admonition "not to suffer men to build slight cottages as heretofore hath been there used and to remove from place to place only to plant tobacco." Also tradesmen and handicraftsmen were to "be compelled to follow their several trades and occupations." [6] By then the early period of extraordinarily high prices for tobacco had long since ended, but enough people still succeeded to keep the possibility of success always open. To the isolated individuals of the colony tobacco seemed the only sure road to wealth, and its appeal remained so strong that in spite of high wages tradesmen could not be kept from becoming planters.

When Berkeley returned as governor in 1662, he carried with him the admonition of Charles II to tell the Assembly to "establish good and wholesome laws and orders and execute them accordingly for the punishment, discountenance, and suppressing of all vice, debauchery, and idleness" and also to "establish all necessary encouragements for virtue, industry, and obedience." The first specific recommendation was to encourage the planters "to build towns upon every river, which must tend very much to their security and in time to their profit." They could not "have a better evidence and example than from their neighbors of New England, who obliging themselves to that order have in few years raised that colony to great wealth and reputation and security." [7] Such advice was hardly offered because the king had any great affection for the American Puritans. He simply concurred in the general agreement that the town-oriented, commercial society of New England conformed to the common conception of colonies. It is significant, moreover, that the establishment of towns and an orderly commercial life constituted the first way by which the king sought to banish idleness and promote industry in Virginia.

The policies of encouraging trade, diversifying agriculture, and promoting "cohabitation" were always linked together, but by the last decades of the century the interest of the Crown in these projects began to flag. Lord Culpeper told the Virginia Assembly in 1680 that the king had "concluded on the necessity of having one or more towns in this country without which no other nation ever began a plantation or any yet thrived as it ought." [8] But the projected remedies of limiting shipping to certain ports and restricting tobacco production met with the firm opposition of the English merchants engaged in the tobacco trade. When it was candidly and repeatedly pointed out that the Crown enjoyed a large and certain revenue from tobacco, which might be lost if the institutional reforms were carried out, people in high places prudently began to withdraw their suggestions. In 1685 the customary clause in the instructions to new royal governors dealing with the promotion of additional staples was left out.[9] In 1691 Governor Nicholson tried again to promote "cohabitation" with a port act aimed at the creation of a few principal towns, but this act was suspended in 1693. Another effort in 1705 failed too, largely because of the opposition of merchants trading in Virginia.[10]

From time to time an ardent critic published his advice on how this odd situation might be corrected. In his *Plain and Friendly Persuasive to the Inhabitants of Virginia and Mary-*

land for Promoting Towns and Cohabitation (1705), the Rev. Francis Makemie did not neglect to appeal to the potentialities of "a country capable of superlative improvement beyond many countries in the world." His astonishment at the absence of towns well illustrates how difficult it was for men of that time to understand what had happened in these colonies. Considering "the antiquity of towns and cities" throughout the pagan and Christian world, he felt "justly amazed to see the unaccountable humor and singularity of Virginia and Maryland." [11] What probably most confused critics like him was the fact that there was not total chaos in Virginia and Maryland. The absence of towns and other aspects of an orderly society ought to have produced the kind of confusion that had existed in the days before 1625. Nevertheless, Makemie was convinced that "towns and cohabitation would render trade universally more easy and less expensive." He also insisted that towns would have a moral effect in that they "would highly advance religion, which flourishes most in cohabitations." [12]

There were also a variety of suggestions and criticisms by people not completely at home in the colonies yet sufficiently attuned to understand the futility of simply demanding the cessation of tobacco culture and the creation of towns. The author of a description of conditions in Virginia in 1649 admitted that the present gain from tobacco put "all endeavors from the attempting of other more staple and solid and rich commodities out of the heads and hands of the common people." His answer was that "the wealthier sort of men must begin and give the example and make the gain of other commodities as apparent to them by the effecting them to perfection, or it will not (as it hath not hitherunto) go forward." [13] Persuasion was to be used for the wealthy, whose achievements would entice the common folk into diversified agriculture. In other words, any successful policy would have to be able to compete with allurement on its own terms. Eight years later Anthony Langston noted that the government had permitted dispersed settlement for some time, "and to draw those off from their now made seats to bring them to a more convenient and secure condition they would think the greatest oppression in the world." Hence "it will be very difficult to settle anything of a town or corporation by the ancient inhabitants." His solution was to begin with new immigrants, who were to be tradesmen required to settle in towns.[14]

William Bullock, writing in 1649, sought to show "how love, profit, and pleasure might be raised and after maintained by a sweet and orderly government."[15] Among the colony's misfortunes he lamented the fact that many come over and live on credit, "idling out their time till their new-contracted debts overtake them and they and their designs are lost." He also blamed conditions on the quality of many of the people induced to emigrate by "spirits," who "take up all the idle, lazy, simple people they can entice." These are persuaded that "they shall go into a place where food shall drop into their mouths, and being thus deluded they take courage and are transported. But not finding what was promised, their courage abates and their minds being dejected, their work is according."[16] Bullock noted, moreover, that God, "the author of all good things, hath not in all this time been pleased to let any man look further than tobacco."[17] Here he was in hopes that a turn of events was about to take place. Unlike critics who looked at the area from the outside and stressed only institutional reforms, Bullock felt himself part of the colony and emphasized that Virginia's plight resulted from moral causes as well. He proposed administrative reforms aimed not at greater coercion but at more local control of colonial government to encourage all to take an interest in the commonwealth. He stoutly condemned the mischief of "sending strangers to govern this country, who neither know the people nor their customs, neither they him."[18]

Actions and statements alike by natives of Virginia and Maryland throughout the colonial period reveal that they recognized the disadvantages of a system dedicated almost entirely to personal economic advancement. In 1632 the Virginia Assembly complained that they "the poor planters of this colony have a long time groaned under the cruel dealings of unconscionable merchants, who have by needless and unprofitable commodities always pre-engaged the inhabitants in debts of tobacco to the value almost of their ensuing crops, whereby we have necessarily been tied to planting of that bad commodity from which otherwise we had willingly declined." [19] However much English merchants helped fix staple agriculture on Virginia and Maryland, this would not have been possible without the co-operation of the planters, whose allegiance to the doctrine of allurement made the one-crop system inevitable. They were only concerned with exploiting their own lands for profit, and most of them utterly lacked the sensitivity to the mechanisms of organized trade and co-operative liaisons all over the empire which would have been necessary if they were to have done their own trading. They produced and produced, whether tobacco was in demand or not.

As early as 1630, when tobacco prices were very low, planters had shown an interest in cultivating grains. Yet "there was never a prolonged disposition on the part of the people of the Colony to abandon for any length of time the culture of the plant and direct their attention to other products. This disinclination was as notable in the closing as in the early part of the century." [20] Although there were campaigns to get away from the sole production of tobacco throughout the colonial period, interest always waxed during periods of declining tobacco prices and waned during times of prosperity. It was observed that "the moment the price of tobacco rises, other produce is laid aside." [21] Often planters felt themselves caught on a treadmill, but a struggle with high stakes in a chaotic economic system was the only thing they understood. In 1685 William Byrd I hoped that "tobacco may do well this year. All agree it's generally better than hath been of late years." [22] Yet the next year he admitted that the large crops endangered the market, "but the case hath been the same these forty or fifty years." He then remarked wistfully,

"I could wish we had some more certain commodity to rely on but see no hopes of it." [23]

The desire of the Crown in the 1680's to limit tobacco production and promote towns was not opposed by the colonists, who were suffering at the time from overproduction. A Colonel Spencer wrote to England that Virginians "are now grown sensible that our present necessities and too much to be doubted future miseries are much heightened by our wild and rambling way of living," and they "therefore are desirous of cohabitation." While the Assembly had passed a law calling for a town in every county, Spencer admitted that it would probably "miss its wished effect if not totally miscarry by the multiplicity of places appointed for towns." [24] In 1688 an Englishman called this situation an example of everyone's "being more solicitous for a private interest and conveniency than for a public," for "they will either be for making forty towns at once, that is two in every county, or none at all." [25] Although natives of the two colonies were aware of their problems, because of their individualism they could not effect any meaningful change in the way things were.

At the same time, the Carolina proprietors were embarking on a scheme of colonization which was not intended to entice the idle multitudes of England to a land of opportunity. They were mainly interested in operating a land office to attract settlers from other colonies. A new assessment of the home situation had brought a reversal of thinking, and men no longer felt that emigration was in the interest of the mother country. Because the proprietors wanted to promote "cohabitation," no seigniory or barony was to interfere with compact settlements and the Fundamental Constitutions provided for port towns.[26] It was almost axiomatic that the model which they sought to imitate was New England. In a letter in 1671 Lord Ashley stressed towns as "the chief thing that hath given New England so much the advantage over Virginia and advanced that plantation in so short a time to the height it is now at." [27] The proprietors wanted to avoid the food scarcities which had resulted in Virginia from the immediate search for profit, and in 1669 they told the governor not to permit the cultivation of staples for export until an adequate food supply was assured.[28] The tension between the goals of profit and community did not, however, take long to develop in South Carolina. The proprietors were also concerned about revenues to pay for supplies, and so in 1677 they suggested that the settlers "be but so industrious as to plant tobacco or any other thing to draw a trade to you until we can furnish you with more profitable plants."[29]

Even though the proprietors did not really object to tobacco, the settlers did not particularly find it attractive after trying it out. As Thomas Ashe explained in 1682, because of difficulties encountered in planting and curing and the fact that the European market was already oversupplied, "they do not much regard or encourage its planting, having already before them better and more profitable designs in action."[30] In fact such profitable designs did not really materialize until rice became the colony's staple after the turn of the century. South Carolina was consequently different from Virginia in that staple agriculture required more than a generation to take hold. Something more was operative in the attitudes of the early South Carolinians than the logic of Ashe's argument concerning market conditions. Tobacco was already beginning to glut the market when Maryland was settled; yet this did not prevent men there from producing it, nor did overproduction stop individual planters from adding even more to the surplus.

If one-crop agriculture and the absence of towns and reciprocal economic relationships can be taken as an evidence of the failure of a sense of community and social purpose, the existence of Charleston and the absence of a single-crop economy for several decades may indicate that some sense of community and of purpose influenced the actions of the early settlers of South Carolina. The initial vision in the tobacco colonies, though apparently more brilliant, had collapsed far more rapidly and spectacularly. It had failed too soon to manifest itself in the outward symbols which Penn had considered so essential to the success of his "holy experiment." South Carolina at least had some of these symbols, for by the 1680's the achievement of Charleston was something Virginia could not even then boast, much less after only a few years of settlement. Thomas Ashe praised the town in 1682 for being "very commodiously situated" with respect to the many rivers of the area, so that "at the tide or ebb the planters may bring their commodities to the town." [31] Doubtless geography figured in the development of Charleston as Ashe's description of it suggests, but it may be argued that Norfolk was almost as well situated with respect to the Chesapeake Bay colonies. Ironically, Charleston represented the climax of an achievement rather than the beginning. No other significant town appeared. Though additional counties were laid out in 1682, the usual machinery of county administration did not develop. Some of the elements of this failure can be found in the proprietors' policy of permitting a reasonable choice in the location of lands, with the result that settlement followed the courses of the rivers and not the orderly plan which they had drafted.[32]

South Carolina had always had elements opposed to the general aims of an organized society. In 1671 Governor West wrote Lord Ashley that he had published some orders "for the better keeping of the sabbath day and for preserving our stock this year. But some hot spirited persons being ambitious of perpetuating their own wicked inclinations, spurned at all order and good government, fearing to be reduced from a sordid beastly life." The reply of one member of the opposition reveals that at the heart of the controversy lay the old problem of defining the conditions of industry in a new settlement. He described West as "feeling authority creeping upon him" and assuring the people that "he would afflict and inflict punishment upon them if they did swear and prophane." Most important, there was "not a word of encouragement to industry and planting." [33] The proprietors had early confronted the problem of idleness in the form of settlers who relied overmuch upon the provisions sent from abroad. In 1679 they informed the governor that they had heard that "many persons who arrive in our province to plant do spend their time idly and consume what they bring with them," and so they are forced to leave. To "excuse their own ill husbandry" they lay "the blame on the country and the nature of the soil, to the discouragement of others." The governor was told to do "as much as you may to discountenance debauchery and idleness." [34]

In 1684 the proprietors complained that "if the inhabitants of Carolina did plant in towns and villages, their lives would be more comfortable and their trade better carried on and be much more secure." [35] In 1694 announcement was made that the Quaker proprietor John Archdale was to be sent as governor, and he would "bring over a good number of industrious people of good stock and of such a reputation here that if they come to be well settled, they will encourage great numbers to follow and be a means to have the country well peopled." Archdale was told to "endeavor the building of a new town or towns in such places as you shall think most healthful and commodious for commerce and trade." [36] Nevertheless, the proprietors failed to check the slow but steady drift away from orderly settlement and "cohabitation." Being less zealous than the leaders of the Virginia Company, they contented themselves more with advice than with elaborate programs and so in practice acquiesced in what was taking place.

Rice production began about 1695 although there was considerable economic diversity as late as 1710. [37] A complaint of the governor in 1720 shows that by then the major planters had come to act in accordance with the psychology of allurement. He lamented the fact that silk and indigo had been abandoned in favor of other commodities which were "found to yield the planters more profit." He also noted that "several useful manufactures might be gone upon in this province to good advantage, but our planters applying themselves almost wholly to the making rice, pitch, and tar, they do not think thereof." [38] As a food product rice never received the criticism that was heaped on tobacco, but many expressed a similar concern about excessive dedication to this staple. There was need "to come off . . . the darling rice" said one planter in the *South Carolina Gazette* in 1747, but that same year "Patricola" argued that only by granting large bounties could sufficient "rewards" be given to induce even "the industrious adventurers" to turn to new commodities.[39] Four years before, some South Carolina planters visiting Georgia "plainly confessed their error in pursuing almost solely the planting of rice for so many years without turning their thoughts to other things which would be a profitable and a proper product of this land and climate. They owned that the market for rice was overstocked in Europe."[40] Unlike the Chesapeake colonists, South Carolinians were able not many years after this to find some relief in a second staple, indigo.[41]

In 1729 the king ordered eleven townships to be laid out in the South Carolina interior in which every settler was to have an in-lot and an out-lot. In the preamble to one of the instructions drawn up by the Board of Trade the acknowledged success of townships in the settlement of New England was stressed. In a few cases, where there was strong ecclesiastical control, the towns maintained some sort of community life for a time, but eventually the rural town system was absorbed by the plantation system.[42] In fact, the period from 1733 to 1760 was marked "by a wild orgy of land-grabbing and slave importation by the planter class, in which the greed for private gain counteracted efforts for the public good."[43]

In contrast to the other southern colonies, North Carolina represented not so much the disintegration and failure of a sense of community and of social vision as the almost total absence of both. According to C. M. Andrews, the early settlers were left largely to fend for themselves. Most were barely able to make a living, and "because of poverty and an almost entire absence of religious institutions and the restraining influences of a settled life, they and the people generally got a reputation for restlessness, quarrels, disputes, and factional feuds."[44] The colony for many years had essentially an iso-

lated small farm economy although there were some plantations.[45] Its first town, Bath, was not founded until 1705, but
the lower Cape Fear settlement actually began in 1727 with
the founding of Brunswick.[46] Although North Carolina
evolved somewhat in the direction of a more organized social
life, observers continued to point to failures in achievement.

Early in the eighteenth century, John Urmstone, a missionary, noted the absence of an organized economic life within
the colony, where instead of reciprocal relationships "all seem
to live by their own hands of their own produce, and what
they can spare goes for foreign goods." [47] Governor George
Burrington in 1732 hoped that eventually such improvements
as silk culture "may be undertaken to increase the trade of
Great Britain." But he confessed to the Lords of Trade that
"the inhabitants of North Carolina are not industrious but
subtle and crafty to admiration." [48] Gabriel Johnston, Burrington's successor, was even more unhappy about the general
disorder and lack of application. He attributed the chaos of
public business "to the want of a town near the center of the
country where all the offices ought to be kept. But the people
both here and in Virginia are very far from being fond of
towns." He was pleased, however, to have "prevailed so far,
though not without great opposition, to get a law passed for
establishing a town on the forks of Cape Fear River." [49] In
1749 he wrote that for fifteen years he had been engaged in "a
very laborious work" of "civilizing a wild barbarous people
and endeavoring at least to bring them on a par with our neighboring colonies." [50]

The southern colonies in the middle of the eighteenth century had certain basic similarities, which they shared with the
sugar colonies of the West Indies.[51] The origins and initial
development of each may have been different, but they had
come to resemble each other more than any of them resembled the colonies to the north. It was not especially easy for
men living in the southern colonies to answer criticisms that
they had failed to develop the institutions their northern
neighbors had, for these men only too willingly acknowl-

edged shortcomings in their own societies. At the same time they had more or less freely chosen to follow the way of life others condemned—indeed they had as passionately responded to its appeals as they had to the beauties of the land where they had settled. If their commitment was ambivalent, this only complicated the need they felt to explain themselves. In the process of articulating their allegiance and their reservations they defined a style of life and a set of values which can appropriately be called Southern.

To the eternal reproach of their laziness

4

The celebration of the triumph of freedom and opportunity —the oldest and certainly the most persistent literary form of the southern colonies—served from the time of Hamor and Rolf to vindicate the doctrine of allurement and hence the way of life of these societies. Since some men were economically successful and enjoyed great freedom in their rise in the world, these expressions cannot be regarded as sheer bombast. They were accurate, potentially, for everyone. A good example of this literature of celebration is John Hammond's *Leah and Rachel* of 1656. The author's purpose was to unite the experiences of Virginia and Maryland by characterizing them as "the two fruitful sisters." He sought as well to refute the aspersion that the country was "an unhealthy place, a nest of rogues, whores, dissolute and rooking persons, a place of intolerable labor, bad usage, and hard diet, etc." [1]

Hammond admitted the truth of these charges as regards the first years of Virginia, blaming the adventurers for their "avarice and inhumanity" in emptying jails, embezzling food, and indulging in wicked practices including martial law. Finally "the bondage was taken off, the people set free and had lands assigned to each of them to live of themselves and enjoy the benefit of their own industry; men then began to call what they labored for their own." After the disastrous

1622 massacre the people again began "to gather wealth, which they rather profusely spent (as gotten with ease) than providently husbanded or aimed at any public good or to make a country for posterity." For several reasons many were discouraged from coming, "who rather cast their eyes on the barren and freezing soil of New England than to join with such an indigent and sottish people as were reported to be in Virginia." Yet all this time the colony was not "without divers honest and virtuous inhabitants, who observing the general neglect and licentiousness there caused assemblies to be called and laws to be made tending to the glory of God, the severe suppression of vices," and the planting of corn. "The inhabitants now finding the benefit of their industries began to look with delight on their increasing stocks (as nothing more pleasurable than profit), to take pride in their plentifully furnished tables, to grow not only civil but great observers of the sabbath, to stand upon their reputations, and to be ashamed of that notorious manner of life they had formerly lived and wallowed in." [2]

It is not entirely clear why profit should have led to such a decline after the massacre and yet have virtually effected the subsequent reform. For while laws did figure in Hammond's scheme, the reform really began in the hearts of the virtuous people who made the laws, and it was carried through by the allurements of gain, the key for Hammond to the successful functioning of the society. "Those servants that will be industrious may in their time of service gain a competent estate," he insisted. Allurement seems actually to have caused a moral change in those who responded to it, for "of such a happy inclination is the country that many who in England have been lewd and idle, there, in emulation or imitation . . . of the industry of those they find there, not only grow ashamed of their former courses but abhor to hear of them, and in small time wipe off those stains they have formerly been tainted with." For the incorrigible, however, there were "severe and wholesome laws and remedies made, provided, and duly put in execution." [3] Like earlier Virginians such as Hamor, Hammond saw economic freedom as a moral good and laws as a punishment of the morally bad.

Indeed economic freedom was considered the substance of the good society and a certain friendliness, decorum, and leisurely activity its form. Servants did not work as hard as those in England, Hammond maintained. Actually "little or nothing is done in winter time. None ever work before sunrising nor after sunset. In the summer they rest, sleep or exercise themselves five hours in the heat of the day. Saturday afternoon is always their own. The old holidays are observed and the sabbath spent in good exercises." The inhabitants as a whole were "generally affable, courteous and very assistant to strangers (for what but plenty makes hospitality and good neighborhood)." [4] This early tribute to Southern hospitality was both a mode of conceptualizing social order and unity and a refutation of the criticisms of institutional shortcomings. Social unity was viewed in terms of the form in which human intercourse took place—not as deriving from laws and formal institutions as it had been for coercionists, nor from a community of belief in God and love for one another as it had been for early Puritans. Such a mode of conceptualization had the obvious utility that it was independent of the formal institutions these colonies were criticized for lacking. It did not matter if there were hardly any inns and public houses. The gracious hospitality of the inhabitants made them unnecessary.

This is not to say that hospitality was a myth. For men to believe that theirs were societies of graciousness and order was in some sense to make them so. More important, this was an ideal or an aspiration—related to the early fascination with a Golden Age of ease and plenty—which men held even though they might often fail to live it. The emphasis upon unlimited opportunity suggested busy lives and economic triumph. At the same time, though paradoxically, the image of graciousness and leisure suggested in its way a certain quality of tranquil aloofness toward such endeavor.

Like its sister colonies to the north, South Carolina also had its celebrants of freedom and opportunity. In 1763 one resident boasted that it had "long thrown off that drooping and languishing state its first fine-spun constitution kept it under, and it is now become one of the most opulent and thriving among the British colonies." [5] The existence of Charleston was of incalculable value to the celebrants of the colony. In the early 1770's another resident described it as "in every respect the most eminent and by far the richest city in the southern district of North America." This writer further related the prosperity of the colony to what he considered the religious and national harmony of the inhabitants, who were from the "beginning renowned for concord, complaisance, courteousness, and tenderness towards each other and more so towards foreigners without regard or respect of nation or religion." [6]

Beyond the necessity of explaining themselves to the world, southern colonists also felt called upon to vindicate America itself—or at least that part which was responsible for alluring them with the opportunities they so much insisted upon. Here it is enlightening to compare their approach with similar attempts at vindication by Pennsylvanians. In 1686 William Penn published several letters from the settlers of the colony as an antidote to "divers false reports going about town and country to the injury of the province of Pennsylvania." In one of the letters Dr. Nicholas More denied the truth of evil reports that people were starving, that the land was "so barren, the climate so hot that English grain, roots, and herbs do not come to maturity; and what grows, to be little worth." It may have been true that "there was an indifferent plenty of most things" when men were just clearing the land, but "since that our lands have been grateful to us and have begun to reward our labors by abounding crops of corn this year." [7] The year before Penn had also asserted that the "earth, by God's blessing, has more than answered our expectation." [8] The reaction of both men was to vindicate the richness of the land by stressing what industry had made it yield. Indirectly this was an assertion of the virtue of their society as the cause or at least the occasion of God's abundantly blessing the land.

The reaction in Virginia and Maryland was generally quite the opposite—to defend the natural fruitfulness of the land independently of those who had settled it. This tendency can already be seen in the dark days of the Virginia Company, when there was really nothing in the way of human achievement to take credit for. In 1612 a writer, describing the desperate conditions before the arrival of aid from England, noted that "the occasion was only our own for want of providence, industry, and government and not the barrenness and defect of the country as is generally supposed." [9] At the time such a defense had great religious significance, for to attribute barrenness to the land was equivalent to denying God's blessings of allurement. The Rev. Alexander Whitaker promised a terrible punishment to "those spirits of slander whom the devil hath stirred up to speak evil of this good land." [10] Even after a degree of prosperity had arrived, writers continued to attribute to the land an independent quality of wealth and worthiness. John Hammond referred to the "odiums and cruel slanders cast on those two famous countries of Virginia and Maryland, whereby those countries not only are many times at a stand, but are in danger to moulder away and come in time to nothing; nor is there anything but the fertility and natural gratefulness of them left a remedy to prevent it." [11]

To stress the worthiness of the land itself, however, only evaded questions about the accomplishments which the blessings of allurement were supposed to have stimulated. At the same time the insistence on its amazing fertility contained a certain ominous suggestion that the very ease of reaping benefits might become a temptation to abandon industry. In the eyes of Robert Beverley the people of Virginia depended "altogether upon the liberality of nature without endeavoring to improve its gifts by art or industry. They spunge upon the blessings of a warm sun and a fruitful soil and almost grudge the pains of gathering in the bounties of the earth." His purpose in calling attention to "this slothful indolence" among his countrymen in his *History and Present State of Virginia* (1705) was to "rouse them out of their lethargy and excite them to make the most of all those happy advantages which nature has given them." [12] Beverley's view of Virginia's troubles was essentially a moral one, and his book was in its way a jeremiad, calling upon men to search the frame of their hearts, repent, and be up and doing. Then the land would validate their endeavors, for the fault lay not in it but in the hearts of the people. If they would "be persuaded to be temperate and take due care of themselves," he insisted, "I believe it is as healthy a country as any under heaven, but the extraordinary pleasantness of the weather and the goodness of the fruit lead people into many temptations." [13] Although Beverley did not phrase his exhortation in theological terms, what he was actually doing was calling upon his readers to use rightly the gifts of God.

In his *History of the Dividing Line betwixt Virginia and North Carolina, Run in the Year of Our Lord 1728*, William Byrd wrote that the first settlers in Jamestown had "detested work more than famine." Later the Company sent more laborers, "who however took care not to kill themselves with work." [14] If sloth was man's basic weakness, no wonder idleness was general among men in southern Virginia and North Carolina, where "the air is so mild and the soil so fruitful that very little labor is required to fill their bellies." To provide clothing made no demands of labor either, for "a very little of that will suffice in so temperate a climate." [15] In his famous description of the "Lubberland" of North Carolina, Byrd treated laziness as a kind of original sin. For him there had been no dialectic in recent history of beginning industry, temptation, and then a fall into sloth; rather " 'tis a thorough aversion to labor that makes people file off to North Carolina, where plenty and a warm sun confirm them in their disposition to laziness for their whole lives." [16] Perhaps Byrd was less optimistic than Beverley about the likelihood of repentance, for he never published this sustained lamentation on the great sin of laziness.

When referring to laziness or indolence in the southern colonies, possibly men simply meant supine lassitude. In his description of Lubberland, Byrd wittily remarked that the people did "not know Sunday from any other day any more than Robinson Crusoe did, which would give them a great advantage were they given to be industrious. But they keep so many Sabbaths every week that their disregard of the seventh day has no manner of cruelty in it either to servants or cattle." [17] Yet in 1715 the North Carolina legislature had enacted a law requiring attendance at divine service and decreeing that no "person or persons whatsoever shall do or exercise any worldly labor, business or work of their ordinary callings or shall employ themselves either by hunting or fishing on that day or any part thereof." [18]

Just as it seems unlikely that many really spent their whole lives lying around, so also it seems doubtful that there was any real problem of idleness in the form of persons without any means of livelihood. This had been the major problem in England which colonization was to have cured. Many of the complaints about idleness during the first years of settlement doubtless referred to confused and ineffectual activity on the part of men whose social displacement at home was compounded by the strangeness of the New World environment. This was particularly true in early Virginia because of the complete novelty of the situation, the general confusion as to what was expected, the physical hardships, and the fact that many brought over to cure their idleness—sons of noblemen particularly—were utterly unprepared to deal with practical matters. In each of the colonies, however, references to this kind of confusion were soon replaced by complaints about the shortage of labor. Conceivably such shortages could have been due to the refusal of the perversely lazy to do anything. Yet on closer examination the problem seems not to have been putting the unoccupied to work, but changing the work patterns of the occupied.

In March of 1756 Governor Arthur Dobbs of North Carolina condemned the efforts of the colonists to avoid being drafted into the militia and accused them of being "so indolent and relaxed by not having the laws executed that they won't submit to government." [19] The previous year he had addressed the colonial legislature on the necessity of a law "to oblige planters who have small properties to bring up their children to industry or to bind out their children to necessary trades, many of whom breed up their children to sloth and idleness, to the public loss of the society." By these means "artificers' wages might be regulated by affording the necessaries of life cheaper, the excessive price of which at present is a great discouragement to the improvement of the province." [20] It seems doubtful that the colonists whom Dobbs criticized for failing to support the militia and enter the artisan class had no kind of livelihood. More likely they were busy with their own projects and were unwilling to forgo them. The distinction between industry and idleness in Dobbs's criticisms was not between inactivity and work, but between socially useful endeavor aimed at the "improvement" and defense of the colony and its opposite.

In his concern with work as a social activity performed in the context of a well-ordered community, Dobbs was simply expressing the common assumption of the age. What had really bothered social critics in England had been the fact that idleness meant large numbers of people having no meaningful place in society and making no useful contribution to it. In each of the southern colonies men were initially concerned about idleness because of the absence of an orderly society in which people knew what to do and performed their tasks accordingly. If in later years many critics tended largely to emphasize institutional reforms—establishing towns and diversifying agriculture—rather than putting the idle multitudes to work, this would seem to suggest that most of the people were busy enough, in pursuing their own advantage.

Coercionists and Puritans would have agreed that the most zealous pursuit of private ends unsubordinated to larger social considerations would utterly fail to qualify as industry. Both freely called such activity idleness. Attractionists, however, included this pursuit within the definition of industry, so that for them idleness meant both the failure to take advantage of opportunities and the failure to perform socially useful tasks.

In accordance with the doctrine of allurement these two aspects of labor should have harmonized with one another. Still, the Virginia Company took no chances when it advised those in charge to "take care that your mariners that go for wages do not mar your trade, for those that mind not to inhabit for a little gain will debase the estimation of exchange and hinder the trade forever after." Yet in June of 1607 the Council in Virginia wrote to London that these men had lost and broken many tools in gathering sassafras roots, "our easiest and richest commodity," besides drawing colonists away from their assigned tasks.[21] In 1610 the practice of seeking private gain was evidently general enough to merit the censure of a commentator, who referred specifically to the "secure negligence and improvidence, when every man sharked for his present booty but was altogether careless of succeeding penury." He cited an "incredible example of their idleness," given by Sir Thomas Gates, who had "seen some of them eat their fish raw rather than they would go a stone's cast to fetch wood and dress it." [22] This incident may be interpreted as an example of ineptitude with regard even to such little things as knowing how to prepare meals properly. It may, however, admit of another interpretation. Conceivably the men were too busy seeking personal gain to be bothered.

It seems clear that many of those accused in the early days of idleness were only idle when judged from a social perspective. They were busily, even frantically, responding to the allurements which the New World offered. The socially disruptive character of such activities became increasingly obvious in the years after 1607, and those who sought to curb them by force were men whose allegiance to labor as the pursuit of personal profit was subordinated to their support of an orderly and regulated social system. Long after he had left Virginia, Captain John Smith wrote that "the desire of present gain in many is so violent and the endeavors of many undertakers so negligent, everyone so regarding his private, that it is hard to effect any public good and impossible to bring them into a body, rule, or order unless both authority and money assist experiences." [23]

While opportunities enticed men in the southern colonies into vigorous activity, it was not into industry which was meaningfully related to the kind of elaborate and orderly society which had been expected and of which men assumed labor must be a part. Where there were few towns or even villages, where there was no busy commercial life involving the interchange of services of many different classes of people, it seemed that everyone must be lazy because there was so little evidence of the fruits that industry ought to have borne. Both Beverley and Byrd, among others, praised beavers for their industry. To Beverley "the admirable economy of the beavers deserves to be particularly remembered. They cohabit in one house, are incorporated in a regular form of government something like monarchy." [24] Byrd praised them as the most intelligent and industrious animals in the world, living "in large societies or communities" and having "a fine organization as well as good police among themselves." [25] How little Virginians were like beavers goes without saying.

Significantly, Beverley's judgment of the first Virginia colonists followed the judgments of early writers like Smith —with the difference that Beverley favored the term laziness in place of the earlier preference for idleness. He severely criticized the first settlers, who, "taking all to be gold that glittered, ran into the utmost distraction, neglecting both the necessary defense of their lives from the Indians and the support of their bodies by security of provisions." Hence, he noted, they were forced to live from day to day off the land like "some of the laziest Indians." [26] The failure in his opinion of the Virginia Company was due to the fact that "the chief design of all parties concerned was to fetch away the treasure from thence, aiming more at sudden gain than to form any regular colony or establish a settlement in such a manner as to make it a lasting happiness to the country." [27]

Repeatedly, Beverley and Byrd indicated their desire for a

more complex social context. Only because they implicitly accepted "cohabitation" and all it suggested as worthwhile standards could they judge the inhabitants of Virginia as lazy for failing to perform labor which accorded with these standards. Beverley specifically related laziness to "the unfortunate method of the settlement and want of cohabitation." This, he had previously indicated, was due to several factors: "The liberty of taking up land and the ambition each man had of being lord of a vast though unimproved territory, together with the advantage of the many rivers which afforded a commodious road for shipping at every man's door, has made the country fall into such an unhappy settlement and course of trade that to this day they have not any one place of cohabitation among them that may reasonably bear the name of a town." [28] In 1737 Byrd zealously sought to promote "cohabitation" with his plan for developing Richmond "in a pleasant and healthy situation and well supplied with springs of good water." [29] Although the jeremiads of these two men represented a desire for the kind of society the age accepted as natural, they were also an admission of how strongly colonists were attached to the way things were. Repentance seemed the only answer since, as the Rev. Hugh Jones, an English commentator, accurately remarked, "neither the interest nor the inclinations of the Virginians induce them to cohabit in towns." [30]

The form of agriculture in the southern colonies, so intimately connected with the scattered settlement, also came in for vigorous attack from Beverley and Byrd. Again it is evident that what they were calling laziness was the failure to establish a diversified economy, not a lack of busyness on the part of the planters in cultivating their money crops. In 1728 Byrd wrote that Virginia had a "happy climate abounding so much with everything that is necessary that it leaves little for industry to do." Then he immediately went on to point out that his "countrymen devote themselves to the making tobacco, to the utter neglect of all other improvements." [31] He was certain that North Carolina flax was the finest in the world, yet colonists there were "so intolerably lazy they seldom take the trouble to propagate it." [32]

The judgment of laziness also derived from the fact that men had certain notions of what the outward manifestations of labor should be—neat houses and barns, orderly fields— and these were generally lacking. Visitors noted that tobacco, for example, was planted in small patches scattered chaotically over large plantations. In the low country of South Carolina and Georgia land was monopolized in large parcels and remained uncleared, leaving the area with an even less cultivated appearance than the Chesapeake country.[33] John Lawson confessed that he had never seen "one acre of land managed as it ought to be in Carolina" and observed that "were they as negligent in their husbandry in Europe as they are in Carolina, their land would produce nothing but weeds and straw." [34] By European standards the inhabitants of the southern colonies certainly did not engage in laborious agricultural practices, but their careless methods of soil exploitation yielded immediate gains—and that was what mattered to them. William Byrd's description of "the happy effects of industry" in a particular family indicates that he too responded to neatness, care, and order as visual evidence of industry. In this family "everyone looked tidy and clean and carried in their countenances the cheerful marks of plenty. We saw no drones there, which are but too common, alas, in that part of the world." [35]

The opinion was widespread that sloth also lay at the root of the practice of importing most of the necessities and (much worse) the luxuries of life. Beverley described Virginians as "such abominable ill-husbands that though their country be overrun with wood, yet they have all their wooden ware from England . . . to the eternal reproach of their laziness." [36] Similarly a French Huguenot observed of the Virginians in the late seventeenth century that with tobacco "they buy land, they rent it, they buy cattle; and as they can get anything they need in exchange for this commodity, they become so lazy that they send to England for clothes, linen, hats," and so on and on. The importation of luxury items by the wealthy, moreover, contributed to the impression that they led idle and self-indulgent lives anyway. To this commentator it seemed that the gentlemen of Virginia spent "most of their time visiting each other." [37] There would seem to be no reason to question the accuracy of this observation, but still one must explain such statements as Hugh Jones's that "tobacco requires a great deal of skill and trouble in the right management of it." [38] In 1704 John Blair wrote that the people of North Carolina insisted that any religious offices be performed on Sunday, "for they won't spare time of another day." [39] What has been said previously about the nature of economic life in these colonies is further evidence that men there were often aggressively, ruthlessly busy in advancing their affairs.

The problem then is to explain why most men in the southern colonies *seemed* to lead idle lives when in actuality they were often very busy. The answer lies in the fact that they were not busy all of the time. Diligent labor of the sort Max Weber has associated with the "spirit of capitalism" is not necessary if men work mainly for gain, for there is no reason why they should be busy during periods when activity will yield no reward. Hunters and herders, as well as farmers and planters, could conceivably have had and did have many periods of free time. This sporadic inactivity would have contributed to an impression of idleness, which belied the underlying reality. With "the great labor about tobacco being only in summertime," the Virginia planters "acquire great habits of idleness all the rest of the year," a description of the colony noted.[40] Money gave the wealthy the means for leisured self-indulgence between periods of activity, and the lesser sort filled their days as best they could. As Lewis Cecil Gray has said of the lower classes, their lives were "characterized by a great deal of laborious work unrelieved by labor-saving devices that might have been provided under a commercial economy, alternating with long periods of leisure." [41]

John Brickell voiced a traditional complaint against laborers in the southern colonies when he wrote that in North Carolina they lived "after a very loose and indolent manner, for if they work two days in the week they generally drink and are idle all the rest (provisions and liquors being so very cheap)." [42] Not only did a person not have to work diligently to attain the level of economic well-being he desired, but the inadequate labor supply and consequently high wages made it possible for those of very moderate ambition to subsist without much effort at all. If a man must work for six days in England to get enough to live on, there was no reason why the laborer in the colonies should not stop after two if he could earn as much in the shorter time. Relatively few, however, seem to have found such an alternative particularly attractive, and those who wanted to better themselves economically had to work hard—but not all the time.

It was the non-rational character of labor in the southern colonies—whether it was aimed simply at subsistence or at economic advancement—rather than the absence of any application at all that made men there seem idle. One cannot help recalling young Benjamin Franklin trudging the streets of Philadelphia in the early morning and his remark that he took great care not only to be industrious but to appear industrious. Orderliness, diligence, careful planning—all the traits which Franklin exemplified and which a great many men of the age would seem to have considered proofs of industry—were not in conspicuous evidence in the southern colonies. The residents of Bertie and Edgecombe precincts in North Carolina betrayed a typical disdain for orderly and careful acquisition of wealth when they wrote Governor Johnston in 1735 that they had settled and improved their lands "with much labor from the barren woods" and at the same time admitted that many had simply trusted "to what providence would lay in our way for food—sometimes a deer or bear and sometimes a racoon and many days nothing, a rare feast for industrious Protestants." [43] The reasons for patterns of industry in a society, as Weber has shown, are not based simply upon economic considerations. None of the southern colonies had either the intellectual climate to favor diligence or the social and economic structure to further it. Byrd was delighted with the pains and good management of one planter who had a fine orchard, "which is not common in that indolent climate; nor is it at all strange that such improvident people, who take no thought for the morrow, should save themselves the trouble to make improvements that will not pay them for several years to come." [44]

The southern colonies were not without examples of industrious people like Franklin, but it was generally observed that by and large most of them were recently arrived foreign Protestants, who usually lived in communities by themselves. The evangelist George Whitefield was surprised and pleased with the colony of Swiss in Georgia and wrote in his journal that "surely they speak not truth who say the Georgia people have been idle, for I never saw more laborious people than are in these villages." [45] In 1752 Bishop Spangenburg of the Moravian Church divided the inhabitants of North Carolina into two classes: "Some are natives of the state; these can endure the climate pretty well but are naturally indolent and sluggish. Others have come here from England, Scotland, and the northern colonies." [46] By this comparison he probably did not mean that all the newcomers were industrious workers, but where immigrants could be identified as groups they remained conspicuous because they were different. Coming after the general patterns of social life had been established, they had the choice of remaining separate and different or of adapting themselves to the ways of the majority. No immigrant group was either large enough or united enough to change the general social context into which it moved. Hence the situation of chaotic self-aggrandizement flourished unchecked for all practical purposes.

The impression of laziness might further have been enhanced by the social disorder which this orientation caused. Doubtless it had the effect of creating bewilderment among many, and this would have increased the ineffectual character of their actions. Eliza Lucas of South Carolina noted in her journal in 1742 that "the poorer sort are the most indolent people in the world, or they would never be wretched in so plentiful a country as this." [47] Such a statement assumed that social conditions can have no limiting influence on the individual in his pursuit of gain and thus that he is solely responsible for his own success or failure. It is not inconsistent to emphasize self-aggrandizement and at the same time to admit that poverty and failure existed in these colonies. The conditions of success were at best uncertain, and many must have fallen by the way. To explain failure of all sorts in terms of laziness was only natural to men accustomed to a moralistic and personalistic outlook. Indirectly it vindicated their way of life by fixing sole responsibility upon those who did not succeed. If opportunities failed to allure, this was simply evidence that the individual was too perverse to respond. One might employ a theological parallel concerning the doctrine of allurement. Early attractionists had assumed that the enticing powers of opportunity were irresistible and irreversible. Rolf and Hamor, Beverley and Byrd, by contrast, were really Arminians. They assumed that men could resist enticements of their own free wills and so remain idle. But if they did, they had no one to blame for their failures but themselves.

The "Secret History" of his experiences while surveying the boundary line between Virginia and North Carolina, which Byrd wrote for private circulation, contains many casual references to situations of social confusion, poverty, and injustice—references which Byrd did not comment on because he evidently assumed that his audience was familiar with these conditions. Yet when he organized the same material into *The History of the Dividing Line*, he felt that explanations were called for in a work intended for publication, and laziness was what he fixed upon. One very poignant example is his description in the "Secret History" of the family of Cornelius Keith, among whom Byrd had "never beheld such a scene of poverty in this happy part of the world. The hovel they lay in had no roof to cover those wretches from the injuries of the weather, but when it rained or was colder than ordinary, the whole family took refuge in a fodder stack." He observed further that the "man can read and write very well" and had a trade, yet he was "poorer than any Highland Scot or bogtrotting Irishman." In the *Dividing Line*, after describing this condition, Byrd remarked that "all his wants proceeded from indolence and not from misfortune. He had good land as well as good health and good limbs to work it, and besides had a trade very useful to all the inhabitants round about." [48] Similarly, the "Secret History" noted that one Andrew Dukes "had lately removed or rather run away hither from Maryland." Many things could have caused Dukes to run away, but the *Dividing Line* explained that he "was lately removed bag and baggage from Maryland, through a strong antipathy he had to work and paying his debts." [49]

All of the external factors which contributed to the impression of laziness were greatly magnified in men's minds. It was not simply that they sensed a want of community and of purposeful, organized social and economic life among themselves, but also that the absence of meaningful external restrictions and guideposts left the individual with no assurance that his labor was purposeful or industrious. Franklin could be certain that his rituals along the Philadelphia streets and in his shop gave him the appearance of being industrious because he knew what he had to do to create such an appearance, and he knew that his audience knew this also. Even if the isolated farmer or planter in the southern colonies had an audience, he neither knew what he ought to do nor had he any assurance that his audience knew either. Nevertheless, the jeremiads called such men to repentance for their failure to develop the kinds of societies which the founders had envisioned.

A generation after the initial settlement in America Puritan preachers too were using the jeremiad to express the sense of their society's failure to fulfill the ends to which it had originally been dedicated. Beverley and Byrd differed from their New England counterparts in concentrating exclusively upon laziness, yet this too has its parallel in the attitudes of the Puritans. In 1652 the Massachusetts General Court expressed a point of view in which "corruption itself now appeared not as a cause but a visitation of wrath." [50] For Beverley and Byrd sin itself was also seen as Virginia's great misfortune, not sickness nor natural disasters as in the case of Whitaker and Smith a century before. Part of the reason why the cry for repentance was so anguished lay in the fact that there had never been a clear vision analogous to the Puritans' City upon a Hill. Neither was there a clear notion about how to proceed in the present—only the sense of having failed, with the conviction that the failure was due to laziness and laziness, to the lush land.

The assertion that the lushness of the land actually caused laziness through the temptations it offered has a certain poetic truth. In enticing men into the pursuit of personal gain by permitting the cultivation of profitable staples, it had, socially speaking, tempted them into laziness. Also some of the careless practices they indulged in would not have been possible elsewhere. Taken as a statement of fact, however, it is difficult to see why conditions should not have affected women as much as men, yet both Byrd and John Lawson largely exempted them from the imputation of laziness.[51] The area, moreover, was no tropical paradise, where ripe fruits dropped into the mouths of contented idlers, as the repeated instances of starvation and near-starvation testify. Nevertheless, the traditional association of southern lands with tropical abundance, upon which the early explorers and propagandists had relied, was still widely accepted. John White had warned the early Puritans of the temptations to sloth in such regions at the same time that he praised the encouragements to industry in the harsh environment to the north. As it came to seem reasonable to Puritans and Quakers to justify their achievements in part by pointing to the natural obstacles they had to overcome in New England and Pennsylvania, so southern colonists came to explain their lack of achievement by pointing to a lush land, which supposedly had posed no obstacles.

At the same time that men were condemning the laziness of their society, they were praising its graciousness, order, and ease. The importance of maintaining allegiance to this ideal was enhanced by the necessity of refuting the criticisms of outsiders concerning the treatment of white servants and slaves. Beverley insisted that because he had heard "how strangely cruel and severe the service of this country is represented in some parts of England," he could not refrain from affirming "that generally their slaves are not worked near so hard nor so many hours in a day as the husbandmen and day laborers in England." [52] Such arguments reflected an obvious lack of assurance about the rectitude of the means that were being used for worldly advancement. At the same time, the emphasis upon ease reinforced the elements of irrationality in men's work patterns as well as their tendency toward self-indulgence. Beverley acknowledged that "here is the most good nature and hospitality practiced in the world both towards friends and strangers, but the worst of it is this generosity is attended now and then with a little too much intemperance." [53]

While it also seemed important to celebrate the opportunities which the area afforded the ambitious, the ambiguous element of minimizing the effort involved to seize these opportunities had persisted. When Byrd sought to induce a group of foreign Protestants to come to Virginia, he waxed eloquent about the "provisions of every kind which may be produced with little labor in the greatest plenty." [54] He argued that in his promotional venture, the Land of Eden, "everything will grow plentifully here to supply either the wants or wantonness of man." [55] In hinting at the attraction of ease and self-indulgence, such remarks further contributed to the atmosphere of uncertainty about the value and meaning of work. At the same time, the assumptions which underlay the jeremiad contradicted the protestations of ease and thus must have made men feel vaguely guilty about them. And so the emphasis upon industry and success became all the more important.

In stressing the theme of success the literature of celebration was as accurate as the jeremiad. The two simply dealt with different things. What the jeremiad lamented was the absence of industry in a social sense. What the literature of celebration proclaimed was the triumph of "industry" in a personal sense. Ironically this distinction was not clearly understood. Consequently, when one attempts to look beneath the lamentations of the jeremiad for any concrete suggestions, the fact emerges that both Beverley and Byrd, along with other commentators, conceived of the inadequacies of the social situation only as deterrents to individual profit. Byrd referred to a piece of property which "would be a valuable tract of land in any country but North Carolina, where for want of navigation and commerce the best estate affords little more than a coarse subsistence." [56] Beverley likewise regretted that the "unfortunate method of the settlement and want of cohabitation" prevented Virginians from making "beneficial use" of such crops as flax, hemp, cotton, and wool, "which might otherwise supply their necessities and leave the produce of tobacco to enrich them, when a gainful market can be found for it." [57] Yet it was useless to suggest the need for a more elaborate social context simply to increase individual profits.

What had happened was that the two historically separate definitions of labor and laziness—social and personal—had become confused in men's minds. What they condemned as laziness was the absence of rational, purposeful, socially oriented labor; and thus far they were following the traditional definition of work. At the same time the newer definition, busyness in pursuit of private gain, was to these men the only meaningful and practical evidence that a man was not lazy. Driven by the specter of laziness, unable to find personal and social goals which were meaningful and satisfying, many threw themselves even harder into the frantic pursuit of wealth to prove their industry. Yet this only increased economic chaos and social fragmentation, and so aggravated the very conditions which contributed to their feelings of laziness. The harder they worked on their isolated plantations, the lazier everyone seemed.

The more idle one felt oneself and one's fellows to be, the more difficult it became to cope with the fact that the pursuit of wealth did not necessarily keep men occupied all the time. But one had to keep busy—which is just what Byrd tried to do. Two entries in his diary—both in 1709—illustrate this. One evening in town he "went to dinner where I ate nothing but mutton hash. After dinner we played at cricket and then went to whist and I lost 30 shillings. I went home about 11 o'clock." Later in the year at home he "settled some accounts and read news. I ate fish for dinner which we catch in great quantity. It rained a little in the afternoon. I settled more accounts and played at billiards with my wife. In the evening I read more Italian and washed my feet." [58] Again the contrast with Franklin is striking. The latter left as a record of his life a public recital of the purposeful pursuit of virtue and advancement intended as an example for posterity. Byrd's record of aimless activities, which revealed his concern with accounting for every minute, was written in code and presumably intended for no one but himself.

Just as frenzied economic activity to avoid laziness only enhanced the awareness of it, so busyness also tended to aggravate the condition it was supposed to correct. These two elements of frustration were well set forth by Byrd in a description of himself entitled "Inamorato L'Oiseaux." He spoke of himself as not having been endowed by nature with a talent for industry. Laziness keeps a man in the degree in which he is born, while "diligence gives wings to ambition by which it soars up to the highest pitch of advancement." Then he went on to suggest his want of "constancy, which is another ingredient to raise a great fortune. To what purpose is it for a man to be always upon the wing if he only fly backward and forward. He must go right out or else he will never go far. He should fix one certain end in his own thoughts, and towards that all his designs and all his motions should unalterably tend. But poor Inamorato had too much mercury to fix to one thing." [59]

If the allurements of the New World had assumed the ambiguous character of beguilements, and if every effort to root out idleness only made men lazier, southern colonists were hopelessly condemned to "fly backward and forward." Yet if they would only repent and make themselves worthy of the land, perhaps it would no longer punish them by deceiving them.

5

In comparing early Virginia with New England, William Byrd admitted that although the saints "may be ridiculed for some pharisaical particularities in their worship and behavior, yet they were very useful subjects, as being frugal and industrious, giving no scandal or bad example, at least by any open and public vices." [1] Yet as early as 1668 this common assumption that Massachusetts represented the most acceptable form of colonial society had been questioned in England by Josiah Child. He reasoned that the mother country profited by emigration to the West Indies because "one Englishman with the blacks that work with him, accounting what they eat, use and wear, would make employment for four men in England." On the other hand, "of ten men that issue from us to New England and Ireland, what we send to or receive from them doth not employ one man in England." [2] Although propagandists since the days of Hakluyt had stressed the importance of settlements abroad as sources of trade, after the Restoration men began to reconsider the role of colonies in the light of the logic of the Navigation Laws. The more they came to examine the society of the saints, the less acceptable it seemed.

What was wanted, theorists reasoned, was not trade-oriented, town-centered societies modeled after English society as observed in New England. These colonies produced many of the same kinds of goods as the mother country and so were niggardly in their imports, while the industrious endeavors of their merchants and seamen took trade away from their British counterparts. By these new standards all the good advice and efforts of critics—including King Charles himself—concerning the southern colonies were entirely wrong. To promote towns in the colonies and to discourage revenue-producing staples was in fact the height of folly. Perhaps the most candid defense of everything the critics of the southern colonies were opposed to was made in 1714 by some customs commissioners in response to an act by the Jamaica Assembly creating new ports of entry on the island. They had no objection to the legislation provided it "will not encourage the inhabitants to reside in towns and there set up manufactures for the supply of their own necessities." Among other things such activity would "take off their hands which might be employed more to the benefit of this kingdom in planting and raising sugars and other commodities of that island." [3]

According to these criteria the southern colonies were not the failures they had been accused of being. Rather they were models for the saints to emulate. The Board of Trade informed the king in 1721 that "the commodities the people of Carolina take from Great Britain are all manner of clothing, woolen, linen, iron ware, brass and pewter, and all sorts of household goods. Having no manufactories of their own and their southerly situation will make them always dependent on Great Britain." [4] Staple crop production was obviously the most desirable form of activity for colonists to pursue—and the one least likely to lead to economic (and possibly political) independence. Even that horrid weed tobacco was at last redeemed from the ignominy it had labored under since the time of James I. Sir William Keith pointed out that "a great revenue is raised to the Crown of Britain by returns made in the produce of the plantations, especially in tobacco, which at the same time helps England to bring nearer to balance their unprofitable trade with France." [5]

The Navigation Laws became in fact an argument for perpetuating economic conditions in the southern colonies. Governor George Burrington wrote the Duke of Newcastle in 1731 that the colonists in North Carolina should be allowed larger quantities of land, for "if men are obliged to live so near one another, they must make their own apparel and household goods because they cannot raise stock to purchase them brought from England. It is by breeding horses, hogs, and cattle that people without slaves gain substance here at first, not by their labor." [6] That same year the inhabitants of Albemarle County opposed restrictions that Virginia had placed upon the marketing of their tobacco and shrewdly informed English officialdom that unless the law were repealed, many of them would be reduced to poverty "and must either be obliged to quit their plantations or fall upon such useful manufactures for their necessary clothing, etc., as will prevent the sale of considerable quantities of European goods and consequently be prejudicial to the trade of Great Britain." [7]

Strictly speaking, it is not accurate to treat the mercantile system as if it had been an established and generally agreed-upon doctrine. Theorists were constantly debating and redefining the implications of the Navigation Acts, and as early as 1718 some had begun to discard the notion that the New England and middle colonies were injurious to the mother country. In his *Survey of Trade*, William Wood noted that they were markets for British goods and stressed their importance as furnishers and transporters of supplies for the other colonies.[8] This amounted to accepting the northern colonies almost solely in terms of their utility as appendages to the staple-producing areas. Somehow older objections were not entirely answered, such as the complaint of an agent to the Board of Trade that New Englanders were "promoting and propagating woolen and other manufactures proper to England, instead of applying their thoughts and endeavors to the production of such commodities as are fit to be encouraged in those parts." [9] These and the middle colonies were not dependencies in the same sense that the staple colonies were.

Consequently, some men still found it possible to regard the northern colonies as standards and the southern and island colonies as departures from what was most preferable. Edmund Burke admitted that "there is not one of our settlements which can be compared, in the abundance of people, the number of considerable and trading towns, and the manufactures which are carried on in them, to New England." Although the southern provinces were rich and fertile, "New England is the first in America for cultivation, for the number of people, and for the order which results from both." [10] He praised Pennsylvanians as "a people who from a perfect wilderness have brought their territory to a state of great cultivation and filled it with wealthy and populous towns." [11]

It is in the context of this debate on the role and make-up of colonies that the early history of Georgia can best be explained. The image of a noble, philanthropic venture seems at first glance to place it quite outside social reality elsewhere in the southern colonies. In terms of the vision of its founders, Georgia most recalls the attempt in Virginia more than a century before to serve God and benefit the commonwealth and its subjects. As Benjamin Martyn, propagandist for the colony and spokesman for the Trustees, argued, if there are any poor in a nation "who do not or cannot add to the riches of their country by labor, they must lie a dead weight on the public; and as every wise government, like the bees, should not suffer any drones in the state, these poor should be situated in such places where they might be easy themselves and useful to the commonwealth." [12] Thus any person considered useful at home was not eligible to be sent off, and so the Trustees restricted their "charity to such only as fall into misfortunes in trade and even admit none of these who can get a subsistence." They did not intend, moreover, to provide for all of these, for Georgia was to be open to absolutely "none who have the character of lazy and immoral men." [13] By common agreement this left essentially two groups of people. The first were those who "cannot add to the riches of their country by labor," the unemployed but industrious poor, "who by idleness might have been debauched and by want emboldened to injure" others.[14] The second were those "who do not," persons not yet hardened in idleness, who "might be seasonably rescued or reclaimed from that extravagance to which idleness and ill example had exposed them." [15]

Being very much aware of the failure of previous efforts to create organized societies, the Trustees were prepared to employ fully such restrictions as they considered necessary to foster conditions which would set everyone on paths of industry. Martyn noted that they recognized the inconvenience of allowing individuals to possess large quantities of land "by which means the greatest part of it must lie uncultivated and they are thrown at such a distance that they can neither assist or defend one another." Hence "the Trustees settle the people in towns a hundred families in each and allot no more land than what can with ease be cultivated and yet will afford a sufficient and handsome maintenance." Settlers were forbidden to alienate their lands without permission so as to prevent speculation and monopolizing of holdings. Because "they will be settled in such a frugality, none who can live here will think of going thither, where though they will have a sufficient and plentiful maintenance, they will have no room for luxury or any of its attendant vices." [16]

Though its aims were more modest than those of Virginia, Georgia was still a visionary scheme designed in part to meet the challenge of idleness in England. At the same time the Trustees consciously conceived of their undertaking as fully contributing to the ends of mercantile colonial policy. The semi-tropical crops which they wanted grown were intended not to compete with the staples of the other southern colonies.[17] Obviously they were in sympathy with what these colonies represented, for, as Martyn pointed out, Virginia had "grown so great a province that the revenue is increased 100,000 pounds for duties upon goods that are sent yearly home from thence." [18] Much was said about the value of Georgia as a frontier defense against the Indians, thus freeing the planters of South Carolina from danger and enabling them to produce more staple crops. Hence one finds an interesting duality in the aims of the Trustees. Although they wanted to establish a colony that differed conspicuously in social organization from the other southern colonies, they also wanted one that resembled them in many respects. "England must be the market for the greatest part of her produce," Martyn argued, and "her people must send to England for all their manufactures." [19]

While the Trustees were concerned with orderliness and control in Georgia, they earnestly sought to provide such freedoms as liberty of conscience, so that, as Martyn noted, "a well regulated government in a country so temperate, so pleasant, and so fruitful will draw thither many of the distressed Salzburghers and other persecuted Protestants." [20] Although such a liberal sprinkling of the rhetoric of allurement may seem at first surprising, Martyn also drew upon its magic attraction to extricate himself from the objection that the city poor, to whom the Trustees limited their English recruits, would be unable and unwilling to work as farmers abroad. He had already admitted that farming in England was too laborious to attract them, but he argued that in Georgia "their fatigue unless at first will not be so great, as the climate is so much kinder and the soil so much more fruitful." Though "a laborer's hire" would not attract a city man to the English countryside, yet in America "he will not repine at any fatigue when it is on an estate of his own and his gains from this estate will rise in proportion to his labor." [21] General Oglethorpe's celebrations of the country equaled anything the propagandists for Virginia produced; the poor would be given land "so fertile" that they would "receive an hundred-fold increase for taking very little pains." [22]

Unfortunately the allurements of Georgia proved no more certain guarantees of success than anywhere else in the southern colonies. Evidently there was need to clarify the meaning of the preachments of allurement—that the land needed to be *worked* in order to yield the great benefits spoken of. As Francis Moore reconstructed the situation a few years later, he wrote that the Trustees informed "those that they had chosen that they must expect to go through great hardships in the beginning and use great industry and labor in order to acquire afterwards a comfortable subsistence for themselves and families." [23] The Rev. William Best insisted in 1742 that there had never been any intention to fulfill the ends of colonization in Georgia "but by the labor of those that were willing to be employed in it. And without labor it would not produce a maintenance for themselves or make a provision for their posterity. Neither was it to be conceived that any large profits would instantly arise to the first occupiers." [24]

This increased emphasis upon work was accompanied by a growing concern over the problems of establishing a functioning society in the wilderness. Benjamin Martyn admitted in 1741 that "the difficulties which attend the beginning of a settlement are very great, especially beginning it with low and necessitous people. It is hard to form these into society and reduce them to a proper obedience to the laws." He also lamented that because these people "have never been used to look forward, they live but to the present day and are unwilling to labor for anything but an immediate subsistence." [25] There were evidently many in Georgia who shared with other inhabitants of the southern colonies a non-rational attitude toward work, but the Trustees still intended to solve the problem of idleness mainly through the creation of a society which would make work meaningful, control its conditions, and punish the indolent if necessary. Martyn admitted that sending over a great number of needy people was not a good way to begin a settlement, but he remained optimistic about their prospects thereafter—provided not too many were sent at any one time: "When they see a society formed and a government ready established at which they cannot have a shadow of reason to repine, when they see others who had been in the same condition with themselves living happily upon the fruits of their industry and have evident and ocular proofs that they may soon arrive at the same, and when they will not have numbers to countenance them in their idleness, they will in all likelihood be more incited to labor." [26]

The Trustees had not relied exclusively on needy Englishmen. Finding "that many of the poor who had been useless in England were inclined to be useless likewise in Georgia, they determined that these embarkations should consist chiefly of persons from the Highlands of Scotland and persecuted German Protestants." [27] Like their counterparts to the north, these small groups were conspicuous since they showed more industry and settled in a more orderly manner. To defend the policies of the Trustees, Martyn published in 1741 several accounts of these industrious people. One letter reported that in the "neatly built" town of Ebenezer "they have no idle, drunken, or profligate people among them, but are industrious, many grown wealthy; and their industry hath been blessed with remarkable and uncommon success, to the envy of their neighbors." [28] Armed with such evidence, the Trustees were vindicated in their praise of the fruitfulness of the land. Martyn had already pointed out that the many foreign Protestants and Highlanders sent to the colony, "being accustomed to hardship and labor, were not afraid of it in Georgia, and they live by it very comfortably." [29]

Those whom the Trustees were directly concerned with refuting were settlers, mostly from South Carolina, who had come at their own expense and who chafed under the restrictions imposed upon them. Stigmatized as "Malcontents" by those who disapproved of them, many eventually left. These men, Martyn noted, "being too sanguine in their hopes or idle in their dispositions, formed romantic scenes of happiness and imagined they could find the conveniences and pleasures of life without any labor or toil." [30] The secretary of the colony, William Stephens, reported triumphantly to the Trustees in 1742 that things had not gone too well for those Malcontents who had left for South Carolina, where "many of them who had nothing to trust to but their labor were pointed at as a pack of lazy fellows." [31]

One of the major grievances of the Malcontents was the prohibition against Negro slaves. A director of the Royal African Company, Oglethorpe had no moral objection to slavery, nor had the other Trustees. In countering the complaints of the Malcontents, they argued that if those sent over on charity were given slaves (and they could not own them otherwise), this "would be a charge too great for the Trustees to undertake, and they would be thereby disabled from sending white people." Also "it was thought the white man, by having a Negro slave, would be less disposed to labor himself and that his whole time must be employed in keeping the Negro to work and in watching against any danger he or his family might apprehend from the slave." If only those who could afford slaves were allowed to purchase them, this would foster "a greater propensity to idleness among the poor planters and too great an inequality among the people." [32] The opposition of the Trustees to slavery was therefore pragmatic and designed to further the stated ends of the colony—to limit, not to encourage the existence of idleness among the populace.

One of the most important statements of the position of the Malcontents was *A True Historical Narrative of the Colony of Georgia* by Patrick Tailfer and associates. Its clever satire expressed supposed hurt and outrage at being duped by the Trustees, who had assured them that "the soil will produce anything with very little culture." [33] Still, the Trustees could point in answer to the success of the industrious Protestants, and so the Malcontents were in a sense trapped. Only a frontal assault could save them. They challenged directly the very premises of the doctrine of allurement, assuring their readers that "the land, then, according to the present constitution," was not "capable to maintain the settlers here." [34] They were not, however, arguing that the situation was hopeless and the land ought to be abandoned because of its lack of fertility. Slaves were the golden key to prosperity for the Malcontents. To account for the "singular circumstance" of the prosperity around Augusta, Tailfer gave two reasons: "The first is the goodness of the land, which at so great a distance from the sea is richer than in the maritime parts; the second and chief one is that the settlers there are indulged in and connived at the use of Negroes, by whom they execute all the laborious part of culture." [35] The other side was not slow to perceive the relationship between slavery and the promise of allurement. The Rev. William Best told the Trustees in 1742 that although Tailfer and his associates argued "that they were deluded both by poetry and prose into a better opinion of it than it deserved, we have a confession from their own mouths that they nowise question the possibility of advancing even such improvements of Georgia as the fertile imagination of the poet (who had so much abused them) had described." [36]

The Earl of Egmont, one of the principal Trustees, commented at length on Tailfer's arguments in his personal copy of the narrative. These comments make it quite clear that what Egmont most objected to in the Malcontents was precisely the style of life which they shared with other inhabitants of the southern colonies. When Tailfer lamented that men in Georgia were deprived of "the liberties and properties of their birthright," Egmont wrote that "what he clamors for is the use of Negroes, the liberty to sell and take up land at will when and where he pleases, the choice of magistrates independent of the Trustees, etc., in a word to be on the foot of the other American colonies—all of them inconsistent with the peace and welfare of this infant and frontier province." He considered that among the real motives of the Malcontents were their desires of "being eased of labor themselves" and their "intention to follow the raising of rice, . . . which yields more immediate profit." [37]

In the light of the strong support which the Trustees had shown for the aims of mercantile colonial policy and their liberal use of the rhetoric of allurement with its connotations of freedom and opportunity, Egmont's comments were, at best, not wholly consistent. Thomas Stephens, the disloyal son of the secretary of the colony, could argue with some justification that "if the liberties of former colonies had really prevented or even retarded their own increase and prosperity or their benefit and advantage to Great Britain, some political reasons at least might have been alleged for them; but when

94

the very contrary is self-evident," the bad circumstances of the people of Georgia must be owing "to the want of that liberty which has enriched and established the neighboring colonies and extended the British trade and empire in proportion." [38] The fundamental difficulty of the Trustees' position stemmed from their dual allegiance to the aims of mercantilism and the desire to establish a real society in Georgia. If they had wanted solely the latter, the policies which they followed might have been more single-minded. If they had wanted simply another southern colony, there would never have been any conflict with the Malcontents.

The parallel with the early history of Virginia is obvious, for the leaders of the Virginia Company too were divided between the goals of an orderly society and one based upon economic freedom. Only in Virginia and Georgia had those in power been so torn between these alternatives, had the rhetoric of allurement figured so prominently, had there been such lofty notions of possibility and such fervent celebrations of intentions, had the confrontation between broader social goals and individualistic desires been quite so dramatic and so quick to develop, had the original vision collapsed so rapidly and so completely. Long before the two decades of the trusteeship had passed, slavery had become a reality in Georgia, and the colony was rapidly becoming indistinguishable from its neighbors to the north.

The confrontation between the Trustees and the Malcontents was simply another of the several conflicts, although perhaps the most dramatic, between the two divergent definitions of labor which were a part of the intellectual heritage of the southern colonies. What the Trustees wanted was diligent personal application to tasks which would further the aims of the enterprise. The Malcontents opposed these policies solely because they prevented the individual planter from maximizing his wealth. They were convinced that Negroes could be used much more profitably than white men, and as early as 1735 they had sent a petition to the Trustees "for the use of Negroes, signed by about seventeen of the better sort of people in Savannah," which "set forth the great disproportion betwixt the maintenance and clothing of white servants and Negroes." [39] "Besides," Thomas Stephens later argued, "our neighbors, having such an advantage as the privilege of Negroes, can always undersell us in any manufacture or produce." He condemned the Trustees' prohibition of the importation of rum, "though from whatever moral motive," as being "greatly prejudicial to trade and injurious to the particular circumstances of the people." [40] Behind this whole argument was the assumption that work is performed solely for the sake of gaining wealth, and hence that course of action leading most directly to affluence is the best one to take. The Malcontents were denying the validity of the social limitations placed by the Trustees on work for profit. They were not asking to live in inactivity.

Still, Stephens felt he had to answer the presumption "that the admitting and substituting Negroes to the laborious parts of culture, etc. would make the white men grow idle and lazy." He reiterated the Malcontents' conviction that whites could not perform the work necessary for rice production, asking then if "others may be found much fitter and abler for this work and who besides doing it better shall save a man all the trouble and put money into his pocket, is this a criminal or unreasonable piece of luxury?" He was convinced that there was still work for whites to do since "the labors of the field here supply but a small share of that variety and stock which goes to answer the common necessary demands." From the perspective simply of personal profit Stephens's argument made sense, yet even he felt the need of adding, however vaguely, a social justification for the endeavor of the whites, who could "be still industrious and to better purpose, each man furnishing that part for which he is best qualified." [41] Here was yet another reason for fearing the men in the southern colonies were lazy. As long as labor carried with it connotations of diligent personal application, the labor system of the region could never be considered an example of the white slaveowners' dedication to industry.

William Byrd had in a sense acknowledged this in a letter to Lord Egmont praising the decision to prohibit slavery in Georgia. Slaves, he noted, "blow up the pride and ruin the industry of our white people, who seeing a rank of poor creatures below them detest work for fear it should make them look like slaves." [42] Ironically, as Byrd bequeathed the honors of the family name and fortune to his son in 1744, the great experiment which he had commended was falling into ruins as complete as those left after the disintegration of the Virginia Company.

For the punishment of idleness and vice

6

Ever since George Percy's account of early Virginia, with its alternate views of the beauties of the environment and the sufferings of the first colonists, the South has presented a dual image. On the one hand, it represents graciousness, harmony, easy living, and beneficent nature—on the other, violence, hate, cruelty, ruthless acquisitiveness, and exploitation of men and natural resources. The readiest explanation for these contrasting images would seem to be that chaos, violence, and exploitation have been the reality—reflecting the ineffectiveness of the kinds of controls which have checked men's disorderly instincts elsewhere—and that the contrary image is simply a façade to hide the essential ugliness. Such a view, however, does not do justice to either half of the image. It dismisses the protestations of order and graciousness as unreal, if not self-consciously fraudulent. It ignores their importance to men and their effect in influencing irrational attitudes toward work by lessening its significance. Conversely, to dwell upon violence and chaos as elemental may be attractive to an age which relishes a dark view of human nature, but it ignores the dynamics of these factors. If in any sense it was important for men to believe in the possibility of disorder or violence, then one needs to be very cautious about thinking simply in terms of dark realities they were seeking to control. Here, as in the area of order and graciousness, what they thought may have influenced what was. This would mean that both sides of the image are true—when and where men have made them true.

The constant shortage of labor in all the southern colonies and the very small number who remained tradesmen amply reflected the impact of the doctrine of allurement. Logically it could only be expected to appeal to independent operators. For a man to work for or in co-operation with others was contrary to the notion of personal independence implicit in the concept of freedom of opportunity. Moreover, co-operative endeavor did not promise the large and ready profits that staples were reputed to bring. If the doctrine of allurement offered no real basis for making use of the services of others, the only meaningful alternative was the old notion that because idleness and violence are inseparably connected, coercion may be necessary to enforce the discipline of labor and thus prevent social disorder.

In 1619 the Virginia Council decreed that a large number of new arrivals were to be placed as tenants under older planters. Among several reasons given for this action, it was stated that experience had proved that where "abundance of new men are planted in one body they do overthrow themselves either by contagion of sickness or by the mother and cause thereof, ill example of idleness." [1] Two years later the Company in London noted acidly "that it is here reported that contrary to the public faith given, not the sick but the ablest men are let out to hire and their provisions converted to private uses; and where it is pretended this placing them with old planters is for their health, they are so unmercifully used that it is the greatest cause of our tenants' discontent." [2]

Because it was difficult to obtain servants, hired labor was the exception rather than the rule throughout most of the seventeenth century in Virginia. Probably two-thirds of the landowners did their own work. [3] The whites who could be obtained as indentured servants proved generally disappointing because they constituted a class upon whom the use of force was inherently self-defeating. Compulsion may have worked for a time in the early years, but it could hardly have encouraged more servants to come to America. In order to attract them masters were increasingly required to specify exact terms of service and in effect fell back upon the arguments of allurement. With land so abundant and cheap this only encouraged the servants to set up on their own as quickly as they could. The futility of the whole process made it quite clear that if force had to be used (and it appeared that it must), it was necessary to find some other means of insuring a dependable labor supply.

The obvious solution was the use of Negro slaves, for emigration from Africa had never been subject to the uncertainties of personal choice. Thus there was no reason why coercion could not be used fully and therefore effectively. Virginia planters were eager to purchase blacks throughout the century. Slaves were difficult to obtain, however, first because the Dutch controlled the trade and later because the sugar islands pre-empted most of the laborers the Royal African Company could supply. Thomas J. Wertenbaker has suggested that the severe depression in tobacco prices beginning about the time of the Restoration and lasting into the early 1680's hastened the decline of the independent yeoman farmer in Virginia. After the world market had stabilized itself, he has further argued, the margin of profit was too narrow to permit a planter to cultivate tobacco exclusively without the use of slaves.[4] Nevertheless, men could have lived comfortably by engaging in generalized farming or following trades, but most did not. The margin of profit simply made slavery more desirable than ever to the tobacco farmer, and the fact that the supply of slaves opened up about the same time that the market improved was mainly a happy coincidence. Had there been no depression, planters would still have hastened to take advantage of an opportunity they had sought for years.

Perpetual slavery became almost inevitable when men did not really expect others to work for them unless compelled to. The situation would only have been different if slave labor were not a possible alternative to working for oneself, but the most ambitious Virginians were never willing to reconcile themselves to the limited economic possibilities of the latter course. Ironically, the doctrine of allurement inflamed men's expectations at the same time that it largely eliminated one of the most elementary means of advancement—the capacity to utilize the labor of others. In a limited way slavery remedied this defect. Negro servitude did not make the southern colonies different from New England and Pennsylvania. They were different first. That is why slavery became so widespread there. The presence of a small number of slaves in the northern colonies did not change the essential conditions of life there either. That is why the number remained so small.

Whether one regards the degradation of the Negro and his full slave status as a condition which rapidly appeared or whether one chooses to see the process as a more gradual one, the fact remains that men turned sooner or later to slavery to solve a problem which arose from the very nature of their societies.[5] Eventually in all of the southern and West Indian colonies Negroes proved to be relatively cheap, available, and dependable workers. Whites were not. As the Rev. Peter Fontaine computed the costs of hiring a common laborer in Virginia in 1757, he concluded that it required nearly twenty pounds a year "for a lazy fellow to get wood and water;" and "add to this seven or eight pounds more and you have a slave for life."[6] This solution seemed logical enough, but not everyone was able to take advantage of it. There were only the Indians, free Negroes, and other whites to fall back upon if slaves could not be secured. One can point to more than one instance in which aspiring whites who needed laborers found them among free men who were ostensibly being punished for idleness and violence.

In the mid-1670's the Indians in Virginia began daily to commit "abundance of unguarded and unrevenged murders upon the English, which they perpetrated in a most barbarous and horrid manner." A champion in the form of Nathaniel Bacon arose to defend his fellow colonists against these savages, for whom he "had a perfect antipathy."[7] One of his first acts was to "terrify" the Pamunkeys. According to Wilcomb E. Washburn, Bacon and his followers were not primarily concerned with defending the frontiers. They "did not kill a single enemy Indian but contented themselves with frightening away, killing, or enslaving most of the friendly neighboring Indians, and taking their beaver and land as spoils." There is good evidence, Washburn also argues, that Bacon used a particular attack to obtain Indian slaves.[8] The commissioners sent by the Crown to deal with the rebellion were convinced that friendly Indians were the best guards of the frontiers, and they sought to persuade the whites to remain content with what they had "and not still covet and seek to deprive them of more out of mere itch of luxury rather than any real lack of it."[9]

In 1739, it might be noted in passing, when troops were needed to fight in defense of the English colonies, the Virginia Assembly impressed all idle vagrants into military service, exempting indentured servants and those who could vote. The colony was even gracious enough to give its neighbors its surplus vagrants, and so "all the idle fellows" were carried "out of a country settled only by planters."[10] In early 1740 a Major Otway wrote William Byrd that Virginia had "raised five hundred men in this colony very soon after the war was declared, which was the quota expected from us; for though we do not abound in people, yet it can be no great loss to part with such as are idle and vicious."[11]

Perhaps the best example of the relationship of idleness, violence, and the need for labor occurred in South Carolina in connection with the Regulator movement. In the middle 1760's many who considered themselves the respectable elements of the backcountry complained that the lower classes did not work but lived off the industrious by pilfering and thievery.[12] "The country swarms with vagrants, idlers, gamblers, and the outcasts of Virginia and North Carolina, nor can the industrious obtain any redress, so that they are an heavy clog on the community," a Remonstrance stated, adding significantly that "if you want to hire a fellow to work you'll not raise one for money, but make a dance or a frolic and you'll see an hundred turn out." [13] The Regulators introduced a "plan of regulation" one provision of which was designed to put the "reclaimable" to work. Richard Maxwell Brown, in his recent study of the movement, interprets this as an attempt to solve the perennial labor shortage of the backcountry. The same thing had been done a generation before in North Carolina, where justices of the peace in some counties without authorization bound out free Negroes and mulattoes.[14] Of course some of those termed idle were indeed guilty of socially undesirable behavior. Still, the Regulators, who were propertied men with economic aspirations, moved to stamp out idleness and violence at a time when they were very much in need of labor themselves.

In the early days of colonization authorities in England had followed the practice of putting the idle to work, but the situation there was very different. Great numbers of people were living without performing any socially useful tasks and often without means of adequate support. To prevent violence, which it was feared idleness would generate, work had to be found. Obviously there was no labor shortage at the time, and those who were bothered about the problem had no stake in the potential violence of the idle. Violence was always held out as a future possibility and every effort made to prevent its occurrence. In the southern colonies the situation was quite the opposite. A need for labor preceded the discovery of idleness and violence. Make-work projects were not concocted to keep people out of mischief. Instead the idle were seized upon to fill a critical need for workers. Labor was to be a punishment, not simply a means of preventing violence. In England the problem was solved when the idle had been made busy. In the southern colonies the problem became acute or disappeared as the need for labor increased or decreased. In Virginia, when the quota for the troops had been met, there ceased to be a problem.

It is illuminating to contrast this concern with idleness and violence with that expressed in Boston in 1752 by the Rev.

Charles Chauncy in a sermon on the idle poor. While he did indicate that idleness could generate crime, he saw this as a remote possibility. Work directly contributes to the public good, he insisted, "for there cannot be a flourishing people without labor." Therefore, "it is indeed a great hurt to a community when private persons dispense their charities to such among the poor as keep themselves so by an indulgence to idleness while yet they are able to work." [15] Chauncy instead approved of a society which had recently been formed to promote industry by establishing a linen manufacture. Happily, this project would both put the idle to work and reduce the colony's trade deficit, in part the result of purchasing foreign linens. Many thousands of the poor would "be employed in this single manufacture and taught not only to support themselves but to become useful and valuable members of the community." [16]

Evidently people giving alms to the poor were not especially concerned about imminent violence. Explicitly, Chauncy's program was an affirmation of the social role of labor and an insistence that the idle contribute to the well-being (or at least what he, as one of the wise and good, thought was the well-being) of society. The impression that the sermon leaves is that linen manufacture was intended as a response to the already existing problems of idleness and trade in the colony. It does not seem simply to have been a device for keeping the poor out of mischief, and so it differs from many of the schemes in Elizabethan England. Laborers would not actually be needed until the project was perfected. By contrast, in South Carolina the workers were needed at the very time that idleness was discovered among the lower orders. In both cases work was viewed as a means of social control, but with an important difference. Chauncy addressed himself specifically to the furthering of social ends by means of a community undertaking involving extensive planning, co-operation, and organization. He did not propose coping with violence through providing individual employers with needed laborers.

Obviously those in the southern colonies who could obtain

slaves were indeed fortunate. Once slavery was firmly established, it ought to have meant that there was one group of people upon whom allurement need not operate. Yet there was always anxiety as to whether Negroes were indeed indifferent to opportunity. Defenders of slavery tried to assimilate this institution into a scheme of enticement, but it could be as readily argued that if opportunity makes men want to work, compulsion could be assumed to cause only resentment and rebellion. "What could be expected from creatures thus doomed to endless labor and deprived of the natural rights of humanity and the privileges of Christianity," Alexander Hewit, a former South Carolinian, asked, "but that they should snatch at the least glimmering hopes and prospects of a better state and give their taskmaster reason to dread that they would lay hold of some opportunity of forcing their way to it?" [17] Slavery's association with violence was one reason why the Trustees had tried to keep Negroes out of Georgia. Benjamin Martyn argued that it might be "imagined that by gentle usage the Negro may be made a trusty servant; this cannot be depended on. Every man is naturally fond of liberty, and he will struggle for it when he knows his own strength." [18] Similar reasoning led Hewit to conclude that although all slaves were dangerous, the most dangerous were household slaves. They had ready access to firearms, were intimately acquainted with the affairs of the household, and could easily get ideas from the talk of plots which they often overheard.[19]

Not surprisingly, owners agreed that slaves were dangerous and idle, but they saw the danger as greatest where hard work was most needed—among the field hands. In 1713 the South Carolina clergy accused the planters of opposing conversion of their slaves because "they must allow them some reasonable time for their instruction, and this would consequently be a hindrance to their work and an abatement of the master's profit." Slaves were allowed to till their own ground one day a week in order to free masters from the necessity of feeding and clothing them, which the planters "endeavor to justify, saying that if they were not obliged to work that day, they would be employed in that which is worse." [20] Thus hard work and profit went hand in hand with curbing idleness and violence among the slaves. A South Carolina widow in 1711 wrote that "here is good encouragement for handicraftsmen or for husbandmen that can manage the land and get a few slaves and can beat them well to make them work hard." [21] Slaveowners had to believe that their Negroes were lazy and rebellious to justify using them as they did. They were conscientious in the exercise of discipline, and their slaves worked very hard indeed. The evangelist George Whitefield observed that the "poor slaves" of South Carolina whom he saw were "very civil, diligent, and laborious." [22]

That the conditions of servitude might foster a certain amount of "laziness" among slaves is self-evident. They may have worked hard, but hardly willingly or conscientiously. Thus experience confirmed slaveowners in their commitment to coercion and punishment, yet in this commitment they had to control not only the slaves' presumed violence but their own as well. The Rev. Peter Fontaine, Jr., wrote in 1754 that "it is a hard task to do our duty towards them as we ought, for we run the hazard of temporal ruin if they are not compelled to work hard on the one hand and on the other that of not being able to render a good account of our stewardship in the other and better world if we oppress and tyrannize over them." [23] Some two decades earlier William Byrd had written that one of the unhappy effects of many slaves was "the necessity of being severe. Numbers make them insolent and then foul means must do what fair will not." Although treatment of slaves in Virginia was more humane than in the sugar islands, "these base tempers require to be rid with a taut rein or they will be apt to throw their rider. Yet even this is terrible to a good natured man, who must submit to be either a fool or a fury." [24]

Byrd's diaries demonstrate how this Virginia gentleman was constantly struggling to deal with laziness in his slaves—and the curious relationship of this effort to his own fears of laziness and violence in himself. One night in 1711 he "had several people whipped for being lazy in the morning." In April of the next year he was "a little out of humor this morning and beat Anaka a little unjustly for which I was sorry afterwards." [25] Perhaps the most suggestive of these entries is that of June sixth of the same year. In the morning he "was very lazy and did only settle some accounts before dinner." In the evening he "took a walk about the plantation and returned some time before it was dark out of pure discretion and found Prue with a candle by daylight, for which I gave her a salute with my foot." [26] One wonders whether the possibility, and on occasion even the actuality, of violence did not function as an affirmation of vitality in a man who desperately wanted to prove that he was not lazy.

Admittedly, the point that Byrd in some sense found violence attractive is conjectural. Still, a similar fascination pervades the thought of his contemporary and fellow Virginian, Commissary James Blair. Blair came to Virginia in the late seventeenth century and served for over fifty years as director of the ecclesiastical affairs of the colony. His long career evidenced a steady accommodation to the views of the planters and a willingness to adapt his policies to the local situation. Logically his position as commissary should have placed him on the side of the royal governors and in support of policies for strengthening the power of the Church and regularizing its procedures, but it did not. In 1719 Governor Spotswood accused him of being more inclined to countenance "disorders in the worship of God" than to "redress the same." He had seen Blair "present in the church while a layman, his clerk, has read the divine service to the congregation." Blair defended himself by arguing "that the country is so used to this practice that long before I knew it," it was permitted by law.[27]

One of the most interesting aspects of Blair's protracted quarrels with one royal governor after another is the degree to which he accused his opponents of violence and disorder. In 1704 he stated in an affidavit that because of Governor Nicholson's tactics "the country now is exceedingly divided and inflamed, to the destruction of good neighborhood and the hindrance of the public business." [28] Yet in 1703 Col. Robert Quarry complained to the Bishop of London that Blair was really the violent party in the quarrel because he had described the whole populace as ready "for an insurrection or rebellion" and intimated "that nothing prevented it but the interest and prudence of some gentlemen that were the Commissary's friends." [29] It is not easy to square these activities with Blair's later condemnation of the notion that "it was everyone's business to reform abuses and corruptions, not only in their own station, which would have been right, but by invading the stations of others—magistrates, legislators, princes, and governors—which is the highway, instead of peace, to drive all things to anarchy and confusion." [30] Perhaps he considered himself as always having acted within his station, or perhaps he was more deeply divided on the question of disorder than some of his statements would imply.

This plea for order was included in a long series of sermons on the subject of *Our Saviour's Divine Sermon on the Mount.* In analyzing the mentality of the multitude to whom Christ spoke, Blair stated that they had carnal notions of the Kingdom, "that it was to be like one of the temporal kingdoms of this world for wealth and grandeur, ease and pleasure, conquest and revenge." "Was it not natural," he asked, for a hearer "to feed himself with the fancy of living a jovial, sensual life as to eating, drinking, building, purchasing, and all the utmost gratifications of luxury? . . . Was it not natural for him, instead of applying himself to the honest but laborious and tedious ways of providing for himself and his family by way of a lawful calling, to apply himself to the unjust quick ways of conquest and getting by the power of the sword?" Gratifying "their lusts and carnal appetites" would involve "subduing the flourishing Roman Empire . . . by wars and tumults, insurrections and rebellions." [31] To attribute such grandiose and violent desires to the simple folk of Palestine seems almost incredible, and it cannot be denied that Blair was fascinated by this picture of chaos, coming back to it again and again in the course of his sermons. If one substitutes the Virginians of his day for Palestinians, he makes more sense, although this still does not explain his fascination with chaos and violence.

Blair's association of violence and ease is worth noting. Ease meant to him not passivity, but the frantic pursuit of pleasure and disorder. To ameliorate this frenzied activity his sermons strove to set forth an ethic of purposeful, orderly endeavor: "He that would be just and honest should be diligent in the business of his lawful calling; for idleness brings want, and want is a great temptation to injustice and dishonesty." [32] Although he praised sobriety and temperance because they wean men "from those pleasures which luxurious men propose to themselves," he immediately went on to insist that possessions and enjoyments are not forbidden so long as "we keep within the bounds of moderation and sobriety; no more than under the first beatitude we found it unlawful to possess wealth, so that we do not set our hearts upon it." [33] Such a statement would have been interpreted by Puritans simply as an argument for "weaned affections," but in Blair's context it was more an abstract plea for decorum and orderliness in the tradition of the literature of celebration. Meekness was described as "a right government of the passion of anger and especially a bridling and restraining that headstrong unruliness which is incident to it." Blair also spoke of this virtue as an "inward tranquility of mind," which "shows itself in an outward affable, courteous, kind, and friendly behavior to men." [34]

What obviously concerned Blair was not the danger of violent revolution on the part of the masses, but the chaos resulting from the frantic pursuit of affluence on the part of his aspiring parishioners. In his description of unworthy aims, beginning with immoderate concern for wealth and leading through extravagance in possessions and self-indulgence to the desire for warfare and violence, he was setting forth his fear of and fascination with the loss of self-control. His sermons were moralistic, personal pleas to people to control themselves, not outlines of a course of action by which the wise and good might check the turbulence of the lower orders. Yet absolute tranquility was not an answer. Christ did not talk "as if in forbidding anxiety here He forbad all care and diligence about our ordinary callings, all forethought and contrivance, industry and frugality, and as if we should take no thought at all about anything but let all things run into as great disorder as carelessness and negligence will drive them." Later Blair noted that it was not the design of his text "to persuade you of the needlessness of your own labor about clothing, as if you were to give up yourselves to idleness and expect that God will clothe you by nature as he does the herbs and flowers." [35]

For Blair idleness and riotous ease were not the same thing at all. The latter obviously meant vigorous activity, while idleness meant the absence of activity—a state of not caring about anything. To Blair, Christ was as concerned—perhaps more concerned—that people not fall into this state of listless indifference and inactivity as that they give up their pursuit of riotous ease. Thus economic busyness, properly moderated and associated with a certain reserve and decorum, was the only meaningful refuge for Blair. But like Beverley and Byrd, his vagueness about the form and content of labor and about concrete limits upon economic activity made his efforts at once a plea for order and a stimulus to the kind of acquisitiveness which would undermine that order. For him as for Byrd, coping with idleness was essentially a personal matter, and so was dealing with violence. Their preoccupation with self-control can thus be equated with the efforts of the South Carolina Regulators personally to punish the idle by putting them to work for individual planters.

However indirectly he expressed the notion in his sermons, Blair suggested again and again that his fellow Virginians found violence appealing. He was not alone in this belief. When the evangelist Samuel Davies sought to inspire the Virginia troops with courage in 1755, he warned that this was "not a savage, ferocious violence . . . not the fury of enflamed passions broke loose from the government of reason, but calm, deliberate, rational courage." [36] Samuel Quincy, a South Carolina minister, voiced a somewhat similar concern about those who resorted to duelling, noting how common it was "to fly into the greatest excess of passion, to be filled with fury and rage, and threaten if not to execute the most bloody revenge." [37] There is no particular warrant for assuming that, in cautioning against violence, Davies and Quincy were betraying a personal fascination with it. Indeed their perspectives differ markedly from Blair's. They concentrated upon situations much more credibly violent—duelling and war—than Blair's portrayal of the simple folk of Palestine as would-be bloodthirsty conquerors or his equation of this desire with the pursuit of economic aggrandizement.

In Blair himself there is a striking disparity between speculations and reality. In his quarrels with the colonial governors he painted a picture of imminent social chaos all out of proportion to what was evidently the actual situation. Personally he does not seem to have been a violent man. In effect, then, he found the image of violence more compelling than acting it out, and to this extent he followed his own admonitions in behalf of order and self-restraint. Violence was not either in his life or in Byrd's or in the lives of the people referred to by Davies and Quincy an elemental reality existing without purpose and without provocation. The possibility of violence fulfilled a need just as the desire for order and self-control fulfilled a contrary need. The latter represented an antidote to frenzied acquisitiveness and the confusion it entailed. Conceivably it helped to limit disorder within society and within men's lives though it did not eliminate it. Yet in idealizing tranquility men had come dangerously close to Blair's conception of idleness, as his and Byrd's stress upon activity perhaps indirectly acknowledged.

With its overtones of pointlessness and drift, idleness most of all called attention to the need for meaning and purpose in a society where there was no meaning or purpose, and no ideal of order and quiet could fulfill this need. Blair's effort to define purposeful endeavor was no solution, given the realities of life in Virginia, and so the fear of idleness remained. As with Byrd, one cannot help feeling that the fascination with the possibility of violence and disorder lay precisely in their aggressive, active character. Doing something was better than doing nothing at all. However much both men may have consciously feared violence and loss of self-control, they unconsciously feared meaningless idleness even more. Conscious fears may have successfully checked actual violence much of the time, but there must have been occasions when the desire to escape meaninglessness could not be satisfied except by such forms of action as whipping idle slaves. Ironically, Byrd and Blair simultaneously affirmed and denied passionate self-assertion, and by affirming they helped create an important part of the dual image of the South.

7

In 1672 and again in 1748 the Virginia Assembly sought by law to deal with the problem of idleness and vagrancy, and in 1764 Georgia passed an "act for the punishment of vagabonds and other idle and disorderly persons." [1] Aside from the question of the need for laborers, it is of interest to note that compulsion rather than exhortation was invoked. Colonial laws on idleness and vagrancy were framed upon English models drafted by men who had long advocated the use of force in the mother country. Though leading southern colonists remained proponents of individualism and moral exhortation, other men, who felt equally at home in America and did not regard themselves as displaced Englishmen, strongly advocated the use of force in combating idleness.

John Stewart, a late-seventeenth-century South Carolina Indian trader, wrote a friend that in Carolina "plenty and riches of a certain expectation almost surcharges and overflows our hopes." [2] He also found the prospect of staple crop agriculture very attractive, arguing that he would "rather buy corn than wear out my ground with that savage grain maize, reserving the land's fertility for cotton next year, a staple of profit and that may expect a certain market." [3] While he was not in sympathy with the abstract formalism of the Fundamental Constitutions, he did have his own project for improving the country, including "inland towns and frequent villages everywhere begun which will prove the seeds of towns and cities in time, awful obedience to magistracy indoctrinated, vice and laziness discouraged, ingenuity and merit encouraged." With such prompting, everyone would work cheerfully, and "genius will put himself forth in actions of industry, plenty, and riches until we become a fruitful Canaan, the wonder and admiration of America." [4] Stewart would thus compel men to be virtuous and industrious. Force was both a means of changing their outward behavior and of altering their inward disposition.

A few years after the turn of the century the Rev. Francis Le Jau, Anglican convert from French Protestantism, arrived as a missionary in South Carolina. Almost immediately he felt himself at home in "the finest climate" he had ever seen, where "the soil produces everything without much trouble" and where anyone who was industrious would have plenty. Yet in April 1708 he observed that many cattle had died the previous winter "to punish the laziness of our people, who never did provide hitherto for their beasts against winter." These "little losses" he hoped would "make us laborious." [5] Le Jau was greatly troubled by the fact that "all vice reigns here scandalously and without any notice taken of vicious men." [6] One of his favorite schemes was an association for a "reformation of manners." Although he felt in 1710 that "such a thing would be of great use in town," he was convinced it would encounter much opposition and could not "foresee any good effect till our chief men stand for us." The next year he was even more pessimistic, for "the evil cannot be stopped for want of authority to repress it, and we of the clergy have hardly the liberty to speak, and our chief men are little inclined to compel men to be less scandalous." [7]

These men differed from English critics, who were never at home in the New World and viewed authority and coercion mainly in terms of regulating and controlling the outward form of men's behavior. The difference can be seen by comparing Le Jau with his contemporary, Commissary Gideon

Johnston of South Carolina. While Le Jau readily adapted to America, Johnston always dreamed of England and Ireland and felt himself an exile from home.[8] Like Le Jau, he was distressed at conditions in the colony, and he noted that he had done his utmost "to promote a general prosecution of those that are guilty of immorality and prophaneness in this province." One of his main concerns was the creation of outward conformity to the Established Church. This "must be carried on by slow steps and gentle and easy method," for Johnston acknowledged his unwillingness to oppose himself "to the sentiments of others or to run the least hazard of any division or misunderstanding" among the clergy.[9] In contrast to Le Jau's anguish over the absence of local support for his schemes of moral reform, Johnston used careful negotiation to gain the support of his fellow clergymen. When the colonial governor proved a poor ally in furthering the cause of the Church, he appealed directly to the source of authority in England to create the formal structures of power which would foster the growth of the Church in America. In 1713 he wrote the Society for the Propagation of the Gospel that it was useless "to think of sending bishops abroad till the episcopal power and jurisdiction be settled upon a better foot among" the colonies. It would be "almost impossible to persuade some people to do this till they are forced to it by one general law here at home." [10]

To find views similar to those of Le Jau and Stewart expressed by a Quaker further illuminates the peculiar nature of the indigenous opposition to the established order in the southern colonies. William Borden had come from Rhode Island in 1732, and in 1746 he wrote *An Address to the Inhabitants of North Carolina.* This treatise dealt with the effects of corrupt governments, and his basic assumption was that if men choose poor representatives to govern them they are largely to blame for what must inevitably happen. At the same time he vested representatives with power and authority to create conditions of industry and morality. Using the image of the ubiquitous bee, he noted that when young swarms "through loss of their native guide or want of proper aid get shattered, confused, and become useless in the creation," they are likely to "grow lazy, contentious, and quarrelsome." The remedy for the situation lay in the recognition on the part of the bees themselves that this effect "was owing to a poisonous disposition in their unnatural guides by which they have suffered themselves to be governed." They would then be ashamed of their past conduct "and consult better measures to establish their hive in a peaceable and better settlement for the future." When a hive is not disrupted through want of effective leaders, Borden insisted, the work of everyone conduces "to the mutual advantage of their little community." Hence he considered the "revival and preservation of a sinking government" the "only remedy and means whereby both province and people in their distressed state and condition may be rebuilt, repaired, and recovered." [11] This would stimulate industry because good leaders would make the people become what presumably they could not become by themselves—industrious.

Like Beverley and Byrd, Borden blamed individuals for the sin of laziness, but the need for external controls was largely alien to the thinking of the other two men, who assumed that moral exhortation was the best means of social reformation. Moreover, lamentations expressed and in a sense satisfied their feelings of failure about their societies and themselves, but did not suggest any specific actions that might fundamentally alter the structure of power. The jeremiad by itself was thus eminently a socially conservative device. Those who wanted any changes would have to be more definite and more purposeful. Stewart and Borden proceeded upon the assumption that authority must be used not only to make men virtuous and industrious, but to establish the kind of organized communal life lacking in the southern colonies. This is not to say, however, that their approaches were identical. Borden's Quaker concern for personal responsibility, democratic selection of leaders, and the importance of example was not the same as Stewart's passion for stern punishment. What they shared was the fear that without strong governmental controls laziness and violence would destroy society.

Opponents of the status quo in the southern colonies were thus required to advocate institutional forms, just as English critics had done. In other words, a revolutionary in the colonies was forced to become an advocate of control. Ordinarily rebellions, revolutions, and even protest movements are expressions of men's belief that those in authority are abusing their positions. The initial aim is to destroy or at least reform established power, thus widening the area of freedom, however much control and consolidation of power may later be necessary. Conversely, the guardians of public order have traditionally taken as their first line of defense the sanctity of established institutions. In 1768 the Rev. George Micklejohn, an Anglican missionary who had come to America only two years before, preached on the duty of submission to lawful authority in condemning the actions of the North Carolina Regulators. "Was it not for this necessary power which has been committed to them by the Almighty, everything must soon be involved in the most dreadful anarchy and confusion," he insisted.[12] As the Regulators saw things, however, there would have been no need for an uprising if these assumptions about the structure of power in the colony had been correct.

In defending the Regulators against the accusation that they were rogues, their spokesman Herman Husband pleaded that "if we are all rogues there must be law, and all we want is to be governed by law and not by the will of officers, which to us is perfectly despotic and arbitrary."[13] The Regulators were thus demanding law and order and legislative responsibility. To them the colony was not controlled by a strong government under which corrupt local officials exercised, however unjustly, constituted power. Instead an ineffective government seemed to give these officials unlimited freedom to oppress and exploit. They were the ones who stood for individual liberty and seemed to have little need of strong laws, a powerful government, or elaborate social controls. It was the insurgents who needed and wanted law and control. The Regulators constantly advocated the proper use of power to provide order and promote industry among the populace. A plea to the colonial legislature condemned the policy of allowing "so many thousands of poor families to bestow their all and the labor of many years to improve a piece of waste land with full expectation of a title" only "to deny them protection from being robbed of it by a few roguish individuals, who never bestowed a farthing theron." [14] Control and law were especially important to "the wise men among the Regulators," who "had all their influence exercised in moderating the people and keeping them from violent outbreakings, nor was their influence always sufficient." [15]

Those who challenged the established order were especially at a disadvantage because they felt they had to place limits upon the freedom of opportunity which had long been so widely celebrated. If the challengers had economic aspirations, their dilemma was compounded by the fact that the limitations they advocated could become restrictions on their own freedom once they had become successful. This would seem to account for their rather ambivalent attitude toward the uses of power and their uncertainty as to how extensively it should be exercised. The desire to establish controls and to create order by force was evidence of a much greater anxiety about disorder than Blair and Byrd felt. Even more, it indicated a far greater fear of loss of self-control. To succeed men had to prove that their opposition was based upon a strong enough sense of unity of purpose to make controls work, for force alone could not create what was lacking. In fact it could easily become simply violence to curb violence. In this regard two other revolts—Bacon's Rebellion and the South Carolina Regulator movement—deserve to be considered. Both were aimed at curing some form of idleness and violence, yet both reflect the curious fascination with violence which has been previously discussed.

Like other critics of existing conditions Bacon and his supporters condemned the government's failure to create an acceptable social fabric.[16] Governor Berkeley was castigated "for not having during the long time of his government in any measure advanced this hopeful colony either by fortification, towns or trade." [17] Moreover, in moving against the Indians Bacon's avowed purpose was to act in the absence, as he saw it, of effective protection from the colonial government. As for controlling violence, he seems to have had increasing difficulty in keeping order among his own troops. He was greatly troubled by the looting and plundering of plantations where they were quartered.[18] Although the later report issued by the Royal Commissioners must be accepted with reservations, it is still an eloquent statement of the way in which violence to curb violence rapidly led to increasing confusion. Near his end "Bacon now begins to show a more merciless severity and absolute authority than formerly, plundering and imprisoning many and condemning some by power of martial law." Among other things he proposed a "committee to be always with the army" in part "to regulate the rudeness, disorder, spoil, and waste of the soldiers." [19]

According to one historian, there was really no society in the South Carolina backcountry in the 1760's, but rather a mixture of various racial and religious elements with few unifying influences.[20] The inhabitants themselves traced the Regulator movement to the Cherokee War early in the decade. Since that time, according to a petition in 1769, "these back settlements have been in a state of anarchy, disorder, and confusion." [21] The Regulators saw themselves as a small number of virtuous and industrious settlers surrounded by men whose idle and disorderly conduct utterly destroyed the conditions of industry in the backcountry. As the Rev. Charles Woodmason, Anglican missionary and spokesman for their cause, wrote in a Remonstrance issued in 1767, "in our present unsettled situation, when the bands of society and government hang loose and ungirt about us, when no regular police is established but everyone left to do as seemeth him meet, there is not the least encouragement for any individual to be industrious, emulous in well-doing or enterprising in any attempt that is laudable or public spirited." [22] By using force to suppress vice and idleness, order and industry would be restored. Hence the Remonstrance requested "that court-houses, jails, and bridewells be built in proper places and coercive laws framed for the punishment of idleness and vice and for the lessening the number of vagrant and indolent persons who now prey on the industrious." [23]

Disregarded by the government in Charleston, the Regulators "rose in arms, pursued the rogues, broke up their gangs, burned the dwellings of all their harborers and abettors, whipped and drove the idle, vicious, and profligate out of the province, men and women without distinction." [24] As in North Carolina there was concern that the effort of Regulation might lead to violence and excesses. Woodmason told the Regulators that he hoped they would "act as becometh gentlemen—not when you have been kindly entertained in a plantation to make waste and do damage, to lie with the Negro wenches and servants, to debauch the daughters or pervert the wife, or any other such ungodly practices." [25] In fact violence and excess grew more from the zeal of the Regulators as they attempted to control labor, the family, and other forms of social life. They became increasingly rash in their selection of victims, and on one occasion a beating was administered to the accompaniment of a drum and fiddle. The excesses of these efforts at punishment and social control led many of the most powerful settlers of the backcountry to form what they called a "Moderator" movement in the spring of 1769, and a real battle between the two groups was only narrowly averted.[26]

It seems clear that what the Regulators were really concerned about was the chaotic and individualistic economic struggle taking place on the frontier. They did not find the absence of effective controls an evidence of freedom and opportunity. Indeed they wanted laws not simply to control the lower classes, but to control themselves as well. As Woodmason wrote Henry Laurens in 1769, "we believe this to be the only country in the world where people pray, entreat, beg to be made honest, wise, virtuous, and industrious and where their superiors labor to depress and injure their bodies and keep their minds in a state of servility and insensibility." [27] However, the efforts of all those who advocated force to establish order and promote industry in the southern colonies had been essentially foredoomed. The freedom and individualism of these societies had been based upon the premise that compulsion had failed. Victory over laziness could only come about through men's dedication to a meaningful ideal and their willingness to work to fulfill it. A generation before the Regulator uprisings, the evangelists of the Great Awakening had preached such an ideal.

In the years after 1740 ministers consistently exhorted men to diligence and activity. The Christian's work, said Isaac Chanler, a South Carolina Baptist, is "a laborious work," and therefore Christians "must not be slothful in a business of such grand importance." [28] The great Presbyterian evangelist Samuel Davies echoed these sentiments, pointing out how worthless in the work of salvation were the "languid endeavors" of his listeners. Though God is the agent, His "assistance is not to be expected in the neglect or careless use of means, nor is it intended to encourage idleness but activity and labor." [29] Obviously these preachers were concerned here with a different definition of labor from that which had occupied men earlier. Their interests were explicitly religious, and the activity they stressed was diligence in spiritual matters.

In 1760 Josiah Smith referred to "a lazy and a worldly inclination" among those who make excuses for their lack of diligence.[30] His coupling of laziness and worldliness was consistent with the spiritual emphasis of the evangelical preachers. Worldliness in their scheme was laziness—evidence of a disinclination toward spiritual labors. In 1740 Smith had considered it a point of praise that the great Whitefield had so "charmed" the people of South Carolina "with his manner of address that they shut up their shops, forgot their secular business, and laid aside their schemes for the world." [31]

Davies reasoned that "should we form a judgment of the faculties of human nature by the conduct of the generality in religion, we should be apt to conclude that men are mere snails and that they have no active powers belonging to them. But view them about other affairs and you find they are all life, fire, and hurry. What labor and toil! What schemes and contrivances! What solicitude about success!" [32] Clearly there was no need to encourage busyness.

The vision of the preachers was the communion of the saints, the unity of all the righteous through their love of one another. Because this vision applied to all mankind and was formulated in terms of the sentiment of love rather than of social institutions, they did not have to be concerned with many of the failures which had bothered others in the southern colonies. In fact they were often fairly accommodating. George Whitefield was more than accommodating when he wrote John Wesley in 1751 "that hot countries cannot be cultivated without Negroes. What a flourishing country might Georgia have been had the use of them been permitted years ago!" [33] In 1756 Davies referred to the "fields which were wont to loom green and flourishing with our staple commodity on which our trade so entirely depends," fields "prepared with labor and pain." [34] His main concern about slavery was that the Negroes be given Christian instruction, and he called upon masters to discharge their duty by making profitable use of the leisure hours "which both you and your slaves now spend in trifling or sinning." In fact, a master's own interests inclined him to teach his slaves, who would thereby become "good servants, faithful, honest, diligent, and laborious." [35] Davies admitted "that religion should by no means be made a pretense for idleness in masters or servants and that moderate industry in your lawful callings is as much your duty, in its place, as the religious instruction of your domestics." But he dismissed all objections to instruction by placing matters in perspective, asking "are not the affairs of eternity of infinitely greater importance to you than those of time?" [36]

The evangelical ministers had a compelling and clear conception of the good society; they were not searching for one. Their purpose was neither to change the southern colonies through institutional reforms nor to lament their differences from New England in the vague expectation that repentance would result in identity. While they shared with Beverley and Byrd a moral approach to social issues, they exhorted their followers to become, by laboring in God's cause, members of a community which already existed, the righteous community of love. It was open to all men, who had only to strive diligently to become, through God's grace, a part of it. In the secular sphere, the preachers simply assumed that every man must fulfill himself through society and that this was as possible in the southern colonies as anywhere else. Davies insisted that a good Christian "is not only a dutiful servant of God in matters purely religious, but he is an useful member of every society to which he belongs and makes conscience of justice, charity, and all the good offices due to his fellow creatures." [37] Even though they did not stress industry in the secular sense, ministers could speak of it as meaningful because they did not think of its being dependent upon any particular institutional context. It should also be pointed out that Davies came from the middle colonies, and Isaac Chanler published his sermons in Boston with introductions by New England clergymen. As a group, moreover, these ministers spoke and acted upon the assumption of an intercolonial union of the faithful which transcended all local differences.[38]

When the colonial wars diverted the religious emotions of the Great Awakening into a more secular channel, the vision of the community of love became the glorious community of all patriotic Englishmen in America. Industry in doing God's work became industrious exertion for country. In 1756 Davies lamented the fact that a "spirit of security, sloth, and cowardice evidently prevails in these southern colonies, and nothing great is so much as attempted, much less executed." He had already noted that "a brave spirit seems to prevail" in New England.[39] Even though New Englanders led the way, there was no reason why men in the southern colonies could not become as patriotically industrious if they would only bestir themselves. Unlike Beverley and Byrd at an earlier time, Davies at this juncture had a specific program of action to usher Virginians into the land of industry—vigorous support of the wars both at home and on the battlefield. In his most famous patriotic sermon, *The Curse of Cowardice* (1758), he told the Virginia troops that "the mean, sneaking wretch that can desert the cause of his country in such an exigency . . . sins against God and his country and deserves the curse of both." [40] The imperatives of patriotism demanded an end to "prodigality squandering her stores, luxury spreading her table and unmanning her guests, vanity laughing aloud and dissolving in empty unthinking mirth, regardless of God and our country, of time and eternity." [41] Patriotism was therefore a call to vigorous activity which would banish idleness and sloth.

It was also a definition of social solidarity as the framework for this activity and in terms of which it would have meaning. Here was a major difference between the calls to repentance of the preachers and those of Beverley and Byrd. In 1745 John Evans in South Carolina reminded his listeners that on the occasion of a fast day every man "ought to consider himself as a member of the province and the province itself as a sinful member of a sinful nation." [42] A decade later Davies asked Virginians whether they had a right to prolong their lives "by mean or unlawful ways, by a cowardly desertion of the cause of your country and shifting for your little selves as though you had no connection with society." Repeatedly he appealed to broader bases for industrious patriotism: "Virginians! Britons! Christians! Protestants! If these names have any import or energy, will you not strike home in such a cause?" [43]

That Davies and others were moved to substitute patriotic industry for religious industry indicated that the great community of the faithful which they had preached earlier had not become a reality. The wars with the French and Indians provided a very limited arena in which some kind of unified social sentiment could be aroused. Only the future could decide whether the preachers of patriotism would be able to lead the people of the southern colonies finally out of the land of idleness.

Industry, frugality, and temperance
idleness, extravagance, and dissipation

8

It was mostly a fortunate accident that the staple colonies served mercantile theory well. Certainly the Crown could not claim much credit for effective planning and direction. Mercantile theory did not necessarily call for the production of a single staple in any given colony, but merely for the restriction to commodities which England would otherwise have to buy from external sources. Ideally, each colony could rather have grown several staples which fulfilled this requirement instead of a single crop, especially tobacco. The Crown was always willing to encourage such ventures as silk culture, and it granted subsidies and established a public filature at Savannah. The Royal Society of Arts, which was founded in 1754 to advance "arts, manufactures, and commerce," joined in encouraging additional staples. The intent of the Society was obviously to operate within the framework of the mercantile system, for the products it sought to promote were based essentially on considerations of Board of Trade lists of imports into England.[1] Sugar and tobacco culture was not given premiums because this was felt to be unnecessary.[2] Most planters in the colonies, however, found any sort of diversification highly uncongenial. New crops were introduced into the West Indies with very limited results because planters did not want to imperil sugar production.[3]

If it was difficult in practice to improve on the mercantile system, still nothing could go seriously amiss as long as colonists concentrated on producing staples and left other economic pursuits alone. Actually most of the Royal Society's efforts were centered in the mother country, where it was perfectly appropriate to stress an integrated development of commerce, manufactures, and agriculture because Great Britain was an independent nation—just as it was appropriate to stress only agricultural matters within the colonies because they were merely appendages. Nevertheless, mercantile theorists had not succeeded in settling conclusively the question of the role of the colonies, and this became increasingly a source of debate in the years preceding the American Revolution.

In 1751 Benjamin Franklin assured the English public that America's great increase in population was no threat to the mercantile system. An abundance of land meant that the danger "of these colonies interfering with their mother country in trades that depend on labor, manufactures, etc., is too remote to require the attention of Great Britain." Then with masterful subtlety he went on to suggest that the American demand for British manufactures would soon become so great that the mother country could not supply all that would be wanted. Hence "Britain should not too much restrain manufactures in her colonies." [4] Again in 1760, this time in the role of an anonymous English supporter of the acquisition of Canada, Franklin insisted that the additional territory would guarantee that Americans would remain an agricultural people "and thereby free us at home effectually from our fears of American manufactures." As in the earlier period he was aware that the northern colonies did not measure up in all respects to the British standards of model colonies, yet his task was to make them appear so and still allow for a certain deviation. To the objection that the North American colonies had the same climate as England and so produced the same things, he categorically asserted that this was not true "of the countries now likely to be added to our settlements; and of our present colonies the products—lumber, tobacco, rice, and indigo, great articles of commerce—do not interfere with the products of England." [5] The fact still remained that when examples of truly acceptable colonies were needed, it was necessary to look southward.

When men in the southern colonies responded to the British efforts to tighten the imperial system in the 1760's by alternately defending the power of the mother country to control the external affairs of the colonies and denying any authority over internal affairs, they were making a distinction peculiarly relevant to their own situation. They were essentially dependent upon outside sources for marketing their staples and supplying them with what they could not be troubled to produce for themselves. At the same time they had enjoyed a large measure of local autonomy, so that they were accustomed to viewing the imperial connection in terms of mutually advantageous trade relations and little more. Convinced of the importance of the (southern) colonies to Great Britain, Daniel Dulany of Maryland in 1765 could stress their economic dependence at the same time that he refused to recognize any right of the mother country to impose taxes for revenue. "The produce of their lands, the earnings of their industry, and the gains of their commerce," he noted, "center in Great Britain, support the artificers, the manufactories, and navigation of the nation, and with them the British landholders too." [6] He admitted that England could regulate the colonial trade because it was from the colonies that "her greatest wealth is derived and upon which her maritime power is principally founded," but he emphatically denied that she had "a right to impose an internal tax on the colonies without their consent." [7] Richard Bland of Virginia was convinced that Great Britain's profits from the colonies more than made up for any expenses she incurred in their protection. He summed up the imperial connection by arguing that, long before the original Navigation Acts, Virginians "were respected as a distinct state, independent as to their internal government of the original kingdom, but united with her as to their external polity in the closest and most intimate league and amity, under the same allegiance and enjoying the benefits of a reciprocal intercourse." [8]

While southern colonists seem thus to have accepted the premises of mercantile colonial theory, many still showed a certain allegiance to the old ideal of an industrious society. In a letter to a London correspondent in 1765 George Washington noted that "our whole substance does already in a manner flow to Great Britain and that whatsoever contributes to lessen our importations must be hurtful to their manufacturers." Yet he then went on to say that "the eyes of our people, already beginning to open, will perceive that many luxuries which we lavish our substance to Great Britain for can well be dispensed with whilst the necessaries of life are (mostly) to be had within ourselves. This consequently will introduce frugality and be a necessary stimulation to industry." [9] In accordance with such reasoning the citizens of Savannah in 1769, "being destitute of all hope of relief from our multiplied and increasing distresses but by our own industry, frugality, and economy, firmly resolved never to be in the least accessory to the loss of any privilege we are entitled to" and further resolved to "encourage and promote American manufactures and of this province in particular." [10]

These and subsequent threats and resolutions contained an interesting contradiction. Though men could wax eloquent about the virtues of industry and frugality, yet the avowed purpose of the measures they adopted was to force Britain to give in so that they could become idle and luxurious once again. This is no more than to say that many who opposed British policy, notwithstanding misgivings about luxury and idleness, were basically committed to the way things had been. Nevertheless, the various non-importation agreements in the southern colonies referred to the propagation of industry and frugality by means of manufactures so frequently as to suggest that some men did expect concrete changes. In 1774 the Virginia delegates at Williamsburg pledged themselves to stimulate by example "the greatest industry, the strictest economy and frugality, and the execution of every public virtue." They called upon the citizenry as well to refrain as much as possible from the production of tobacco and to "apply their attention and industry to the cultivation of all such articles as may form a proper basis for manufactures of all sorts." [11] The Georgia deputies in 1775 resolved to "encourage frugality, economy, and industry, and promote agriculture, arts, and the manufactures of America, especially those of wool," and to "discountenance and discourage every species of extravagance and dissipation." [12]

A random comparison of similar resolutions in two of the northern colonies reveals no such expectations of social and economic change. The Massachusetts Provincial Congress in 1774 prefaced its recommendation with the argument that "the happiness of every political body of men upon earth is to be estimated in a great measure upon their greater or less dependence upon any other political bodies; and from hence arises a forcible argument why every state ought to regulate their internal policy in such a manner as to furnish themselves, within their own body, with every necessary article for subsistence and defense." The Congress sought "to encourage agriculture, manufactures, and economy so as to render this state as independent of every other state as the nature of our country will admit." [13] Economic independence was thus seen as the appropriate policy of an industrious society, not as a means of creating one. In Philadelphia in 1775 a proponent of cloth manufactures in the colony argued that "a people who are *entirely* dependent upon foreigners for food or clothes must always be subject to them." Rather than hoping that this program would make men industrious, he saw it as the result of "the habitual spirit of industry and economy for which we are celebrated among strangers." [14] Men everywhere agreed on the utility of domestic manufactures, but in the northern colonies this program did not seem at the time to involve a major break with the past.

There were certain groups in the southern colonies, particularly the Charleston mechanics, whose interest in the encouragement of American manufactures was directly related to their desire to escape the inconveniences of the mercantile system.[15] There was also active support of the measures to resist Great Britain from the members of the evangelical clergy, who joined the struggle as a crusade in behalf of the moral reformation of the populace. In 1769 the Rev. Hugh Alison insisted that while "you mutually run into measures of economy, frugality, and industry in order to defeat the acts of Parliament and promote a general repeal, much more should you adopt another kind of economy and industry as absolutely necessary in order to defeat the empire of sin in your souls and to promote your own salvation." [16] Doubtless many failed to reach the spiritual heights Alison called for, but there was widespread sympathy for the more immediate goal of religious liberty in the southern colonies. Even many members of the Established Church saw advantages in a freer religious atmosphere. In 1774 James Madison contrasted the debilitating effect of religious bondage in Virginia with the freedom his correspondent enjoyed in Pennsylvania. To the north "the public has long felt the good effects of their religious as well as civil liberty. Foreigners have been encouraged to settle among you. Industry and virtue have been promoted by mutual emulation and mutual inspection; commerce and the arts have flourished." [17]

Those who demanded religious liberty as well as those who championed the non-importation agreements looked forward to changes in the southern colonies which would eliminate the conditions which had given rise to the concern about laziness. This kind of resistance aimed logically at a type of social organization quite different from what mercantile colonial theory contemplated. While there were many who were reluctant to follow this pattern of resistance to its logical conclusion, they were unsuccessful in inducing Britain to return to the ways of the past. Because they viewed the tie with the mother country in terms of economic advantage, it seemed less and less meaningful to resist the impulse toward separation as the connection appeared more and more disadvantageous. Also, few of the zealous supporters of industry and patriotism saw clearly where their efforts were leading until war actually broke out. Neither did the evangelical ministers. Like their predecessors in the days of Samuel Davies, they expected industrious service in religious matters to result from the measures taken to deal with the imperial crisis. Although they were aware of the worldy dimension of their appeals to industriousness, they tried to keep these concerns subordinate to religious matters. As in the days of the colonial wars, however, distinctions between religious and secular definitions of industry became blurred, and the logic of events tended increasingly to emphasize the secular aspects. Opposition to Great Britain thus found a common denominator in allegiance to industry.

The call to industry was in essence a vision of the good society, an ideal for which all men in the southern colonies could fight. It derived neither from the tradition of the jeremiad nor from the tradition of protests in behalf of control, yet it was an answer to both. No one could explicitly take a stand against it without becoming an advocate of laziness. Because it was an ideal, it avoided demands for institutions to limit freedom and compel men to be industrious. As a secular version of the message of the preachers of the Great Awakening, it was a promise to lead all men in the southern colonies out of the land of idleness. Hence it had, especially in the eyes of the truly inspired, the appeal of a religious crusade. This is not to say it was a major cause of the Revolution. It does indicate, though, how such exhortations against laziness helped to bring together various elements of the population.

The author of a letter to the people of Charleston in 1774 argued that "one great soul of harmony should animate this whole continent and dispose each one to consider an injury offered to any part as offered to himself." He then demanded: "Let us begin by abolishing all parties and distinctions, abandoning luxury and pleasure and establishing economy. Let us nobly determine to make a willing sacrifice of our private interest to this glorious cause." [18] By 1776 American union had become the larger context for all industrious efforts within the former southern colonies. Hopes for change thus became part of the larger vision equated with independence and allowed men to share common ideals with patriots in New England and Pennsylvania, New York and New Jersey. And so they would cease to be different. National unity involved change in the southern states, and change presupposed national unity.

Jonathan Boucher, a native Englishman and inveterate Loyalist who served the Church of England for many years in Virginia and Maryland, was most willing to discredit the notion of an American union. In 1775 he wrote the deputies in Congress from the southern colonies that if independence came about, "wholly unable to defend ourselves, see ye not that after some few years of civil broils all the fair settlements in the middle and southern colonies will be seized on by our more enterprising and restless fellow colonists of the north!" He was shocked at the possibility of such "a monstrous and an unnatural coalition" and would as soon expect "the wolf and the lamb to feed together as Virginians to form a cordial union with the saints of New England." This argument accepted the fact that the southern colonies were "exceedingly different from the northern colonies" and also that they were economically dependent upon an external source.[19] Consequently, Boucher saw no possibility of a union of equals since the southern colonies would suffer from a consolidation that would end the separate relation of each to England. They would no longer be able to enjoy such fruits of luxury and ease as their loose economic ties with the mother country had permitted.

For those who believed the southern colonies would soon be changed, Boucher's fears seemed baseless. They considered complete unity highly desirable. In the late summer of 1775 a young minister named William Tennent, whose forebears had taken such an important part in the Great Awakening, accompanied William Henry Drayton into the South Carolina backcountry to drum up support for the American cause. Tennent filled his journal with enthusiasm over the prospects of the area. "This country affords the greatest number of fine falls for mills of any I have ever seen," he wrote. "The soil is rich and the best foundation seems to be laid by nature for manufactures that can be conceived." He also speculated on the possibility of extending the navigability of the Savannah River another hundred miles.[20] The next year he angrily denounced the "lazy and the deep-pocketed gentry" of South Carolina for their unwillingness to contribute to the defense of the state. He further extended his opposition to established power by supporting religious liberty, arguing in a speech before the House of Assembly in early 1777 that "religious establishments discourage the opulence and cramp the growth of a free state. Every fetter whether religious or civil deters people from settling in a new country. Take off every unnecessary yoke and people of all denominations and professions will flock in upon you with all their arts and industry." [21] In this way, he implied, South Carolina would come to resemble a state like Pennsylvania.

That same year Chaplain John Hurt told the Virginia troops camped in New Jersey that because all men's blessings spring from society and their love of it, society imposes certain obligations. Among them is support of the cause of liberty. "If liberty be destroyed," he warned, "no particular member can escape the chains. . . . If then we have a true affection for ourselves, if we would reap the fruits of industry and enjoy our property in security, we must stand firm to the cause of liberty and public virtue." [22] His sermon was also a condemnation of the harmful social effects of self-indulgence, for "if out of a luxurious vanity we consume the manufactures of other countries to the detriment of our own, if our profusion in extravagant expenses render us less able or less willing to assist the public, we violate the most sacred of all social duties and become flagrant transgressors of the will of our creator." [23] This sermon is a good example of the way in which the various definitions of industry merged, so that spiritual endeavor and patriotic exertion were combined with promoting manufactures. While Hurt seemed to be directing his attack directly at the upper classes, he was equally concerned that lesser men distinguish industry of all sorts from self-indulgence and the selfish pursuit of wealth.

Tennent's associate William Henry Drayton had been firmly on the side of the British in the 1760's. A wealthy aristocrat who married into more wealth, he claimed that the Intolerable Acts had caused him to change sides. While there is evidence that disappointed ambition may also have figured in his conversion and that shrewd political sense dictated his willingness to side with the workingmen of Charleston, few men of high social position in the colonies were willing to take such a radical stand.[24] Even if one chooses to question Drayton's sincerity, he should be given credit for understanding his audiences. Two months before the Declaration of Independence he told the Charleston Grand Jury that the union of the American people was "as astonishing as unprecedented when we consider their various manners and religious tenets, their distance from each other, their various and clashing local interests."[25] He praised the new state constitution, which was "wisely adapted to enable us to trade with foreign nations and thereby to supply our wants at the cheapest markets in the universe, to extend our trade infinitely beyond what it has ever been known, to encourage manufactures among us," and to promote the happiness of the people by permitting the poor to "arrive at the highest dignity."[26] The next year he exhorted the people of South Carolina to make effective preparations for defense against the British and to "cease by your languor in the public defense and your ardor after private gain to invite them to turn their steps this way and seize your country as a rich and easy prey."[27]

Surprisingly, after several years of preaching union, patriotism, and industry, Drayton criticized the Articles of Confederation in early 1778 as an undue restriction of the sovereignty of the states. "When I reflect," he argued, "that from the nature of the climate, soil, and produce of the several states a northern and southern interest in many particulars naturally and unavoidably arise, I cannot but be displeased with the prospect that the most important transactions in Congress may be done contrary to the united opposition of Virginia, the two Carolinas, and Georgia—states possessing more than one-half of the whole territory of the Confederacy and forming, as I may say, the body of the southern interest." [28] He died the next year; so it is impossible to know whether he would have altered his views. But it is noteworthy that such a strong insistence upon the distinctiveness of the southern states should have come from someone who had so eloquently supported the cause of union and patriotism.

Others in the state, particularly Dr. David Ramsay, remained more sanguine about the prospects for an independent America. In a Fourth of July oration in 1778 he dwelt on the rising glories of the new nation. In contrast to the pride, luxury, and extravagance of monarchies, "republics are favorable to truth, sincerity, frugality, industry, and simplicity of manners." "It was the interest of Great Britain to encourage our dissipation and extravagance for the twofold purpose of increasing the sale of her manufactures and of perpetuating our subordination," he noted. Efforts to oppose this were vain, and if South Carolina had "continued dependent, our frugality, industry, and simplicity of manners would have been lost in an imitation of British extravagance, idleness, and false refinements." [29] Ramsay's hopes for the future were evident in his assertion that "union with Great Britain confined us to the consumption of her manufactures and restrained us from supplying our wants by the improvement of those articles which the bounty of Heaven had bestowed on our country." But independence, he further observed, "repealed all these cruel restrictions and holds forth generous prices and public premiums for our encouragement in the erection of all kinds of manufactures." [30] He forecast the expansion of the nation into the remote lands of the west and a great increase in population, the growth of which had been uneven in the past. "Pennsylvania and New England, though inferior in soil, being blessed originally with the most free forms of government, have outstripped others in the relative increase of their inhabitants." [31] South Carolina was to share equally with the rest of the nation in this glorious prospect.

The year the war ended, a treatise on law and government was published in Charleston which, amidst hopes and plans for the future, contained a quite different and yet portentous comment. "The same glowing sun which quickens the vegetable creation so instantly into life also induces us to relax from our labor," the author suggested in invoking the notion of the easy life nature permitted in the southern states to encourage men to abandon frenzied activity. The sun, "performing by its rays the office of invigorating the plant, saves us the degree of toil necessary in other climes and invites us to indulge in the enjoyment of what we have already gained, and not to persevere in an eager and useless pursuit of riches." [32] It remained to be seen whether the struggle for independence had truly ushered the southern states into the land of industry. If men had not forsaken mere busyness, then perhaps they should be encouraged to seek the respite of leisure.

9

Efforts were made in the early 1780's to further the cause of manufactures in the southern states, but despite high hopes travelers still filled their accounts with the same judgments that visitors had been making for over a century.[1] The rapid reappearance of a pattern of dependence upon outside sources for marketing and supply caused many men to reconsider and finally to redefine the terms and conditions of industry which had been advanced during the Revolution as desirable goals.[2] What amounted to a definite scaling down of earlier expectations is seen perhaps most graphically in David Ramsay's *History of the Revolution of South Carolina* (1785). In 1778 he had described British rule as an elaborate scheme to prevent the growth of colonial manufactures and make the colonists idle and luxurious. Now he noted that after South Carolina became a royal colony "the inhabitants enjoyed the protection of Great Britain, and in return the mother country had a monopoly of their trade. Great Britain received great benefit by this intercourse, and the colony under her protecting care became great and happy." Conditions were even better after 1763. The number of inhabitants soon doubled, and "wealth poured in upon them from a thousand channels. The fertility of the soil generously repaid the labor of the husbandman, making the poor to sing and industry to smile through every corner of the land. None were indigent but the idle and unfortunate." The people found peace at home and abroad and so were "completely satisfied with their government and wished not for the smallest change in their political constitution." [3]

Even after the conflict began, most South Carolinians would have rejoiced at the possibility of reconciliation, and only the cruelties and brutalities of the British and their Indian allies transformed these peaceable inhabitants "from planters, merchants, and mechanics into an active, disciplined military body and a well regulated, self-governed community." [4] Ramsay did not go into the postwar situation except to pay tribute to the pursuit of opportunity by noting that the "farmer redoubled his industry from the pleasing conviction that the produce of his labor would be secured to him without any danger from British bayonets or American impress-warrants." [5] In essence the book established the halcyon days before the Revolution as a standard by which to judge the present and perhaps on which to model the future. While his history was neither an apology for British colonialism nor a plea for returning to a state of subservience to that country, Ramsay had accepted and even praised a condition of economic dependence because it stimulated the blessings of allurement. Thus his references to work and wealth seem less to resemble his 1778 oration than the traditional literature of celebration.

During these postwar years James Madison was becoming increasingly critical of the commercial situation in Virginia. In 1783 he complained to Jefferson that Virginians paid a tribute of 30 to 40 per cent on exports and imports to and from Europe above costs in such ports as Baltimore and Philadelphia. The next year he actively supported a plan to limit all commerce in the state to the ports of Norfolk and Alexandria, but, as he later admitted, three other ports had to be added in order "to gain anything and to restrain to these ports foreigners only." [6] He had thus placed himself among the numerous proponents of regulating the economic individualism of the

Virginia planter. Like the earlier attempts to control the size of tobacco crops and confine trade to a few major ports, his efforts met with no success. By early 1786 he was writing Jefferson that it was more important than ever that commercial relations among the states be harmonized because "the local efforts to counteract the policy of Great Britain, instead of succeeding, have in every instance recoiled more or less on the states which ventured on the trial." Two months later he noted significantly that "most of our political evils may be traced up to our commercial ones, as most of our moral may to our political." British credit, unfortunately, was more than "enough to perpetuate our difficulties unless the luxurious propensity of our own people can be otherwise checked." [7]

Madison was therefore willing to support a national government which could deal with the chronic problem of economic disorder resulting from unrestrained acquisitiveness. Judge Henry Pendleton of South Carolina was too. In 1786 he lamented that "no sooner had we recovered and restored the country to peace and order than a rage for running into debt became epidemical; instead of resorting to patient industry and by slow and cautious advances" restoring South Carolina to its former condition, "individuals were for getting rich by a *coup de main*, a good bargain. A happy speculation was almost every man's pursuit" and this led to a burden of debt and the repeated use of stay laws.[8] The next year he dwelt on Britain's efforts "to hold fast the commercial advantages which our avidity for her Negroes and manufactures hath given her." He thus advised that South Carolinians must seek "to live within our income, to secure a balance of trade in our favor, and to urge the federal government to such general regulations as shall secure us from the infamous vassalage into which we are hurrying." [9] Amidst such concerns it is not surprising that it was a southern state, Virginia, which issued a call for a meeting among the states in Annapolis "to consider how far a uniform system in their commercial regulations may be necessary to their common interest and their permanent harmony." [10]

In 1785 James Monroe had objected that the southern states would be surrendering too much if they turned for relief to the northern states because they had no ships of their own. Madison assured him that the present system would never "give the Southern states bottoms; and if they are not their own carriers, I should suppose it no mark either of folly or incivility to give our custom to our brethren rather than to those who have not yet entitled themselves to the name of friends." [11] While the term "Southern" had before 1775 been applied at times even to New York and Pennsylvania, those seeking to adjust opposing sectional interests during the war had acknowledged many of the differences between the states south of Maryland and those to the north.[12] By the time that Madison answered Monroe's objection the distinctiveness of the whole South as a staple-producing area based on slave labor was widely enough acknowledged to make the objection meaningful. It seems appropriate, therefore, to use the terms "South," "Southern," and "Southerner" from this point on, even though a fully articulated sectionalism would not emerge until the antebellum controversy over slavery. But Southerners had no clear conception of a North. Sometimes the Southern states were contrasted to the Northern ones, at other times to the Eastern (New England) states. Whether these differences were a bar to national union or simply an evidence of regional variations common to all large countries was another question—one which figured prominently in the Constitutional debates.

When Charles Pinckney of South Carolina spoke to the members of the Constitutional Convention of the necessity of a stronger government, he said little about the power of commercial regulation because the need for it, he felt, was so generally accepted.[13] Supporters of the Constitution in the Southern states agreed with Madison that the regulatory powers of a new federal government were desperately needed, and they spoke repeatedly of the importance of the proposed reforms in promoting industry. John Marshall argued: "That economy and industry are essential to our happiness will be denied by no man. But the present government will not add to our industry. It takes away the incitements to industry by rendering property insecure and unprotected." [14] Edmund Pendleton also assumed "that there can be no political happiness unless industry be cherished and protected and property secured." [15] Explicitly the Southern Federalists were critics of existing conditions and therefore presumably reformers. Yet even as critics they remained the spiritual heirs of Beverley and Byrd. Acting within the framework of the jeremiad, paradoxically, meant that they were essentially committed to the way of life they were apparently seeking to reform. They perpetuated the old confusion between personal and social definitions of labor by their insistence that the ills of the society would largely be at an end once the conditions of economic advancement were made orderly and predictable.

Not surprisingly, the message of the jeremiad seemed as relevant as ever. In a Fourth of July oration in Savannah in 1788, Major William Pierce argued that after the Revolution, "allured by false schemes of commerce and tempted by luxuries which we had for many years before been deprived of, we plunged without reason or discretion into habits of expense and idle speculation that have so entangled and disordered the economy of our affairs as to make us neglectful of every public concern." [16] The combination of erratic, disruptive, and socially disoriented activities to which Pierce referred had bothered many men since early colonial days, and from time to time they had made desultory attempts to deal with these conditions. To judge from the reports of the postwar period this situation had become predictably worse. Even the weak controls of the British government had provided some element of order and stability. The difference in the degree of confusion dovetailed with the fact that the general atmosphere of the 1780's favored attempts to reduce the endemic economic disorder of Southern life by strengthening the Confederacy—a course of action unavailable in the days of Beverley and Byrd.

Doubtless this atmosphere owed much to the ideas of Northern Federalists, whose passion for social order seems to have influenced Southerners like Pierce. In his oration he also recommended "the cultivation of harmony and good order in society," telling his listeners to "cherish a spirit of industry as the means of doing it; abandon all idle extravagance; introduce economy; love your country; and dismiss ill-founded animosities." [17] One of the Federalist publications, *The Massachusetts Magazine*, illustrates not only this outside influence, but the more extensive concerns of men in New England, who looked to the new government to promote industry in its broadest connotations of social utility and tranquility. The first volume of the magazine in 1789 contained the argument that "every man who thinks at all knows that it is his duty to be industrious, for he cannot but see that should indolence prevail the human race must soon sink into poverty, wretchedness, and ruin." The same volume also included a political thermometer on which such virtues as politeness, liberality, urbanity, justice, economy, industry, and patriotism were listed in ascending order. Idleness was depicted among the domestic evils in association with party spirit, and the public calamities under this party spirit were mobs, luxury, rebellion, anarchy, and tyranny.[18]

In redefining the conditions of industry to meet the demands of the postwar period, Southern Federalists had in effect abandoned any practical expectations of fundamental change and were seeking to make the economic dependence of the Southern states as workable as possible—to eliminate the inconveniences which their agricultural systems fostered and thus to re-create the general pattern of prosperity which David Ramsay had celebrated in his history. In early 1787 Madison had said "that manufactures will come of themselves when we are ripe for them." [19] This rather distant prospect would obviously not influence his actions. He had sought and in promoting the Constitution would continue to seek only to bring about a more orderly economic situation in the South, not to advance manufactures and commerce there. In the various state conventions supporters of the Constitution were often quite candid in insisting that the Southern states were entering into a dependent economic relationship and that it was to their advantage to do so. Governor Beverley Randolph pointed out that if Virginia faced foreign nations alone, it was powerless to prevent their monopolizing its trade because "we have no manufactures, depend for supplies on other nations, and so far are we from having any carrying trade that . . . our exports are in the hands of foreigners." [20] In the South Carolina convention Charles Cotesworth Pinckney was explicit about the economic concessions granted the New England states in return for protection. These had little fear of attack, and so "if our government is to be founded on equal compact, what inducement can they possibly have to be united with us if we do not grant them some privileges with regard to their shipping?" [21] In a way he was saying that the Union would be a business arrangement in which the Southern states would grant economic privileges in return for services rendered—services which Southerners could not perform for themselves.

The willingness of Southern Federalists to accept a dependent economic relationship with the Northern states involved an acceptance also of the distinctiveness of the Southern states. These men saw no incompatibility between Southern distinctiveness and a national government precisely because they conceived of the new nation, like the colonial relation, as a rather loose economic alliance based upon mutual convenience. In fact they were convinced that any differences could be resolved on the basis of each section's need for the other. Essentially they were saying that the new nation would be held together largely by the efficacy of allurement, just as men felt Southern society was. Beyond the area of economic cohesion they were somewhat vague in their view of the extent and actual content of national union. David Ramsay argued that although Congress could forbid the importation of Negroes after twenty-one years, it probably would not because "the more rice we make, the more business will be for their shipping. Their interest will therefore coincide with ours." Ramsay's patriotism also reflected, however, the influence of the revolutionary preachers. He asked Carolinians to "consider the people of all the thirteen states as a band of brethren speaking the same language, professing the same religion, inhabiting one undivided country, and designed by heaven to be one people." [22] This conception of patriotic unity had still, as it had in the time of Samuel Davies, its own kind of vagueness. In Ramsay's case it was quite compatible with the emphasis which he placed upon the economic aspects of union.

Madison too told his readers in *The Federalist* to "hearken not to the unnatural voice which tells you that the people of America, knit together as they are by so many cords of affection, can no longer . . . be fellow citizens in one great, respectable, and flourishing empire." [23] Still, in 1781 he had written Jefferson that a national navy would not only be a defense against foreigners, "but without it what is to protect the Southern states for many years to come against the insults and aggressions of their northern brethren?" [24] Madison's famous argument in *The Federalist*, Number Ten, on the nature of faction, far from advocating an extensive union, based on affection or otherwise, was really an attempt to make permanent differences the cornerstone of national unity. As he said in an earlier statement of the same doctrine, a large republic is better "because a common interest or passion is less apt to be felt and the requisite combinations less easy to be formed by a great than by a small number. The society becomes broken into a greater variety of interests, of pursuits, of passions, which check each other whilst those who may feel a common sentiment have less opportunity of communication and concert." [25] That a nation founded on such a unity of permanent disunity would actually hold together does not seem at all certain unless one concedes the binding force of mutual economic advantage as well as a generalized patriotism. If Madison's concept of unity were accepted, it guaranteed Southern distinctiveness. One might even argue that because the new government would restore conditions of industry to the Southern states, it in a sense fulfilled the expressed hopes of the jeremiad. Because it would do so in a way which guaranteed the existing situation, it fulfilled the tacit expectations of the jeremiad.

At the South Carolina convention Charles Pinckney advanced the argument that "all government is restraint and founded in force" and that in a republican government "a greater degree of force and energy will always be found necessary than even in a monarchy." Monarchies have the sovereign as an attractive force, but republics must depend upon public spirit. Because a public spirit sufficiently willing to sacrifice partial interests to the good of the whole will only prevail in moments of excitement, the inadequacies of the system must be "remedied by a strong government." [26] In dealing with the nature of the Union later in the convention, Pinckney noted that the New England states were different by origin, "pursuits, habits, and principles" from the Middle and Southern states; "but striking as this is, it is not to be compared with the difference that there is between the inhabitants of Northern and Southern states." By Southern he meant "Maryland and the states to the southward of her. Here we may truly observe that nature has drawn as strong marks of distinction in the habits and manners of the people as she has in her climates and productions. . . . The inconveniences which too frequently attend these differences in habits and opinions among the citizens that compose the Union are not a little increased by the variety of their state governments." [27] Presumably national unity would be effected by the coercive powers of the central government, which would nullify local differences. Yet there is the same vagueness as in Madison and Ramsay when one attempts to ascertain precisely the nature of this unity.

After restating the Madisonian doctrine of interests, Pinckney argued that a large republic would allow "the more temperate and prudent part of the society to correct the licentiousness and injustices of the rest." Like his cousin, Charles

Cotesworth Pinckney, he stressed the relative weakness of the Southern states and their need to grant trade concessions.[28] He did not, as some of his statements on the use of force might seem to indicate, expect a national unity through the emasculation of local—that is, Southern—interests. On the contrary, it did not appear to him "that the commercial line will ever have much influence in the politics of the Union." Rather "all the great objects of government should be subservient to the increase of agriculture and the support of the landed interest." [29] Obviously Pinckney believed that the South would have a meaningful say in the affairs of the nation, but this expectation was not based on any clear conception of the extent of national unity or the way in which consensus was to be achieved. National power would simply eliminate divisions without destroying Southern distinctiveness because the South was a major component of the nation's landed interest, and the government was to favor this interest. Why this should be can only be answered by assuming, as with Madison, the potency of economic interest operating upon Northerners. The Southern states would be too useful to them for their demands to be refused or their interests ignored. Yet one must also say that while Pinckney called attention to regional differences, the vagueness of his concept of national unity was actually an assurance that these differences were not really important.

Alexander Hamilton's argument in *The Federalist*, Number Nine, that a firm union would function "as a barrier against domestic faction and insurrection," [30] perfectly points up the difference between his views and those of Pinckney and Madison. Hamilton thought in terms of a united country. Even more important, his thinking was based on a national perspective and a clear view of how national ends were to be furthered. "Under a vigorous national government the natural strength and resources of the country, directed to a common interest, would baffle the combinations of European jealousy to restrain our growth," he argued in essay Number Eleven.[31] He was not talking about a vaguely defined power which would bring order to the chaos of self-aggrandizement through the perpetuation of differences, but a national power which would regulate all the affairs of the country to further national ends. Because both Madison and Pinckney rejected Federalism in the 1790's, this distinction between them and Hamilton may seem unnecessary and even misleading. But in 1787 and 1788 Madison thought he was on Hamilton's side, and Pinckney talked as though he were too.

There were some expressions of support for the Constitution in the Southern states which more nearly resembled the views of Hamilton. Most conspicuous as a group were the mechanics of Baltimore and Charleston, who had a direct interest in becoming part of a national system of manufactures. One must not overestimate, however, the significance of these groups within Southern society.[32] In his "Circular Letter" to the governors of the states in 1783 George Washington insisted that "it is indispensable to the happiness of the individual states that there should be lodged somewhere a supreme power to regulate and govern the general concerns of the confederated republic, without which the union cannot be of long duration."[33] Various comments in the following years show him a rather thoroughgoing critic of things Southern. In 1785 he argued against dispersed settlement of western lands (a policy for the Northwest Territory advocated by the Southern states and opposed by the Northern states in favor of townships) on the grounds that "compact and progressive seating will give strength to the Union, admit law and good government and federal aids at an early period."[34] He wrote Arthur Young, the English authority on farming, that "there is perhaps scarcely any part of America where farming has been less attended to than in this state. The cultivation of tobacco has been almost the sole object with men of landed property, and consequently a regular course of crops have never been in view."[35]

In 1787 Washington wrote his nephew Bushrod that "it does not lie with any one state or the minority of the states to superstruct a constitution for the whole. The separate interests as far as it is practicable must be consolidated, and local views must be attended to as far as the nature of the case will admit. . . . If then the union of the whole is a desirable object, the component parts must yield a little in order to accomplish it." [36] Washington was not ignoring regional differences, but neither was he looking to the efficacy of allurement to protect them. Perhaps the most striking aspect of his thought is his attitude toward work itself. The month he died he wrote the manager of his farms that a careful evaluation must be made of how to utilize the work force to the best advantage, for "when no plan is fixed, when directions flow from day to day, the business becomes a mere chaos." [37] He therefore went on to insist that "it becomes the indispensable duty of him who is employed to overlook and conduct the operations to take a prospective and comprehensive view of the *whole* business which is laid before him, that the several parts thereof may be so ordered and arranged as that one sort of work may follow another sort in proper succession and without loss of labor or of time." Indoor work was to be saved for bad weather "so as to suffer no waste of time or idleness." [38] Washington thus concerned himself with labor and idleness in the context of a comprehensively conceived and carefully supervised pattern of effort in contrast to William Byrd's pervasive fears of laziness throughout Virginia and North Carolina society and his inability to define any similar pattern of effort.

Another group of Southerners had more in common with Washington than with Madison in some respects, yet they were the opponents of both in the ratification controversy. Foremost among these were Patrick Henry and another prominent Virginia Antifederalist, Richard Henry Lee. In a 1766 political paper Henry had professed himself unable to understand why Virginia with its happy situation—"blessed with a soil producing not only the necessaries but the luxuries of life, full of rivers, havens, and inlets that invite the visits of commerce for the products of industry, and bordered with extended plains that instead of lonely scattered huts might be covered with magnificent cities"—should want even the necessities of life. By contrast the situation was much better in Pennsylvania, "the country of the most extensive privileges with few slaves." "A general toleration of religion" seemed to him "the best means of peopling our country and enabling our people to procure those necessaries among themselves, the purchase of which from abroad has so nearly ruined" Virginia.[39] In his passionate desire for change Henry threw himself into the conflict with Britain, telling the First Continental Congress that "the distinctions between Virginians, Pennsylvanians, New Yorkers, and New Englanders are no more. I am not a Virginian, but an American." [40]

In his first speech before the House of Burgesses in the early 1760's, Richard Henry Lee had dealt with the evils of the slave trade, noting "that some of our neighboring colonies, though much later than ourselves in point of settlement, are now far before us in improvement." The reason was "that with their whites they import arts and agriculture whilst we with our blacks exclude both." [41] In 1777 Lee wrote Henry that "our enemies and our friends too know that America can only be conquered by disunion; the former with unremitting art had endeavored to fix immoveable discord between the Southern and Eastern colonies." With respect to Virginia and New England specifically he was "at a loss to know wherein their interests clash." [42] At the end of the war Henry was optimistic enough about Virginia's prospects to speak in behalf of allowing Loyalists to return as part of a general policy of encouraging immigration. Virginians were destined to become "a great agricultural and commercial people." The best way to fulfill this promise was to "encourage the husbandmen, the mechanics, the merchants of the Old World to come and settle in this land of promise; make it the home of the skilful, the industrious, the fortunate, the happy, as well as the asylum of the distressed." [43] While Virginians should also trade with England "during the infant state of our manufactures," [44] it was only a matter of time before the state would be truly a land of industry.

Several years before this, however, Lee had already begun to have doubts about the likelihood of change in Virginia. In October of 1779 he had written John Adams of his personal interest "in the establishment of a wise and free republic in Massachusetts Bay, where yet I hope to finish the remainder of my days. The hasty, unpersevering, aristocratic genius of the South suits not my disposition and is inconsistent with my ideas of what must constitute social happiness and security." [45] In 1780 he wrote Samuel Adams that the "confederation alone can give us system, strength, and respectful consideration" by the European powers.[46] Yet five years later he insisted that "so essential is the difference between the Northern and Southern productions and circumstances relative to commerce, that it is not easy to adopt any general system that would well accord with all." [47] What may at first seem simply a reversal of attitudes on Lee's part—from a critic of Southern ways and a patriotic advocate of a united country to a champion of the South and an opponent of union—was the product of a simultaneous desire for national unity and a fear that the South as it stood was too different to enter the Union on equal terms with the North.

In his Antifederalist *Letters from the Federal Farmer* Lee discussed at length the problem of adequately representing the various segments of the population. The "Eastern states are very democratic and composed chiefly of moderate freeholders; they have but few rich men and no slaves. The Southern states are composed chiefly of rich planters and slaves; they have but few moderate freeholders, and the prevailing influence in them is generally a dissipated aristocracy." [48] This distinction, which was hardly flattering to the South, along with a later discussion of the problem of faction, revealed Lee's deep concern about sectional rivalries. In speaking of conflict between aristocratic and democratic elements within the nation, he clearly had in mind discord between the North (especially New England) and the South. In any government, he argued, "not only the efforts of these two great parties are to be balanced, but other interests and parties also." [49] Both in his notion of two great opposing interests and his belief that the government must actively compose and balance interests instead of letting them balance themselves, Lee obviously did not agree with Madison's notion of a unity of disunity nor with the idea that national unity could be based on some kind of loose economic alliance for mutual advantage.

"Force and opinion seem to be the two ways alone by which men can be governed," he told Edmund Pendleton in 1788; "the latter appears the most proper for a free people, but remove that and obedience, I apprehend, can only be found to result from fear, the offspring of force." [50] In modern terms, he was saying that some kind of consensus or basic agreement must be a precondition of forming a just government. What the Constitution proposed seemed to him to assume the existence of a consensus which he no longer felt the South would subscribe to, even eventually. Because the concept of a national union involved more for him than it did for Madison, he could not accept the Constitution and still acknowledge the distinctiveness of the Southern states. A more limited association was still possible, however, provided its conditions were precisely spelled out. In becoming a defender of Southern distinctiveness, Lee had not ceased to be critical of his region. If he still wanted change, he had nevertheless chosen to remain loyal to it as it was.

Lee did not participate in the Virginia ratifying convention, but Henry did—and most conspicuously. His almost endless arguments are filled with a tone of anger and frustration because Southerners had failed to answer the wartime calls for industry and social reformation. He rejected the notion, so dear to the hearts of supporters of the Constitution, that a change in governmental structure would solve the problems of the state, for "no nation ever paid its debts by a change of government without the aid of industry." He told the delegates that "at present you buy too much and make too little to pay with. Will this new system promote manufactures, industry, and frugality?" Since Henry had not given up the hope of change, he obviously interpreted the meaning of industry in a way quite different from his opponents. Their conception of an economic alliance with the North hinged upon the acceptance of a definition that did not imply the kinds of changes with which manufactures were associated. Henry believed that "the evils that attend us lie in extravagance and want of industry and can only be removed by assiduity and economy." [51] Like Lee, he placed much emphasis upon the importance of men's attitudes, yet there was a certain irony in this emphasis. By themselves calls to industry addressed to men who really did not understand its broader social meaning had not in the past and would not in the future change existing conditions. Henry seemed to recognize this in noting that the states "are naturally divided into carrying and productive states. This is an actual existing distinction which cannot be altered." [52] His desire for the South to resemble the North and his fears that it never would are most evident in the apparent contradiction between his implied call for manufactures and industry and his assertion of the unalterable differences between the sections.

Perhaps the most poignant of Henry's arguments against the Constitution dealt with the question of slavery. Here again one can see both his sense of the distinctiveness of the South and his oscillation between impassioned defense and angry criticism. He warned the members of the convention that another period of crisis like the Revolution might result in freeing the slaves, for "slavery is detested; we feel its fatal effects; we deplore it with all the pity of humanity." These and other considerations would at some future time cause Congress to realize that it had the Constitutional power to free the slaves: "And have they not, sir? Have they not power to provide for the general defense and welfare? May they not think that these call for the abolition of slavery?" [53] This whole argument assumed that, if the Constitution were accepted unaltered, the Northern states would have the right to bring the Southern states into harmony with their way of life; and Henry sympathized with this course of action as much as he feared it.

In the Constitutional Convention George Mason insisted that "slavery discourages arts and manufactures. The poor despise labor when performed by slaves. They prevent the emigration of whites, who really enrich and strengthen a country." [54] At the Virginia state convention he objected to the clause in the Constitution permitting importation of slaves for twenty years at the same time that he criticized the document's failure to guarantee slavery where it already existed. "It is far from a desirable property," he noted, "but it will involve us in great difficulties and infelicity to be now deprived of them." [55] One can simply dismiss Mason's whole position as the hypocritical effort of a man who was himself a large slaveowner to further an internal slave trade based in Virginia, as one Northern Federalist did.[56] This would account for his opposition to the foreign slave trade; yet if this were really Mason's intent, he need not have spoken of slavery's depriving a society of such symbols of industry as manufactures. Such a strange combination of criticism and calls for guarantees reflected his own hopes for change together with his misgivings about how it was to come about. Other Southern Antifederalists in the various state conventions expressed the same split attitude, and their castigation of the new government both as a threat to slavery and as a means of perpetuating it was not lost on the opposition. One Federalist professed that he found in this an utterly inconsistent attitude toward New England. "They tell you that the admission of the importation of slaves for twenty years shows that their policy is to keep us weak, and yet the next moment they tell you that they intend to set them free!" [57]

Although the Antifederalists may have been inconsistent, the fact remains that their opponents really could not appreciate their fears because the two groups defined the nature of the Union in basically different terms. To Federalists the South was offering the North an alliance for profit, and they could not believe that Northern businessmen would endanger such an advantageous arrangement by offending the South in any way. In reply to the persistent Antifederalist arguments that the Northern states would condone foreign control of the Mississippi to the detriment of the Southern states, Madison argued in the Virginia convention that if "interest" should continue to operate on the carrying states, how could their commerce "be so much extended and advanced as by giving encouragement to agriculture in the western country and having the emolument of carrying their produce to market?" William Grayson's answer seems strange unless one realizes that the Antifederalists were talking about much more than a limited economic alliance. To him the issue was not economic but political, involving the creation of new states in the Southwest. It was a great national contest "whether one part of the continent shall govern the other. The Northern states have the majority and will endeavor to retain it. This is therefore a contest for dominion, for empire." [58]

The Antifederalists' cry of distinctiveness must not be mistaken for mere concern over special regional interests. They invoked this concept in issue after issue upon which no sectional cleavage could be reasonably expected. When Timothy Bloodworth in North Carolina expressed fear that the more populous Northern states would outvote the Southern ones on the issue of paper money, James Iredell pointed out that on many issues a state like North Carolina could expect support from some Northern states, particularly New Jersey and Connecticut, which also imported through adjacent states. Bloodworth's only answer was that "when I was in Congress, the Southern and Northern interests divided at Susquehannah. I believe it is so now." [59] Not all Antifederalists in the South were so concerned about Southern distinctiveness. Some had trifling objections to the Constitution, and others objected only because they felt their own local positions threatened. But among some of the most articulate this concern did express itself. They seldom made a direct equation of distinctiveness with laziness, although Henry implied it when he rejected the notion that the new government could cure evils caused by indolence.

Some Northern Antifederalists, however, seized upon the idea of Southern laziness as an argument against trying to make that region part of a strong union. For example, James Winthrop of Massachusetts felt that it was impossible to make laws which would conform to the needs of all the different citizens of the nation because the "idle and dissolute inhabitants of the South require a different regimen from the sober and active people of the North." [60] What Southern laziness meant to him was not what Northern activity meant to Southern Antifederalists. To the latter the danger was that the North would compel the South to fit into the Union. To Winthrop the problem was that the Southern states would not fit. In New England and the Middle states there was much less feeling than in the Southern states that the interests of the entire section were in jeopardy.[61] Indeed Winthrop's concern was solely with an independent Massachusetts. His argument for its separateness was based on the conviction that his state, which Lee had so much admired, met all the accepted standards of industry. Hence if the Constitution were rejected, "we must remain as we are, with trade extending, resources opening, settlements enlarging, manufactures increasing, and public debts diminishing by fair payment." [62]

After his ardent opposition to the Constitution, Patrick Henry's support of Federalism in the 1790's may seem a betrayal of his earlier radicalism. Actually he was quite consistent. Feeling a deep commitment to national unity in 1788, he feared bringing the Southern states into the Union without explicit provisions to protect a way of life which he no longer believed would change. When the Constitution was ratified, Henry supported the new government much more seriously than many of those who helped create it. In 1795 he wrote Washington that "if my country is destined in my day to encounter the horrors of anarchy, every power of mind or body which I possess will be exerted in support of the government under which I live and which has been fairly sanctioned by my countrymen." [63] Both in his opposition in 1788 and his support in 1795 Henry acted from the belief that, if a truly national government were given extensive powers by the people, it would have to be supported—no matter how painful this might some day be to the South.

Given the assumptions of the supporters of the Constitution, painful situations ought not to occur, and they, after all, had won the debate in the South over the nature of the Union. This debate was in fact a continuation of the dialogue, which had gone on since the founding of Virginia, between those who accepted the Southern way and those who wished to change it. Now, however, something new had been added to the situation. In the past there had been no one to challenge effectively the notion of a society based upon allurement—a notion which seemed to work within the South as well as within the empire. But the Antifederalists warned that it would not work once the South became part of a united nation. Doubtless some Northerners would have been only too pleased to perpetuate indefinitely the South's condition of economic dependence without interfering with the Southern way—just as many Southerners would have been only too pleased to accept such terms of union. The problem was not that a union based upon economic convenience was unworkable, provided everyone consented to it. The victors in the South, however, had promised to sell some of their freedom in return for the advantages of economic regulation. Once they had agreed to these conditions of union, the question was who would adjudicate if Northerners decided some day that the nation was more than a league for mutual advantage. Perhaps the time would come when economic concessions could not purchase freedom to pursue the Southern way.

10

The victory for the Southern way signified by the adoption of the Constitution did not destroy the hopes for change, one expression of which was the repeated criticism of slavery. In 1792 David Rice of Kentucky condemned the institution as "the national vice" of Virginia and rejoiced in the fact that his new state need no longer participate in this guilt if its citizens chose to exclude slavery. The social basis of his argument was that "slavery produces idleness, and idleness is the nurse of vice. A vicious commonwealth is a building erected on quicksand, the inhabitants of which can never abide in safety." [1] Rice was convinced that with abolition "the children of the slaves, instead of being ruined for want of education, would be so brought up as to become useful citizens. The country would improve by their industry; manufactures would flourish; and in time of war they would not be the terror, but the strength and defense of the state." [2]

St. George Tucker of Virginia was perhaps more realistic and in a way more Southern when he tied a plan for gradual emancipation to a program providing "that these people must be *bound* to labor if they do not *voluntarily* engage therein." This followed from the fact that the interests of society "require the exertions of every individual in some mode or other; and those who have not wherewith to support themselves honestly without corporal labor, whatever be their complexion, ought to be compelled to labor." [3] Rice and Tucker actually represented the two Southern postures toward labor and its social context—Rice the hope that freedom would produce an industrious society, Tucker the fear that only force finally could accomplish this end. And so slavery remained as evidence that neither force nor freedom had created the society men had hoped for.

These comments on slavery cannot fail to bring to mind the famous condemnation by Thomas Jefferson, in his *Notes on the State of Virginia*, that "the whole commerce between master and slave is a perpetual exercise of the most boisterous passions, the most unremitting despotism on the one part and degrading submissions on the other." He also associated it with the destruction of industry, "for in a warm climate no man will labor for himself who can make another labor for him." [4] Jefferson did not, however, tie his condemnation of slavery to an explicit plea for change. He did predict that Norfolk "will probably be the emporium for all the trade of the Chesapeake Bay and its waters," and he spoke of a canal to link the town to the Albemarle region of North Carolina. Yet he had already explained Virginia's lack of "towns of any consequence" as a result of its geography. There were many places where "the *laws* have said there shall be towns; but *nature* has said there shall not, and they remain unworthy of enumeration." [5] To invoke nature in this way was equivalent to bestowing an almost cosmic justification upon the society. With respect to manufactures Jefferson neither excused their absence nor hoped for their eventual appearance. Quite the contrary, here again he elevated the facts of Virginia life into an ethical system: "Those who labor in the earth are the chosen people of God if ever He had a chosen people." Thus he insisted that "while we have land to labor, then, let us never wish to see our citizens occupied at a workbench or twirling a distaff. Carpenters, masons, smiths are wanting in husbandry, but for the general operations of manufacture let our workshops remain in Europe." [6] Virginia need not be ashamed of its lack of tradesmen, for, as he wrote John Jay in 1785, he considered "the class of artificers as the panders of vice and the instruments by which the liberties of a country are generally overturned." [7]

Jefferson's ideal was not a self-sufficient agricultural society, but simply the South glorified—growing only staple crops and allowing all its commercial and manufacturing activities to be performed by others. If such an arrangement were to work, the crops cultivated would have to be readily marketable, yet in the *Notes* he looked forward to the time when increased tobacco production in the West would force the people of Maryland and Virginia to give it up: "And a happy obligation for them it will be. It is a culture productive of infinite wretchedness. Those employed in it are in a continual state of exertion beyond the power of nature to support. Little food of any kind is raised by them; so that the men and animals on these farms are illy fed, and the earth is rapidly impoverished." He felt the area should turn to the cultivation of wheat, which, he hoped, would eliminate these conditions and diffuse "plenty and happiness among the whole." He also suggested cotton and hemp.[8] There was no proof, however, that wheat would enable Virginia and Maryland to continue to rely upon Europe for economic and commerical services. Although cotton could not readily be raised in these states, hemp offered possibilities of establishing a staple crop economy not radically different from tobacco. At the same time Jefferson's idyll did not precisely square with the facts of Southern life. Although it relegated almost all the economic processes of organized society to Europe, it seemed to contemplate that everyone in the South would be personally busy tilling the earth.

Jefferson was concerned about personal laziness in a characteristically Southern way. In 1787 he wrote his daughter Martha that nothing would make for her future happiness more "than the contracting a habit of industry and activity. Of all the cankers of human happiness none corrodes it with so silent yet so baneful a tooth as indolence." Later that same year he again wrote: "Determine never to be idle. No person will have occasion to complain of the want of time who never loses any." [9] It is noteworthy that he was advocating simply keeping busy rather than purposefulness. Interestingly enough, that year he wrote a foreign correspondent that "among many good qualities which my countrymen possess some of a different character unhappily mix themselves. The most remarkable are indolence, extravagance, and infidelity to their engagements." He considered the abolition of all credit the only cure for the situation.[10] It is not entirely clear whether he was talking about all Americans or simply Virginians, yet in this instance, as in his formulation of a pastoral idyll, his ideas were mostly illustrative of his own part of the country.

Jefferson was aware of the parochial nature of his dreams. In 1785 he admitted that although he would prefer that every American devote himself to agriculture, he recognized that "our people have a decided taste for navigation and commerce." [11] Like Patrick Henry, he was torn between what he sensed as special in the South and what he felt was the genius of the American people as a whole. This concern prompted him in 1792 to urge Washington to run again for the presidency to prevent the "incalculable evil" of the disintegration of the Union. Referring to "the mass which opposed the original coalescence," he noted that "it lay chiefly in the Southern quarter" and "that the Legislature have availed themselves of no occasion of allaying it, but on the contrary, whenever Northern and Southern prejudices have come into conflict, the latter have been sacrificed and the former soothed." [12] Only Washington's presence would preserve the nation intact.

A growing awareness of the realities of national and international politics doubtless explains Jefferson's subsequent support of the style of life he had previously condemned. In 1793 he spoke of the necessity of the country's protecting its citizens, "their commerce and navigation," by means of duties and regulations and of promoting arts and manufactures as a means of preserving America from foreign domination.[13] By the time of his first annual message as President in late 1801, he was speaking of "agriculture, manufactures, commerce, and navigation" as the "four pillars of our prosperity." [14] He still felt by the end of his second term that "the situation into which we have thus been forced has impelled us to apply a portion of our industry and capital to internal manufactures and improvements." [15] But he had broken with an exclusively Southern pattern to advocate all the different kinds of activity which men of the period associated with an industrious society.

During the Revolution the evangelical ministers in the South had preached a union of industrious patriotism that included all Americans. Framed in terms of an appeal to personal commitment, their call had much in common with the moralistic position of Beverley and Byrd. David Ramsay and James Madison combined these two approaches, but the more seriously the message of patriotic union was taken, the more men abandoned purposeless busyness and the notion of a national union based on the power of allurement. In essence both the religious and later the patriotic message of the preachers had always stood less for actually changing the South than for leading its people into a new land of industriousness. First it had been the community of the faithful, later the national union—but always somewhere beyond the South. In a strictly Southern context the exhortation to industry and union did not produce the changes that Patrick Henry had hoped for, but for those who could commit themselves to the cause of American nationalism it had the effect of transcending all local differences.

On Thanksgiving Day of the year that the Constitution went into effect, Oliver Hart, formerly of South Carolina, preached a sermon in which he reminded his listeners that of all revolutions the American certainly "claimed the patronage and agency of the Divine Being." In spite of local divisions, differences of religion, and personal interests the members of the Continental Congress had "all united as one man in the common cause of their country." [16] He dwelt on the vast extent of America, with its capacity to produce all kinds of agricultural products and its "raw materials in abundance suitable for all kinds of manufactures." Praising the Constitution as "open, free, and generous although energetic," he noted that under its influence "religion, agriculture, manufactures, trade and commerce, and the more liberal arts and sciences will all flourish." [17] He affirmed that "if love be the bond of our union, the cement of our social compact, we shall be more happy in ourselves and more formidable to our neighbors." Being blessed with so many advantages, "usefulness should be everyone's aim. Slothful, inactive persons are a dead weight on society. Such drones merit to be stung out of the hive of the commonwealth." If everyone were to try to be of use to his community, "America would form a mighty army of useful individuals." [18] Thus Hart had a context—American nationality—in which to speak meaningfully of industry. It takes on added significance to note that he had originally come to South Carolina from Pennsylvania,[19] and that his sermon on union was delivered in Hopewell, New Jersey.

Other Calvinist ministers in the South continued to celebrate the glories of the Union and to derive from this concept a rationale for industry in their society. In 1795 George Buist, minister of the Presbyterian Church in Charleston, told supporters of the local orphan house that "by enuring these your adopted children to habits of activity, industry, and virtue, you lay the surest foundation of national prosperity." [20] The next year Richard Furman, minister of the Baptist Church in Charleston, spoke to the same group about the prospects of the orphans. "Thus after acquiring the rudiments of useful learning, accompanied by habits of industry, frugality, honesty, and love to their benevolent country, and above all by the knowledge of God and religion," he affirmed, "they will be fitted to enter on regular, useful professions to their own advantage and the public benefit." Their field of endeavor was a land of "agriculture, commerce, manufactures, and arts in a flourishing state." [21] His repeated use of such references as "citizens of Charleston and of America! Venerable patriots!" [22] testified to the fact that he was not concerned about local differences. A man did not have to be if he was willing to look all over the nation for elements of the good society. The more a person's concerns focused on the realities of Southern life, however, the less easy he found the acceptance of a definition of nationality and industry which could only be maintained by ignoring these realities.

In his treatise on agriculture, *Arator* (1803), John Taylor of Caroline turned his attention to the charge that "the mass of those we should call planters or farmers are ignorant, uneducated, poor, and indolent," pointing out that the "agriculturists had the sagacity to discover that the English system of creating an order of capitalists was levelled directly at our prosperity and the magnanimous perseverance to get rid of its authors." Unfortunately, the tyrant had been destroyed but the tyranny remained: "And why should we agriculturists be called ignorant and indolent when we are only gulled, just as mankind in general . . . are gulled?" [23] There had been some disposition before the Revolution to blame English mercantile policy for conditions in the Southern colonies, but Taylor was really the first Southerner to develop a whole philosophy of the South as an exploited victim of the outside forces it had always depended upon. The *Arator* was consequently a call for an oppressed interest to defend itself. His arguments were expressed in behalf of farmers in general, but it is obvious that his concern was with Southern agriculture. "So long as the laws make it more profitable to invest capital in speculations without labor than in agriculture with labor," he argued, "and so long as the liberty of pursuing one's own interests exists, the two strongest human propensities, a love of wealth and a love of ease, will render it impossible" to change men's habits. [24] If there were wise and effective laws, therefore, lazy Southerners (who sought only ease and wealth) would not be encouraged in their laziness. Their only alternative would be to work.

Taylor was convinced that agricultural improvements were

absolutely essential because the relatively poor soil of America (something the advocates of allurement had been unaware of) demanded such techniques as fertilizing and crop rotation. For these to be employed, however, Southerners would have to change their attitudes. He was sure that "the slaveholding states have been deterred from making agricultural improvements and establishing any tolerable system of police for the management of slaves by the lazy and hopeless conclusion that the destruction of their lands and the irregularities of their Negroes were incurable consequences of slavery." [25] Taylor's purpose therefore was as much to induce Southern planters to repent of ways, which he himself called indolent, as it was to demand the removal of external oppressions. He insisted that crop rotation was not enough, and he feared that "all will prefer the ease and profit of annual tillage as a mode of fertilizing the earth to the labor and delay of resting land, reducing tough swards, and raising and applying manure." Nevertheless, he warned that "industrious effort and not lazy theory can only save our ruining country." [26]

Ultimately Taylor's argument rested upon the conviction that his system was more profitable for the individual. To tell planters frantically engaged in the pursuit of gain that "great profit depends on great improvements of the soil, and great improvements can never be made by penurious efforts" may have meant something to those who occupied the worn-out tobacco lands of eastern Virginia. For others in the South the advice was meaningless. The social theory upon which Taylor based his arguments was that "the use of society is to secure the fruits of his own industry and talents to each associator. Its abuse consists in artifice or force for transferring those fruits from some partners to others." [27] What Southerners had long before proved was that it takes very little in the way of society to achieve these ends and even less in the way of partnership.

In the decade before the appearance of Taylor's work, Federalist spokesmen had been assuring Southerners that these ends had in fact been achieved. His fears by implication were excessive if not groundless. These men praised the situation which the new government had created and the part which the Southern states played in the nation's commercial scheme. "A flood of prosperity bursting upon the country on the revival of confidence has flowed into every quarter of the Union and fertilized almost every hamlet with its salubrious streams," Henry William Desaussure wrote in 1798.[28] Two years later, in giving advice on the 1800 election, he argued that "agriculture has been encouraged by the increased demand for the productions of our country, shipped with facility in consequence of our neutrality. The prices of our articles—rice, cotton, and tobacco—are advanced and the planters are wealthy." [29] In other words, the Constitution and the national government were vindicated because they had permitted the Southern way to flourish—not because there had been any change in that way of life.

Statements made in 1799 by Charles Pinckney, who had long since become a Jeffersonian, show a difference of emphasis but the same acceptance of the Southern way. He called for an amicable working out of the problems between America and England and asked where Great Britain had "so excellent a customer" as America: "They a great manufacturing people, we a nation of planters sending them our valuable materials and productions and taking from them in return their manufactures and superfluities." While a Federalist like Desaussure chose to depict the Southern way in commercial terms, a Jeffersonian like Pinckney chose agricultural terms and tended to view the whole nation as a vast plantation. Americans could purchase manufactures more cheaply than they could make them, he insisted, "and the rapid extension of their agriculture will prove the most solid means of promoting the strength and riches and protecting the morals of their citizens." [30]

Viewed from the perspective of its potentialities for individual gain, the South had always seemed a land of promise. A work published in 1802 by William Henry Drayton's son John indicated the literature of celebration still had a base. *A*

View of South Carolina celebrated the freedom there from all the restrictions existing in Europe. As a result its soil was "possessed by the people in a manner the most encouraging to industrious labors." Dealing with the fact of soil exploitation, Drayton admitted that the ease of cultivating lands "has of course led to a slovenness in husbandry, which to an experienced farmer would bespeak ignorance and inattention." He hastened to assure his readers that "this, however, is not the case, as the crops generally produce good returns." [31] Any failures in achieving the social goals of the kind his father, among others, had talked about during the Revolution were not failures at all: "Where agriculture is so much attended to in Carolina and the means of engaging in it are so easy, it is not surprising that few direct their attention to manufactures." This followed from the fact that "the inhabitants of this state find it more convenient to import them from foreign countries than to produce them by their own labor, which they believe can be otherwise more independently and profitably bestowed." [32] Drayton admitted candidly of slavery that "had not this agricultural strength been furnished South Carolina, it is probable in the scale of commerce and importance she would have been numbered among the least respectable states of the Union." [33] His picture was completed by praising the order and decorum of the people, who "are polite and affable, not resenting things as affronts which are not offered as such." Interestingly enough, this notion of order was related to the underlying threat of violence in the form of the duel. To it "may be ascribed many forbearings, which take place between individuals rather than resort to this last extremity." [34]

Seven years after Drayton's book appeared, David Ramsay brought out a two-volume history of South Carolina, which stands in relation to Drayton's work as the jeremiads of Beverley and Byrd stand to the earlier literature of celebration. Ramsay again affirmed, as in his earlier history of the Revolution, that under Great Britain "it was for the advantage of the province as well as the mother country to export the raw materials and import the goods manufactured." [35] Although such a view had underlain in large part his support of the Constitution and the new government, Ramsay still had retained much of the fervor of the Revolution for patriotic unity. In a Fourth of July oration in 1794 he dwelt on the increase of trade and population in America and the fact that "new ports are daily opened and new towns and cities lift their heads in all directions." Not surprisingly, he also stressed the fact that "industry, frugality, and temperance are virtues which we should eminently cultivate. These are the only foundation on which a popular government can rest with safety. . . . Idleness, extravagance, and dissipation of every kind should be banished from our borders. It is from the industrious alone that we can gather strength." [36] This aspect of Ramsay's thought is important, for laments over laziness had always proceeded from an expectation—however vague—that the good society ought to have certain characteristics which were lacking in the South.

In his 1808 history Ramsay noted that "the time is distant and a great revolution must take place in the manners of the inhabitants before they clothe themselves completely from their own resources. Their workshops will probably long remain in Europe or the more northern states; but as the country abounds with the suitable materials, they may whenever they please become a manufacturing as well as an agricultural state." [37] Near the end of his book Ramsay turned to lamentations over laziness. Specifically he found the explanation in the climate, for a "warm, moist, unelastic air fosters habits of indolence." This, combined with leisurely meals and smoking cigars, diminished "incitements to activity and energy of character." [38] Along with the argument that a "propensity to indolence is common in Carolina as in other warm countries and seasons" and the fact that "the exceptions to it are comparatively few," he mentioned that "the Carolinians are not easily roused. When roused, they are active and ardent but not persevering." [39] Ramsay differed from Beverley and Byrd not so much in describing the manifestations of laziness as in attributing it mainly to the climate. What had once been a land of such amazing richness that it tempted people into sloth had now become a country which was too hot and humid to stimulate men to industrious endeavors.

Ramsay was also concerned about the condition of the lower classes, who could not afford slaves. In the past "without the incitement of profitable industry to stimulate their exertions they seldom extended their labors beyond the point which would supply their daily wants in the plainest style of living. Much idleness and consequently vice was attached to their character." He noted of late a considerable change for the better. "To these people the culture of cotton holds out strong inducements to personal industry. It rewards their labors with a large share of the comforts of life without the degradation which must have often attached to them while laboring, not for themselves, but as appendages to planters or large farmers and as fellow laborers with their slaves." He admitted as well that Methodism had an influence in inducing these people "to engage in regular active industry." [40] Yet he returned again to the fact that "in estimating the value of cotton, its capacity to excite industry among the lower classes of people and to fill the country with an independent, industrious yeomanry is of high importance." [41] Groping for a specific solution to the problem of laziness, Ramsay, like Beverley and Byrd before him, found the answer only in more and more hard work in pursuit of profit. This time it was cotton which would usher in the golden age of industry, if only people would devote themselves busily to its cultivation—which they did.

A matter of labor and profit alone

11

In 1803 William Wirt, later the renowned biographer of Patrick Henry, wrote of the Virginia of Jefferson and Taylor in the persona of a British aristocrat. Included in *The Letters of the British Spy* is the caustic remark that there seems to be only one object, "to grow rich, a passion which is visible not only in the walks of private life but which has crept into and poisoned every public body in the state. . . . Hence Virginia exhibits no great public improvements." The gentlemanly observer further takes note of the "life of inglorious indolence by far too prevalent among the young men of this country," from which state "the transition is easy and natural to immorality and dissipation." [1] A few years later Wirt published another volume of observations, this time employing the persona of the "Old Bachelor," a genial Virginian, who deplores the acquisitiveness and lack of patriotism, not simply of Virginians, but of all Americans. Though he does not despair, he is of the opinion that "it would have been easier indeed at the close of the Revolution to prevent the growth of indolent and vicious habits than it will be now to eradicate them." [2]

While Wirt censured Virginians for their indolence, he also pointed out that "if anything indeed peculiarly distinguishes the Virginian from his confederated brethren, it is a lofty and chivalrous spirit." [3] Beyond this hint of ideas which are generally associated with the later cult of the romantic South, Wirt was both attracted by the idea of nature and at the same time torn between its logic and the logic of civilization. In the *British Spy* he condemned civilization because "wherever it has gained ground [it] has interwoven with society a habit of artificial and elaborate decorum, which mixes in every operation of life, deters the fancy from every bold enterprise, and buries nature under a load of hypocritical ceremonies." The orator must hence forget the habits induced by education and go "back to the primitive simplicity of the patriarchal age." Wirt emphatically praised Patrick Henry as Virginia's one orator of nature.[4] Yet in *The Old Bachelor* he took exactly the opposite tack and criticized Virginians for thinking that oratory was possible without any work at all. Great orators of antiquity "did not, like the visionary youth of Virginia, imagine that all this was to be effected by reposing indolently on the bounties of nature."[5]

In spite of this ambivalence, Wirt in his biography of Henry (1818) vindicated the orator's indolence and lack of formal education. As a youth Henry "was too idle to gain any solid advantage from the opportunities which were thrown in his way. He was passionately addicted to the sports of the field and could not support the confinement and toil which education required." With his faculties almost entirely "benumbed by indolence," young Henry spent his time in the forest, dividing his "life between the dissipation and uproar of the chase and the languor of inaction."[6] Henry emerges as a natural man, whose great skill as an orator bespeaks the power and influence of American nature over the acquired skills of artificial (European) civilization. For "however indolent in his general life, [he] was never so in debate, where the occasion called for exertion. He rose against the pressure with the most unconquerable perseverance."[7] Although Wirt's biography can be seen as a nature idyll,[8] the author filled it with worried reservations about the praise of Henry as a child of nature. The "youthful reader" is constantly warned not to "deduce from the example of Mr. Henry an argument in favor of indolence and contempt of study. Let him remember that the powers which surmounted the disadvantage of those early habits were such as very rarely appear upon earth. Let him remember too how long the genius, even of Mr. Henry, was kept down and hidden from the public view by the sorcery of those pernicious habits." [9]

William R. Taylor has shown in detail Wirt's place as one of the first mythmakers of the Southern plantation legend and the way this legend—adopted by Northerners as well as Southerners—functioned as a judgment on acquisitiveness, exemplified by the Yankee.[10] Both Henry's indolence as a child of nature and his later patriotic exertions can be taken as evidence of indifference to the selfish and acquisitive activities for which Virginians had been condemned in Wirt's two earlier books. This myth-making activity has its roots in the common nineteenth-century juxtaposition of nature against civilization and is thus part of an important shift in the history of American thought. In rejecting the world of Benjamin Franklin, in seeing organized society or civilization as a burden rather than a help, men were breaking with the notions of community which had been held in various forms since the beginning of colonization. Logically this would mean that work is not a positive social contribution but simply evidence of acquisitiveness. Wirt was uneasy about praising Henry's indolence because he was still too much a part of an earlier era to accept fully the consequences of making his hero a child of nature. But he could never have praised indolence at all if men had not begun to question the values of industry and society. From the earliest colonial times many expressed concern over what they called "worldliness," yet no first-generation divine would have objected to the fundamental social premises of Franklin's religion of labor—however much he might have deplored its secularism.

During the early nineteenth century nature and idleness were sometimes even explicitly linked as evidence that there are greater joys in life than trundling one's cart down the streets of Philadelphia to prove one's industry to the world.

Washington Irving meant it as no condemnation of his famous character in *The Sketch Book* when Geoffrey Crayon (himself a gentleman of leisure) tells the reader that "the great error in Rip's composition was an insuperable aversion to all kinds of profitable labor." Rip Van Winkle is perfectly willing to help others, "but as to doing family duty and keeping his farm in order, he found it impossible." It is not surprising, therefore, that "if left to himself, he would have whistled life away in perfect contentment; but his wife kept continually dinning in his ears about his idleness, his carelessness, and the ruin he was bringing on his family." Rip is obviously no hero, but his example is not held up to warn American youth of the baneful effects of sloth. The villain of the piece is his imperious wife, whose demands for labor in the name of civilization finally reduce poor Rip "almost to despair; and his only alternative, to escape from the labor of the farm and clamor of his wife, was to take gun in hand and stroll away into the woods." [11]

The significance for the South of this shift in values was that it was now possible to regard the Southern way of life as superior to that of New England. While Southerners since early times had cautiously stressed a certain element of ease or leisure in their lives as an antidote to frenzied acquisitiveness, labor had been so generally accepted as a social obligation that there had been little point in praising leisure for itself or distinguishing it from laziness. In the nineteenth century even Northerners were uneasy about Yankee values. If New England stood in the decades before the Civil War for industry and hard work as it always had, the South in the plantation legend now stood for the leisurely life of planters resting on cool verandahs and slaves fishing lazily along the banks of streams.

The definition of labor previous to this time had two aspects—personal and social—and leisure now implied the opposite of both. If plantation life really represented not rural society but the negative absence of the impedimenta of civilization, then in this respect the myth was an accurate representation of the South. Personal disdain for material affairs and delight in taking life easy, the aspects of leisure which increasingly interested men, posed certain problems. In the years before the Civil War the economic life of the South was centered in the Southwest, where the picture of "plantation society is one of feverish struggle for wealth, colored by a notable speculative element, and frequently characterized by competitive expenditure." [12] The plantation myth, however, did not deal with the Southwest but with the seaboard South, particularly Virginia and the lowcountry of South Carolina, and Southerners had developed something of a tradition for praising ease which they could now exploit. Also, however frantically men may have been engaged in pursuing wealth, there was often little evidence of affluence. It was easier to think of a planter, who had made and lost vast sums of money and who was often sorely in need of both credit and cash, as somehow less concerned about wealth than a busy Benjamin Franklin, whose total earnings may have been far less but whose person and property glowed with the evidence of virtuous enterprise.

Although the plantation myth was a very appealing defense of the South, writers who used it encountered unforeseen difficulties and ambiguities. In George Tucker's *The Valley of Shenandoah* (1824) the author seems quite unable to suppress the underlying economic realities of Southern life. When Mrs. Grayson is compelled to sell most of her slaves, the buyer, whose father had moved from Virginia to Georgia, tells her "that he himself had been very successful as a cotton planter; and from small beginnings, by means of industry and good management . . . he had made a considerable sum, which he wished to vest in Negroes and thus extend his cotton plantations." [13] The wife of Major Fawkner is increasingly "on the lookout for good bargains in land, Negroes, or bonds." It may be argued that Mrs. Fawkner serves in some sense as a scapegoat, and that Tucker really has to stress the fact that her husband is "naturally generous and high minded" as well as "of an indolent, easy disposition" in observing that "he had insensibly fallen into the views of his wife and had become more bent on making money than had been natural to him." [14] The inability to find any satisfactory middle ground between indolence and the frantic pursuit of gain might explain why plantation novelists so often emphasized failure and careless economic practices on the part of the planters. Edward Grayson tells a friend from New York that easy living among Virginia gentlemen and the resulting plunge into debt means that the best estates are "constantly passing from the hands of those who have inherited them to those whose frugality, or industry, or rapacity furnish the means of their purchase." Grayson dwells significantly not on the new purchasers, but on the dispossessed. If he blames them for "their deplorable incapacity for business or labor and their silly pride," he also has "a lively pity for their humiliation and distress." [15]

Ironically, the same indolence that contrasts to Mrs. Fawkner's energy carries with it an element of pointlessness and meaninglessness. "As our whites who can command the labor of slaves are not permitted to work by their prejudices and their pride," Grayson notes, "for want of other employment they are very much exposed to the seductions of gaming and drinking." [16] In an essay written a few years previously, Tucker had implored planters to become interested in literature so that "many of our fox-hunters and hunters of squirrels and gamesters and tipplers would be spared the sad necessity of flying from themselves." [17] While the reality behind this sense of purposelessness was more complicated than Tucker recognized, the fact still remained that it was very difficult to depict the ease even of a fictionalized and idealized Southern planter without admitting an element of pointlessness into his life. In this respect the celebration of personal leisure had failed to distinguish it effectively from laziness and hence purposelessness. Perhaps the most obvious means of giving direction to the life of the planter was to make him a member of some kind of social or intellectual group, either directly or through his interest in literature and culture. Tucker's greatest praise is bestowed not on the plantation but on Williamsburg in 1796. Though free of the evils of civilized life, the town evidences the advantages of learning, refinement, and social intercourse. He later praises Virginia gentlemen of the old school, whose "luxurious and social habits in which they were educated gave them all that polished and easy grace which is possessed by the highest classes in Europe." [18]

The need to acknowledge the existence of organized society often led the formulators of the plantation myth to associate the lives of Southern gentlemen with aristocracy, cultivation, and civilization. This involved really a different way of defining leisure by using it in its Aristotelian meaning of freedom from the necessity of having to engage in manual labor. Leisure in this sense had traditionally been associated with the lives of gentlemen living off their rents and supposedly devoting themselves to learning and public life. To pretend that the planter was really an English country gentleman had the obvious advantage of positing a style of life which satisfied a desire to condemn labor as the base pursuit of personal gain without denying the importance of society. Scorning mercenary values, leisured Southern aristocrats could presumably interest themselves in all forms of learning and culture and thereby avoid lazy and meaningless lives. Tucker's descriptions of leisure activities, however, indicated how imperfectly the South actually embodied this ideal. By suggesting a resemblance to European culture he invited a comparison which could only be to the South's disadvantage. Many Southerners pointed to the accomplishments of the generation of Jefferson and Madison, yet Tucker unhappily conceded that the type was nearly extinct.[19] Even as ideal aristocrats, these men expressed very little of the South as a society of refinement and cultivation when they participated in national and international culture. To praise Williamsburg as a center of culture called attention to what was least characteristically Southern, the city, rather than what was most Southern, the plantation.

The evocation of aristocratic analogies also failed to solve several problems in regard to idleness. Authentic European aristocracy had long been criticized for this vice. Moreover, it was very difficult to depict Southern aristocrats who avoided meaninglessness because their society lacked the complexity that existed in Europe. Finally, the aristocratic distinction between work (performed by the lower classes) and leisure (enjoyed by those above them), which was alien to both Puritan and attractionist assumptions, had never really taken root in America any more than aristocracy itself had. It was the other meaning of leisure as leisure time, coming in reaction to the notion that men's doings are supposed to be useful to society, which was eventually to gain acceptance.

If it still remained difficult to distinguish leisure from laziness despite aristocratic trappings, John Pendleton Kennedy, like Irving before him, showed what could be done by abandoning the distinction altogether. His novel *Swallow Barn* (1832, 1851) was dedicated to William Wirt as the "first fruit of the labors (I ought rather to say, of the idleness) of your trusty friend." [20] The main character is Frank Meriwether, the proprietor of Swallow Barn, who inclines "to be lazy and philosophical." Moreover, "he thinks lightly of the mercantile interest, and, in fact, undervalues the manners of the large cities generally." [21] A pervasive atmosphere of laziness keeps the turbulence of the lower orders in check. In contrast to the "rude and busy scene" of a Fourth of July celebration "was the voluptuous landscape around us. It was a picture of that striking repose which is peculiar to the tidewater views, soft, indolent, and clear." [22] Kennedy notes with approval that "the gentlemen of Virginia live apart from each other," surrounded "by their bondsmen and dependents," and that "they frequently meet in the interchange of a large and thriftless hospitality, in which the forms of society are foregone for its comforts and the business of life thrown aside for the enjoyment of its pleasures." Their style of living is even compared with "feudal munificence." [23]

Kennedy succeeds largely because of his satirical tone—his playful acceptance of indolence rather than any serious attempt to define a life of leisure. The reference to feudalism is not really meant to be taken seriously, and many of the currently popular symbols of the cult of romantic chivalry are held up to amusement. Because the book avoids seriousness, the reader can accept the values of its lazy and self-contained world without uneasiness. He may smile good-naturedly at Frank's provincialism, but his laziness does not seem pointless because it remains always a bit unreal. Given this mood, Kennedy is able to allude casually to certain economic realities without fear that they will destroy the repose of his world. The narrator admits that "there is a fascination in the quiet, irresponsible, and reckless nature of these country pursuits that is apt to seize upon the imagination of a man who has felt the perplexities of business." Then he adds that he would only like for himself "a thousand acres of good land, an old manorhouse on a pleasant site, a hundred Negroes, a large library, a host of friends, and a reserve of a few thousands a year in the stocks in case of bad crops, and finally a house full of pretty, intelligent, and docile children, with some few et ceteras not worth mentioning." [24] On the subject of slavery Meriwether insists that the Negroes do not work very hard, but he continues: "You gentlemen of the North greatly misapprehend us if you suppose that we are in love with this slave institution or that, for the most part, we even deem it profitable to us." [25]

In all, Kennedy's portrait of Virginia life hardly adds up to a vigorous and impassioned vindication, but its success lies precisely in the fact that it does not. A lifelong Unionist, politician, railroad promoter, and supporter of internal improvements, Kennedy himself was no Meriwether.[26] He was able to have the best of both worlds—his own and Meriwether's—by relying entirely on neither. His one serious reference to romantic chivalry almost undercuts the whole lazy world of the plantation. Captain John Smith is described as a man whose "character was moulded in the richest fashion of ancient chivalry and, without losing anything of romance, was dedicated, in his maturer years, to the useful purposes of life." [27] One can think of many useful activities in which

Smith engaged, but one labors almost in vain to find their counterparts in the world of Swallow Barn.

The laziness so fondly stressed by Kennedy stood for an ineffectual self-indulgence and indisposition to action which were surely meant to assure the North that the South was absolutely harmless and could be safely left alone. The connection between Kennedy's emphasis upon laziness and his Unionism was very direct indeed. The idea of a vigorous, united nation of Frank Meriwethers is too fantastic even to be entertained. This is even more clearly illustrated by James Hungerford of Maryland, whose novel, *The Old Plantation*, was issued two years before the outbreak of the Civil War. The story takes place in the early 1830's, a period of seething political agitation in the South. However, there is almost no reference to these matters and certainly no interest manifested in them. Instead the main characters spend their days fishing, telling stories, and attending parties. In fact the most concerted display of energies in the novel involves planning a large party. Isolation is tempered, as it always had been in the South, by this form of hospitality. The innocuous character of this pleasant world is accentuated by the author's half-serious, half-comic references to chivalry. The narrator is complimented on his courtesy by a reference to the *Morte d'Arthur* and is later told that he rides like a knight. He and his cousin hold a mock tournament for the benefit of the ladies, in which they joust with their riding whips, but they do not really conceive of Maryland as a feudal society.[28] The North could hardly feel threatened by the aggressive chivalry of two boys with riding whips.

If an acceptance of laziness, indeed a vindication of it, worked best in the service of Whig harmony and Unionism, one might expect men of sectional sympathies to have had more trouble dealing with this aspect of Southern character. William Alexander Caruthers's *The Kentuckian in New York* (1834) includes an extended exchange of opinions between a Southern Whig and Unionist and his more militantly Southern friend. Harmony is advocated by Victor Chevillere of

South Carolina, who writes during a trip to the North: "Every southern [Southerner] should visit New York. It would allay provincial prejudices and calm his excitement against his northern countrymen. The people here are warmhearted, generous, and enthusiastic in a degree scarcely inferior to our own southerns." Since harmony is impossible if one side is viewed as completely good and the other as completely bad, he balances this condescending judgment with criticisms of the city's mobs and its poverty on the one hand and of slavery on the other.[29] Chevillere's correspondent is Beverley Randolph of Virginia, whom the South Carolinian gently chides for his provincialism. Randolph is much more deeply concerned about the social situation in the South, where "the very happiest, most useful, and most industrious class of a well-regulated community" is wanting because its place is taken by slaves. Though Randolph insists he is no abolitionist, he cannot deny that slaves "are in incubus upon our prosperity."[30]

To resolve the conflict between loyalty to his section and knowledge of its defects, Randolph looks west. He expresses sorrow for "poor, exhausted eastern Virginia." Though he still loves this area, he finds on the western side of the mountains a scene which is totally different. "There a long and happy valley stretches far as the eye can reach, with its green hills and cultivated vales, neat farm houses, and fragrant meadows, and crystal springs, and sparkling streams, its prosperous villages, its numerous churches, and schools, and happy, happy people."[31] Ironically, this description of the promised land of industry resembles far more the traditional pictures of New England and Pennsylvania than of most places in the South. Indeed the Valley was something of an extension of Northern civilization, though strong Southern influences had modified its social patterns. This vision of a land of industry in the west is set forth even more strongly in Caruthers's subsequent works. As a Whig politically he was not personally committed to an early form of Southern nationalism, nor did his western vision necessarily imply anything exclusively Southern.[32] Yet it is significant that in attempting to solve the problem of laziness rather than simply accepting it like Kennedy, Caruthers found the answer in turning away from traditional Southern patterns to something closely resembling the North.

Nathaniel Beverley Tucker, a militant Southern nationalist, sought, even more fervently than Caruthers, alternatives to laziness. In the novel *George Balcombe* (1836) the young Virginia aristocrat William Napier must endure years of poverty and struggle both at home and in the west to retrieve his family fortune, which has been dishonestly withheld because of the treachery of the villainous Montague. Balcombe, a resourceful Virginian now living in Missouri, insists that this struggle has been worthwhile. Had it not been for Montague, Napier "would have been now drowsing away his existence on the banks of the Potomac, a lazy, luxurious country gentleman. Montague has made a man of him." [33] In *The Partisan Leader* (1836), the purported chronicle of a Southern war for independence, the traitorous Owen Trevor, who sides with the Union, is a man "in whom the pleasures of an idle life and the schemes of ambition had left little thought of the simple joys of his childhood's home." [34] In his quarters "everything betokens comfort and luxury, ease and indolence." He is "indifferent to duty, frivolous, self-indulgent, and mercenary," while his brother Douglas, the soul of Southern patriotism, is "assiduous, discreet, temperate, and disinterested." [35] The reader, however, is given few clues as to what Douglas Trevor and William Napier will be like after the struggles are over and they have settled down to lives (presumably of ease) on their plantations. If Tucker sought activism within a professedly Southern context, he was able to find it only in public or private battles—and the ultimate influence of ease silently outlasts the strenuous phase of his characters' lives.

In his many novels dealing with the American Revolution William Gilmore Simms was able like Tucker to portray in a situation of war heroic and active Southerners such as Willie

Sinclair, who is "prompt, cool, and energetic." [36] Among Simms's characters the noble, though rotund, gourmet Captain Porgy most resembles Kennedy's Frank Meriwether. In battle he is a good officer and a true patriot, but once the struggle for independence is over Simms is unable to depict him with the same assurance as Kennedy treats Meriwether. In fact the aura of disinterestedness evaporates in the harsh glare of the economic realities of Southern life. The vigorous widow Mrs. Eveleigh has done Porgy the good deed of saving many of his slaves from the British by being friendly with men of both sides. "The result," she confesses candidly, "has made me somewhat unpatriotic. I supplied the enemy with aid and comfort, but always, in the phrase of the tradesmen, for a *consideration.* . . . The war, accordingly, which has ruined so many has made my fortune." Porgy has been taken in hand by Sgt. Millhouse, who helps him with his plantation. This economic realist scorns Porgy's lack of concern for what is useful, telling him that real wisdom consists "in making a crop, driving a bargain, gitting the whip hand in a trade, and always falling, like a cat, on one's legs." He terms Porgy's interest in music and poetry "all flummery." [37] Off the field of battle, therefore, it is necessary for Simms to cling to Porgy's amusing and bemused ineptitude in dealing with his affairs as a bulwark against the frantic pursuit of gain.

From earliest colonial times the call to industry had been a condemnation of society and yet at the same time a stimulus to frantic endeavor. Both the condemnation and the effect figure in the various plantation novels—the first in the form of Caruthers's westerners, the second in Simms's Sgt. Millhouse. William R. Taylor has noted the tension in these novels between Cavalier and yeoman ideals.[38] The Cavalier planter exemplified the Southern way, while potentially the yeoman stood for a changed South, a land of small farms and enterprising tradesmen. At the same time the idealized yeoman is different from the real "red neck" (Sgt. Millhouse), whose attitudes are characteristically Southern. The North as the embodiment of mere acquisitiveness had become increasingly suspect as a model through the antebellum period, as had such exemplars of busyness as Sgt. Millhouse. Hence the attractiveness of the ideal of ease, yet for obvious reasons industry, or at least activity, remained equally desirable. Southerners had not really rejected the importance of society, nor had they been able to distinguish leisure effectively from purposelessness and laziness. They could not confidently praise the South as a land of boundless economic opportunity as they once had. Neither could they vigorously defend it as a land of leisure as they would one day. Instead many oscillated between qualified praise of ease and efforts at finding convincing alternatives.

This can be seen in the thinking of other Southerners besides the plantation novelists. In 1857 Governor Henry Wise of Virginia, speaking of the resources and hopes of the state, told how its early pattern of settlement had meant that its people were "segregated and isolated in a way utterly opposed to the concentration of population and capital, to the building of cities and of ships, and to the encouragement of the mechanic arts." [39] But he did not regret this situation: "We have no cities, but we have a meliorated country populace, civilized in the solitude, gracious in the amenities of life, and refined and conservative in social habits." He then added that "we have little *associated* but more *individual* wealth than any equal number of white population in the United States." Virginians could buy utensils from others because "our labor in the past has been and at present is better employed than to manufacture them ourselves." [40]

Based upon this reality, the ideal of leisure never lost its appeal because in the last analysis it glorified the Southern way. Slavery, Wise insisted, "affords a class of masters who have leisure for the cultivation of morals, manners, philosophy, and politics." [41] Yet after this hymn to the distinctiveness of the state he went on to celebrate the effects of diversification of agriculture in eastern Virginia and the various internal improvements which the state was projecting. Virginia would become a funnel of commerce which would rival New York and London, and the result would find her "an empire in herself, in the anomalous condition of an old State with all the undeveloped resources of a new State, and of a new State with all the ameliorations of an old State." [42] Such a combination of industry and leisure would indeed make Virginia unique.

No one was more influential in helping to bring about the agricultural changes in eastern Virginia which Wise described than Edmund Ruffin. He attacked relentlessly the traditional practices of the planters of the seaboard South and spread the gospel of intensive cultivation and the proper use of fertilizers. His concern with changing the old pattern of agriculture was based upon an acknowledgment that the evils of this system were primarily social rather than personal. The error of planters, he said, "in regard to their own interests, great as it may be, is incomparably less than the mistake as to other and general interests not being thus affected." Hence he warned that "with the impoverishment of its soil a country, a people, must necessarily and equally be impoverished." [43] As a militant Southern nationalist, Ruffin attacked the opinion he found in South Carolina that it was cheapest to buy hay, corn, and provisions on the grounds that it was almost impossible "that there can exist anywhere a truly thriving agricultural class, which, as a regular system, buys, instead of raising, the necessary and most important articles of food." [44] This linking of industry, change, social concerns, and an interest in Southern nationalism seems as logical as the absence of such connections in Kennedy's *Swallow Barn*.

In discussing the influence of slavery in 1852 Ruffin admitted that while he had sought to increase agricultural productivity, still if he had to choose, he "would not hesitate a moment to prefer the entire existing social, domestic, and industrial conditions of these slave-holding States, with all the now existing evils of indolence and waste and generally exhausting tillage and declining fertility, to the entire conditions of any other country on the face of the globe." [45] Kennedy's reaction to such a sentiment would have been to insist that the best way to avoid the necessity of painful choices was not to get excited about anything. After all, it would seem logical to suppose that if one wished to be loyal to the South, and indolence with all its effects was intimately a part of the Southern way, the more indolent the more loyal. Of course, this implied certain concessions to the realities of economic life in the United States, but a gentleman of leisure could not be bothered with the trying details that hurried the miserly merchants and manufacturers of Boston and New York into premature graves. If idleness was to be a virtue, it must mean above all not getting excited. The trouble with America was that there were far too many excited people. Let the South relax in the calm assurance that by nurturing an ideal of escape from the vexations and responsibilities of organized social life, it was performing a service as important as supplying the millions of bales of cotton which kept the wheels of the nation's economy turning and the short-sighted hustlers busy.

12

At the height of the Nullification crisis in 1832 Robert Y. Hayne passionately defended the Southern way before his fellow United States Senators. He dismissed the notion that South Carolinians should turn to manufacturing and so "abandon our agricultural pursuits and involve the whole Southern country in desolation and ruin." [1] "In a broad view of the question," he noted later in his speech, "it never can be expedient to introduce into a country the manufacture of any article that cannot be produced as cheaply at home as it can be obtained from abroad." The answer to prosperity lay in "FREE TRADE, in its largest sense," which, next to the Christian religion, he considered "the greatest blessing that can be conferred upon any people." [2]

By the latter part of the decade, however, such Nullificationists as Hayne and George McDuffie had begun to have second thoughts. Beginning in 1837 the first of a series of Southern Commercial Conventions was held and the resolution adopted "that we are called upon by every consideration of interest and of patriotism to throw off the degrading shackles of our commercial dependence" upon the North. [3] The logic behind this change in sentiment was simple. As McDuffie told the delegates, "every political community should endeavor to unite within itself and have under its own control, as far as circumstances will permit, all the elements of national wealth." He justified this plea for self-sufficiency by the stern reminder that Southerners were "distinguished from our Northern confederates by peculiar domestic and civil institutions, which are inseparably identified with our great staple productions and which we hold to be absolutely exempt from all foreign scrutiny or interference whatever." [4]

A decade later James H. Hammond sought to convince his fellow South Carolinians in particular of the wisdom of economic diversification. He was deeply concerned about the shortcomings of Carolina society, insisting that no man of one idea can succeed because "both human affairs and the works of nature are complex, exhibiting everywhere an infinite variety of mutual relations and dependencies." By analogy no nation devoted to a single pursuit can succeed, and thus "those nations only are powerful and wealthy, which, in addition to agriculture, devote themselves to commerce and manufactures." [5] This tribute to the style of life exemplified by the North indirectly acknowledged how far South Carolina (and presumably the rest of the South) fell short of possessing the accepted evidences of industry and hence separate national existence. The persistence of the old belief in the importance of socially meaningful labor was demonstrated by Hammond's reply to the objection "that where manufactures and commerce flourish morals are corrupted and free institutions do not prosper." He admitted that "it is undoubtedly true that when men congregate in cities and factories the vices of our nature are more fully displayed, while the purest morals are fostered by rural life. But, on the other hand, the compensations of association are great. It develops genius, stimulates enterprise, and rewards every degree of merit." [6]

Hammond could not, however, sustain his opposition to the idea of the South as a land of ease, free from the impediments of civilization. His avowed purpose was to recommend cotton manufacturing, and he argued that "God in His bounty has manifestly designed it and all its attendant benefits for the people of the cotton-growing region." Nevertheless, he maintained that he was not "desirous to see the mechanical and manufacturing spirit and influence prevail over the agricultural in this State or in the South." [7] His commitment to the Southern way had already been revealed when he insisted that manufacturing would in no way undermine the free trade principles of the South.[8] Whether coarse manufactures would actually have needed tariff protection is not the point here. Free trade was associated in the South, as Hayne had acknowledged in 1832, with the whole pattern of independent production upon isolated plantations sustained by the services of outsiders. A thoroughgoing program of manufacturing and commercial development would conflict with such an approach, and a much different temperament would be needed to promote new forms of investment.

The vast quantity of literature devoted to industrial and commercial change in the antebellum South embodies this same dichotomy between the Southern way and the notion that the region must expand and diversify its economic activities. It is significant, therefore, that many of the pleas in behalf of this course of action were, like Hammond's, cast in the form of the jeremiad, always the reflection of feelings of confusion, frustration, and divided loyalties despite its overt commitment to change. In a speech in the mid-1840's William Gregg, the South Carolina cotton manufacturer, minced no words in calling upon his lazy brethren to repent for having failed to fulfill the promises of the land. The state was, "to say the least, destitute of every feature which characterizes an industrious people." Like many earlier Jeremiahs, he looked to New England as the example of the model society. A visit there was enough to demonstrate "the difference between indolence and industry, extravagance and economy." Gregg looked upon repentance as a necessary element of action and also as an alternative to political agitation, because "a change in our habits and industrial pursuits is a far greater desideratum than any change in the laws of our government which the most clamorous opponents of the tariff could devise." [9]

Perhaps the most powerful motivation for change stemmed

precisely from Southerners' persistent feelings of inadequacy toward the North. Its economic gains during this period were by comparison so rapid and impressive that J.D.B. De Bow felt compelled to write the members of the Southern Railroad Convention in 1851 that the South had "no time to lose. Every day increases the distance between ourselves and our enterprising neighbors and makes the contest between us a more hopeless one." [10] "This is a period in the history of the world in which advancement is emphatically the order of the day," Rosewell Beebe of Arkansas wrote the same convention. Referring to the impact of the "spirit of improvement," he noted that "where this spirit has prevailed it has overcome prejudice, aroused indolence to energy, supineness to effort, given new impulses to trade, and multiplied the sources of wealth and happiness to the laboring classes." [11]

Obviously men also advocated economic diversification to enable the South to remain equal within the Union in order to defend its special interests and institutions. Like the support of free trade, therefore, the desire to rival the North involved an allegiance to the Southern way which directly conflicted with any consistent commitment to change. It would be very convenient to associate the calls for manufacturing and commerce with the development of a sentiment for Southern nationalism. But this disregards the fact that many advocates of economic diversification, including William Gregg, were supporters of the Union, while convinced Southern nationalists like William Lowndes Yancey and Robert Barnwell Rhett were mostly indifferent to such changes. The picture is very unclear, and with the ambivalent commitment both to the present and to change the results were even less decisive. Certainly there was an increase in industrialization, but achievements were limited, and the problems involved in overcoming the effects of busy idleness were almost insoluble. *De Bow's Review*, the most articulate organ of diversification, was usually printed in New York, where more competent work was done. An important collection of articles on the industrial resources of the South and Southwest, issued by De Bow in

1853, found six times as many purchasers in the North as in the South.[12]

Furthermore, efforts at change tended, as they generally had in the past, to reinforce patterns of economic individualism rather than to create conditions of co-operative activity. In 1854 General M. B. Lamar pleaded with members of the Southern Commercial Convention to abandon local interests and "to unite in the same common action for the common weal of all." [13] Yet this proved impossible. Southerners envied the advantages of New York and Philadelphia, but it was not good enough for them to have one or two commercial centers. Every state must have its own. No integrated railway system developed because, as Charles S. Sydnor notes, "the staples of the region were destined for transatlantic and Northern markets; no part of the South needed much of the product of any other part." [14] Here was the key to the failure of efforts to change the South's economic patterns, and it explains the marked contrast with the integrated production and transportation systems of the North. Work as a social activity had always meant that men needed the services and productions of those around them. Because Southerners did not, the patterns of laziness remained. As in the past, the newest form of the jeremiad only promised an increase in busyness. Hammond argued for the success of cotton manufacturing on the grounds that if necessary "there is no doubt we can extend our hours of labor beyond any of our rivals." [15]

Throughout this period of agitation for economic change a small number of men had been endeavoring to inform the South of the true cause of its inferiority, which they no less than Gregg and Hammond lamented. In the words of Daniel R. Goodloe in 1846, "slavery sits like the Old Man of the Sea upon the necks of the people, paralyzing every effort at improvement." [16] The intimate association of this institution with the most characteristic features of the Southern way lent credibility to the argument that it was responsible for the familiar evidences of lazy inferiority to the North. During the debate on the slavery question in the Virginia legislature in early 1832 Charles J. Faulkner had argued that "there is no diversity of occupations, no incentive to enterprise." Slavery had made labor disreputable; towns were stationary and villages declining. In fact, "the general aspect of the country marks the curse of a wasteful, idle, reckless population, who have no interest in the soil and care not how much it is impoverished." [17] Hinton Rowan Helper was therefore touching Southerners in a very sensitive spot when he too drew upon the jeremiad for his *Impending Crisis of the South* (1857). With a single, though crucial, exception he accepted all the premises of the advocates of progress in the South, arguing that "in ease and luxury we have been lolling long enough; we should now bestir ourselves and keep pace with the progress of the age." [18] The answer was very simple for these critics of slavery. Get rid of it, and magically the South would become a land of industry. As Helper told his fellow Southerners: "Your rivers and smaller streams, now wasting their waters in idleness, will then turn the wheels of multitudinous mills. Your bays and harbors, now unknown to commerce, will then swarm with ships from every enlightened quarter of the globe." [19]

When conservatives in the Virginia debate of 1832 sought to counter the criticisms of their opponents, they insisted that it was "impossible to touch this subject without impairing the value of the property of the slaveholders." [20] This, however, was not responding to the line of attack which the critics had taken. Their arguments were entirely social rather than personal in nature. In fact all of the discussions of the effects of slavery dealt with general social conditions in the South, not with the personal prosperity of slaveholders. After stating that among other things slavery "converts the energy of a community into indolence," Charles J. Faulkner asked: "Shall society suffer that the slaveholder may continue to gather his crop of human flesh?" [21] Clearly slavery could not be positively vindicated simply on personal grounds when social considerations still mattered too much to be ignored. Hence it was necessary for the defenders of the institution to prove that, socially speaking, the South was not a land of idleness.

In discussing the "morals of slavery," William Gilmore Simms insisted that labor "is one of the first elements of religion, as it is the prime element of human prosperity." Man must first labor, and "the desire to escape this destiny is one of the true causes of the present distress of our country." [22] In his natural state the Negro lived, William Grayson maintained, "a careless life of indolence." Slavery was the necessary condition of labor for him because "he is lazy and improvident. Slavery makes all work, and it ensures homes, food and clothing to all. It permits no idleness, and it provides for sickness, infancy and old age." [23] By insisting that labor is essential to civilized life, proslavery theorists transformed the old contention that in order to control idleness slaves must be forced to work into an argument that curbing a slave's idleness helped raise him from savagery to civilization. While Dr. Samuel A. Cartwright of Louisiana felt that Negroes were a separate and inferior order of beings, he rejoiced that the strict regulations of the plantations were "gradually and silently converting the African barbarian into a moral, rational, and civilized being." Work was absolutely the best thing for him, because "experience proves that he is much happier during the hours of labor in the sunny fields than when dozing in his native woods and jungles." [24]

While theorists were immediately concerned only with justifying Negro slavery, many nevertheless suggested elaborate notions of social evolution, which linked slavery of all kinds with the development of civilization. In the late 1830's a prominent South Carolina judge, Chancellor William Harper, insisted that "if anything can be predicated as universally true of uncultivated man, it is that he will not labor beyond what is absolutely necessary to maintain his existence." Harper thus concluded that "the coercion of slavery alone is adequate to form man to habits of labor." [25] Later in his argument he noted that "in early stages of society, when people are thinly scattered over an extensive territory, the labor necessary to extensive works cannot be commanded. Men are independent of each other. Having the command of abundance of land, no one will submit to be employed in the service of his neighbor." One quickly realizes that what was intended as a general hypothesis may more accurately be termed a description of actual conditions in the South, for "if a man has the command of slaves he may combine labor and use capital to any required extent and therefore accumulate wealth." [26]

One difficulty with this line of argument was the fact that slavery did not exist in the most advanced communities of the nineteenth century. The full elaboration of the notion of wage slavery seemed to be an answer, yet in turning to very recent English history for most of their evidence, theorists failed to explain why slavery had never been widespread in the North—why it was that even in the earliest stages of colonization men had voluntarily exchanged services in New England and Pennsylvania. Edmund Ruffin argued that the New England settlers brought with them "habits of industry and artificial wants, which had been produced and cultivated in their ancestors by their former and then extinct old system of slavery," that is, serfdom.[27] Still, the very logic of this argument carried the suggestion that slavery was associated with relatively unadvanced cultures, Rome and Greece notwithstanding. In 1832 Professor Thomas Roderic Dew of William and Mary College had virtually admitted what Ruffin was not quite able to disguise. Dew noted that slavery or serfdom in southern Europe had declined at the end of the Middle Ages with the extension of "commerce and manufactures and the consequent rapid rise of cities, accompanied with a more regular and better protected industry, producing a vast augmentation in the products which administer to our necessities and comforts and increasing in a proportionate degree the sphere of our wants and desires." He was thus compelled to insist that this pattern of development did not apply to Negroes in the South because of "their present limited wants and longing for a state of idleness." [28]

As early as 1826 Edward Brown of South Carolina was arguing that many mutually dependent orders within a society are evidence of an advanced civilization and that anything weakening gradation leads back to barbarism. He then explained that where wages are high and laborers can easily subsist, "that state of dependence which tended to keep them sober and honest no longer existing, they will rush headlong to the gratifications of their passions. . . . The only barrier to this disorganization of civilized society is slavery." [29] Not only was Brown describing a social situation in which men would not work for others unless compelled to; he was using the subordination of a single class, Negro slaves, as a general argument for a structured society. Ironically, many theorists could not refrain from other assertions which directly contradicted the notion of the South as an orderly society of mutually dependent classes. "Jack Cade, the English reformer," said Professor Dew, "wished all mankind to be brought to one common level. We believe slavery in the United States has accomplished this, in regard to the whites, as nearly as can be expected or even desired in this world." [30] Since the argument for a structured society presupposed mutual dependence as an attribute of industry and social differentiation, the notion of absolute equality among whites can be taken to imply the opposite—little or no mutual dependence, even though there might be differences in wealth and power. Moreover, in almost all formal defenses of slavery there is a moment of candor, a frank statement that the institution was necessary for activities requiring the labor of others because there seemed to be no alternative. This admission of the absence of economic interdependence among white men was implied in the theoretical arguments, but it was often stated quite openly. William Grayson maintained that the greatest "difficulty to the master in any exchange of slave for free labor is that in truth he has no choice. It is slave labor with him, or none." [31]

While Chancellor Harper insisted that "all the great and enduring monuments of human art and industry—the wonders of Egypt—the everlasting works of Rome—were created by slave labor," he could only offer the rather faint hope that "there will come a stage in our progress when we shall have facilities for executing works as great as any of these." [32] Try as they might, therefore, proponents of slavery had failed to defend the institution in terms of a coherent theory of labor and society. Ralph E. Morrow has argued that the most important function of the proslavery argument was to bolster the doubts of those within the South who professed no opposition.[33] Moral doubts could in part have been assuaged by justifications in terms of social relevance, and these in turn called for a meaningful definition of the society of which slavery formed a part. Deeper feelings of failure which the jeremiad had always expressed contributed also to the desire to find acceptable answers. Hence the added confusion and moral anxiety for many as they failed to convince themselves that slavery was anything more than a means of self-aggrandizement intimately associated with the traditionally acknowledged shortcomings of Southern society. Like the attempt to find a definition of an industrious society in terms of manufactures and commerce, the effort to evolve a proslavery theory does not bear a relationship to any particular concept of Southern nationalism. Arguments were as vigorously advanced by Union sympathizers like William Grayson as by militant advocates of a separate South like Ruffin. To complicate the confusion the proslavery theory did not really complement the notion of a commercial and manufacturing South. In its critique of the evils of capitalism, in fact, it represented more nearly the opposite.

Perhaps the most ingenious formulation of this theory was suggested by the pioneer Mississippi sociologist Henry Hughes. He divided society into three classes—simple laborer, skilled laborers, and capitalists. Only the first must be compelled to work, or civilly obliged, as he phrased it. The other two classes work voluntarily. It is unnecessary to compel them because they stand to lose financially if they do not add to the labor performed by the slaves. As Hughes described the situation, in perhaps the earliest example of sociological jargon, "all classes are societarily enforced to work; the simple-labor class, civilly; the others, economically. One class are civil obligees; the other, economic; and all, moral and societary obligees." [34] In his own way he was expressing the Southerner's special conceptualization of social unity. Society functioned, he in effect suggested, by a balance between coercion (with respect to the slaves) and allurement (with respect to all other classes). In a sense it did. Ultimately, therefore, the proslavery theory reduced itself simply to a version of the doctrine of allurement, as modified to account for the necessity of coercion.

In his fully elaborated analysis of society and government in the United States John C. Calhoun shared this long-standing Southern faith in the binding powers of economic motives, even though he built his system upon an admission of the absence of industry and unity within Southern society. His early nationalism was both an acknowledgement of Southern distinctiveness and an expression of hope that economic and patriotic ties would effectively unite this different South with the other parts of the Union. In expressing support for a proposed tariff in 1816, he praised American manufactures because such an interest "is calculated to bind together more closely our widely-spread republic. It will greatly increase our mutual dependence and intercourse, and will as a necessary consequence excite an increased attention to internal improvement." He had already protested that his motives were entirely disinterested since he came from the South, which had "no interest but in the cultivation of the soil, in selling its products high and buying cheap the wants and conveniencies of life." Rather his concern was with the security of the country as a whole.[35] On another occasion that same year Calhoun voiced the hope that patriotic dedication to the requirements of national defense would lead to the moral improvement of all Americans, who were blessed with many advantages which "operate on the dispositions and habits of this people with something like the effects attributed to southern climates; they dispose them to pleasure and to inactivity except in pursuit of wealth." Calhoun thus preferred the country to be essentially on a war basis because it made effort necessary to secure liberty, whose "favor is never won by the cowardly, the vicious, or indolent." [36] It is not clear how much he hoped the South might change as a result of such necessities, but he evidently expected Southerners to abandon "inactivity except in pursuit of wealth" and at least in this sense to become more industrious.

The Nullification crisis profoundly and conclusively convinced Calhoun of the distinctiveness of the South. Because he had always been aware of it, he was not disillusioned in the way Patrick Henry and Richard Henry Lee had been after the Revolution. Instead he set himself the task of defining precisely the terms of union which the Federalists in the South had rather too carelessly accepted. He told the people of South Carolina in 1831 that he saw in the "Union, as ordained by the Constitution, the means if wisely used not only of reconciling all diversities, but also the means, and the only effectual one, of securing to us justice, peace, and security at home and abroad." While admitting the importance of the Union to the South, he had already acknowledged the unanimity of the region's commitment to the notion that "its prosperity depends in a great measure on free trade, light taxes, economical, and, as far as possible, equal disbursements of the public revenue, and unshackled industry, leaving them to pursue whatever may appear most advantageous to their interests." [37] His theory of national unity would therefore have to take account of the functioning of allurement and its effects.

Like the proslavery theorists, Calhoun began with the premise that man is a social being, but he balanced this with a belief that man "is so constituted that his direct or individual affections are stronger than his sympathetic or social feelings." What follows from this fact is "the tendency to a universal state of conflict between individual and individual," which, "if not prevented by some controlling power," leads to the destruction of the "social state and the ends for which it is ordained." [38] Calhoun thus shared with those earlier Southerners who had reacted against the conditions of excessive freedom—especially the Regulators—a concern for order. Essentially, however, he stressed, as Southern supporters of the Constitution had done, the need to provide stability in order to facilitate the operation of allurement within society. The effect of insufficient governmental control, he felt, "would be insecurity, and of insecurity, to weaken the impulse of individuals to better their condition, and thereby retard progress and improvement." It is worth emphasizing that Calhoun rejected the notion of human equality not because he believed in fixed and interdependent orders within society, but because equality seemed to him to impede the proper functioning of allurement by implying limitations on men's freedom of opportunity. The main spring of progress is the desire of individuals to better themselves, and "the strongest impulse which can be given to it is to leave individuals free to exert themselves in the manner they may deem best for that purpose, as far at least as it can be done consistently with the ends for which government is ordained, and to secure to all the fruits of their exertions." [39]

The theory of the concurrent majority may be interpreted as an attempt both to give free play to the operation of allurement and at the same time to curb its bad effects. The concurrent majority "is better suited to enlarge and secure the bounds of liberty because it is better suited to prevent government from passing beyond its proper limits and to restrict it to its primary end, the protection of the community. But in doing this it leaves, necessarily, all beyond it open and free to individual exertions." [40] This was precisely how Southern Federalists had interpreted the role of the Federal government under the Constitution—to provide that minimum of order necessary to permit the greatest possible amount of personal economic freedom. In order to achieve this end, however, Calhoun had gone far beyond Madison by making the peculiar Southern fascination with violence and disorder one of the cornerstones of his system. Social order was placed under the constant threat of disorder by giving individual interests within the community the right of veto. Yet this threat of disorder was intended to produce order because of "the necessity which compels the different interests, or portions, or orders, to compromise—as the only way to promote their respective prosperity and to avoid anarchy." [41] Southerners often justified the duel with this same argument that the threat of violence actually promotes social order by making it a matter of self-interest to avoid giving offense. Furthermore, the constant possibility of disorder would have the effect of keeping Southerners alert, for they could never relax into a false sense of security. In his expectation of the South's ability to bring the North to terms by the use of its veto powers, Calhoun clearly retained much of the Federalists' conviction of the region's sheer utility to the North. Otherwise the emphasis placed upon self-interest is not very convincing. He did not follow the analogy of the duel to the extreme by threatening war to force concessions.

The ultimate logic of Calhoun's system was to preserve Southern distinctiveness, and he sought to do so by maximizing the degree of social disunity within the nation. If the states still retained their sovereignty, "instead of being united socially, their citizens would be politically connected through their respective States." [42] This was his answer to Patrick Henry's fears that a united nation would involve extensive and difficult changes for the South. The very notion of state sovereignty took account of disunity within the South itself by permitting a single state like South Carolina to exercise vigilance when only a minority even within that state were truly vigilant. As a theory of government, moreover, Calhoun's view was as much a unity of disunity as Madison's. It sought to neutralize the effect of Northern unity while it protected Southern disunity. It envisaged no slave power within the nation, for there was no provision for concerted minority action. Even the notion of a dual presidency was based on the dubious assumption that a Southern President would guard Southern interests. In fact, a Northerner, Buchanan, would prove a truer friend of the South than a Southerner like Jackson.

In 1838 Calhoun asked in Congress: "When did the South ever place her hand on the North? When did she ever interfere with her peculiar institutions?" [43] Repeatedly defenders of the South insisted that all they wanted was to be left alone, and this was true. Calhoun had no desire to make the North like the South. He simply wanted everyone to live and let live. This meant that each individual was capable of taking care of himself as long as others did not unite against him. The functioning of the concurrent majority would protect the special interests of the slaveholder in the nation, as it did in South Carolina, by using the limited powers of government to destroy all combinations against him—not by giving him exclusive power in his own right. In this way economic freedom could be maximized and the traditional aspects of Southern life forever preserved. While explicitly Calhoun's views were a defense of order, ultimately and more extensively they were a defense of freedom as the term was understood by Southerners. He did not advance a theory of Southern nationalism. Every element of his system was designed to protect the interests of a disunited people who could neither live wholly with nor without the rest of the country. James H. Hammond's observation in 1850 is therefore an accurate one: "Mr. Calhoun was mainly influenced by that deep, long cherished, and I might almost say superstitious attachment to the Union which marked every act of his career from its commencement to its very close." [44]

Beyond the level of theory, Calhoun recognized many kinds of bonds of national union—bonds which by 1850 he feared had all been broken: "Some are spiritual or ecclesiastical, some political, others social. Others appertain to the benefits conferred by the Union, and others to the feeling of duty and obligation." [45] If religion could help hold the Union together in part by giving labor meaning in terms of men's allegiance to society and the nation, doubtless Calhoun understood his section too well to expect it to perform a similar task for an independent South. During the War of 1812, religion had been at the service of patriotism as it had been during the

Revolution. The Rev. Finis Ewing, founder of the Cumberland Presbyterian Church, preached a fiery sermon which was reprinted in 1850 by the editor of a Louisville religious journal in the hope that "in these times of traitorous schemes and treasonable movements on the part of sectional extremists the reading of this sermon can but tend to induce a stronger love of country in those who have not passed through the times that tried men's souls." [46] A few years later Ewing's biographer pointed out that "he who loves his God supremely will also love his country disinterestedly. . . . Being a fellow-citizen with the saints, he is a co-worker with patriots." [47]

Such sentiments vindicate in part Calhoun's judgment of the importance of religion as a national bond, but where matters Southern were concerned one finds no similar sense of patriotic zeal and idealism. Understandably one of the major problems was slavery. It had been possible at the time of the Revolution to participate in a national vision without having to come to terms specifically with this institution. It was not possible any longer. Strong opponents like Peter Cartwright left the region to be free to criticize it. A few other ministers got into trouble for their sentiments, but most voiced no opposition.[48] Many continued to be concerned about the personal welfare of the slave and spoke out especially in the early years against what they considered the abuses of the institution, but beyond the domain of day-to-day conduct clergymen professed to remain aloof from the whole question. In 1838 the Rev. Theodore Clapp of New Orleans counseled those concerned to "let not the character of the clergyman be merged in that of the politician. Let him at all times preach unconditional submission to civil laws and institutions." [49] In 1851 the Rev. James Henley Thornwell of South Carolina insisted that the church "has a *creed*, but no *opinions*. When she speaks, it must be in the name of the Lord, and her only argument is, thus it is written." [50] In practice Thornwell used this distinction, as many clergymen did, to advance scriptural arguments for the lawfulness of slavery and thus to qualify the silence of the ministry on political and social topics. Even if their often reiterated exigeses were fully believed, however, their dry logic was totally devoid of any sense of inspiration. Thus in the years before the Civil War ministers contributed no interpretation of the meaning of labor to the cause of Southern nationalism. In place of the ideal of unity, industry, and patriotism which their predecessors had preached before the Revolution, they could only offer aloofness or scriptural defenses of the Southern way.

When the Rev. F. R. Cossitt, the biographer of Finis Ewing, sought in 1853 to describe the way in which unity and patriotism had supposedly emerged in the Cumberland country of Kentucky and Tennessee, he included no religious reasons. Rather, like Calhoun, he saw much value in the threat of violence. The necessity of defending helpless women and children against the Indians, "while it excited a deadly hatred of the savages, united the inhabitants in the golden bonds of fraternity and friendship, prompting to that kindliness of feeling, courtesy of bearing and reciprocity of good offices which mutual interests and common dangers are calculated to engender." Moreover, it inspired a spirit of patriotism, which "grew into that peculiar species of chivalry which so distinguished itself under General Jackson in the Indian war." [51] Beyond the allusion to fighting as a unifying element within society, it is worth noting the stress Cossitt placed upon personal factors such as local ties, friendships, and direct emotional reponses. Southerners had long conceptualized social unity in terms of personal encounters and relationships.

Calhoun participated to a certain extent in this pattern of thought. In 1838 he said that "the Southern States are an aggregate, in fact, of communities, not of individuals. Every plantation is a little community. . . . These small communities aggregated make the State in all." [52] The leap from the plantation, with its personal contacts so idealized by pro-slavery theorists, to the integration of a whole society is quite amazing and much more imaginary than the view of the plantation as a little community. Calhoun spoke also of the importance of ties of affection in binding the nation together. He hoped that his proposal for a dual presidency to implement the functioning of the concurrent majority "would make the Union a union in truth, a bond of mutual affection and brotherhood." [53] At the time of the Revolution the evangelical ministers had thought in terms of an affectional union, but in stressing industrious service they had demanded of each individual an active commitment to the American cause. Their aim therefore was to transform private feelings and responses into a shared community of belief. Calhoun failed to bridge the gap between individuals and society in part because he failed to define industry in social terms.

Others who engaged in the effort to define a united and industrious society in terms of the home, local ties, and personal affections also never quite succeeded in convincingly transcending the intimate.[54] While many Southerners doubtless had great affection for family and friends and for the localities in which they lived, this did not involve any larger social unity nor any sense of loyalty to the South as a whole—but rather a pervasive particularism. Neither did these attachments give to Southern society a stable and traditional character like that of rural England, which William Gilmore Simms praised in 1842 and contrasted with what he found in the South.[55] Moreover, geographical mobility, which had always been fairly common, made the ultimate meaning of the emphasis upon local ties somewhat ambiguous. Thomas R. R. Cobb of Georgia candidly admitted in 1858 that as far as the slaveowning planter was concerned, "the homestead is valued only so long as the adjacent lands are profitable for cultivation. The planter himself having no local attachments, his children inherit none. On the contrary, he encourages in them a disposition to seek new lands. . . . Such a population is almost nomadic. It is useless to seek to excite patriotic emotions in behalf of the land of birth when self-interest speaks so loudly." [56]

No Southerner celebrated the importance of familial and affectional ties more fervently than George Fitzhugh, yet this insistence must be seen in the context of his other ideas and what they suggest about Southern society. Ostensibly the purpose of his *Sociology for the South* (1854) was to attack free trade and free society, whose principles were the doctrines of Adam Smith "that individual well-being and social and national wealth and prosperity will be best promoted by each man's eagerly pursuing his own selfish welfare unfettered and unrestricted by legal regulations or governmental prohibitions, farther than such regulations may be necessary to prevent positive crime." [57] Presumably this applied to Northern society, but it soon becomes obvious that in terms of this definition the South, of all societies, was the most free. Under a system of free trade, fertile soil and good river outlets become an affliction because "the richness of soil invites to agriculture, and the roads and rivers carry off the crops to be exchanged for the manufactures of poorer regions where are situated the centers of trade, of capital and manufactures." In essence Fitzhugh was saying that the South had been freely allured into staple crop agriculture, and the only hope lay in the elimination of the enticements which free trade offered. Then the South "must manufacture for itself, build cities, erect schools and colleges, and carry on all the pursuits and provide for all the common wants of civilized man." [58] Because of his desire for change, Fitzhugh in effect made the *Sociology* a jeremiad, and as always the North somehow remained the model of the good society. "All great enterprises owe their success to association of capital and labor," he noted. "The North is indebted for its wealth and prosperity to the readiness with which it forms associations for all industrial and commercial purposes." [59]

Three years later in *Cannibals All!* Fitzhugh abandoned the jeremiad to make a frontal attack on the North, and in doing so he turned to the concept of industry and social unity as a function of familial and affectional ties. He dwelt lovingly on the plantation as a happy family, looked back into history to the first family associations, and then blithely concluded that it is "an historical fact that this family association, this patriarchal government for purposes of defense against enemies from without, gradually merges into larger associations of men under a common government or ruler." [60] The concept of the cannibal, one who lives off the labor of others, was a very clever attempt to turn the tables on Northerners by proving that they, not Southerners, were the lazy ones. When Fitzhugh dealt with the common charge against slavery "that it induces idleness with the masters," he referred to hard personal endeavor among small planters, who attended to everything themselves, and to the fact that if large planters "do their duty, their time is fully occupied. If they do not, the estate goes to ruin." Southern women too were very busy while "the rich men in free society may, if they please, lounge about town, visit clubs, attend the theatre, and have no other trouble than that of collecting rents, interest, and dividends of stock. In a well-constituted slave society there should be no idlers." The master and the slave both labor for each other, but the capitalist "lives by mere exploitation." [61] While Fitzhugh's picture of slavery is obviously sentimental and his planters seem more busy than industrious, nevertheless his insight into the fact that labor in the North was losing its social character is important. This only increased the dilemma of the Southerners' search for a meaningful definition of industry during these years.

Like other defenders of slavery, Fitzhugh applied order and subordination in practice only to the Negroes, though he did make rash statements like "liberty for the few—slavery, in every form, for the mass!" [62] He even wrote an article in 1858 proving that the white race was the best slave race, but what he really was concerned about emphasizing was that "too much liberty is the great evil of our age." To make his point he considered "the vindication of slavery the best corrective of the spirit of lawless licentiousness that threatens to subvert society." [63] Perhaps this was so, but he ventured no meaningful definition of an ordered society beyond the plantation. He shared with all those in the South who had sought various definitions of the industrious society during this period—whether in terms of manufactures, slavery, or affectional and familial ties—a failure of accomplishment. If he did not understand Southern society so clearly as Calhoun, he understood it well enough to have deplored Nullification, to dread disunion, and to oppose secession until the last moment.[64]

Fitzhugh revealed his ambivalent attitude toward the function of power in society when he said that "if government be not too much centralized, there is little danger of too much government. The danger and evil with us is of too little." [65] Charles Fenton Mercer, an eccentric Virginian, emphatically agreed with the latter thought as strongly as he disagreed with the former qualification. In 1845 he wrote an attack on the weakness of the national government in which he opposed virtually everything that Calhoun and Fitzhugh upheld except their passion for order. He could not find enough scorn for the followers of Jefferson, whom he equated with all Southern militants, because "they built up the horrid doctrines of State rights, nullification, secession, Federal usurpation and consolidation as counteracting principles or humbugs to alarm the people and paralyze the movements of Federal power." Mercer wanted order. He did not turn to the South to find it, for he expected endless strife and jealousy to be the only result of a separate Southern confederacy.[66] When he said that "man neither is equal, can be equal or ought to be equal," he meant exactly what he said.[67] He was not using this as a justification for Negro slavery and white equality. On the contrary, he considered slavery one of the principal sources of disunion within the country as well as the "blackest of all blots and foulest of all deformities." He regretted that it would long endure, but he was sure that it would because it was profitable to slaveowners.[68] Although he was pessimistic about the future, he still dreamed of a simple consolidated national government. Understandably he insisted: "I would have no slaves, of course, in my republic." [69]

Here was one answer to Fitzhugh and Calhoun, Harper and Hammond, but it was not the answer of a true Southerner. One did, however, speak out in 1854 in an article opposing the commercial conventions in the South. The author was wearied with all the talk of progress, for "no man can now enjoy his *otium cum dignitate*. Whatever his fancies or his inclinations may be, he is forced into the vortex of progress; and he who would cheerfully, if let alone, indulge in the repose of Rip Van Winkle, finds himself perforce acting in a crowd of noisy, brawling, roistering *progressistas*." [70] In his candid vindication of the Southern way with its unique version of the life of ease, this planter revealed again the truth that lay behind the plantation novels—the truth that made the South the perfect embodiment of the attitude toward society symbolized by Washington Irving's famous idler. The writer admitted that Northerners were "necessarily more enterprising, energetic and intelligent," but this was not intended as a compliment to the Yankee proponents of progress. He had no use for all the schemes of improvement. Indeed, his thesis on the question of economic change was that "in all other countries the instinct of capital is unerring in finding its natural operation, and so it is here. The proper occupation of capital in these States is the raising of staple crops; any other diversion of it is unwise and generally unsuccessful." [71] Until such time as a state of mutual dependence among social classes might be achieved, "the South must be regarded only in respect to its planters. They furnish her wealth, the sources of her commerce, and the basis of the whole foreign trade of our common country." Southern civilization was unique, and each man must decide whether it was worth preserving. If "he is satisfied with it, then let him act on the defensive and resist the efforts of those who, dazzled by the splendors of Northern civilization, would endeavor to imitate it. This can be done only by the destruction of the planter class." [72]

The South could not remain Southern and become a land of industry at the same time. All those who had sought to have both industry and idleness, so to speak, had failed. There remained the elaborate and artificial formulation of the nature of the American Union which Calhoun had put forward in an attempt to consolidate the investment which the supporters of the Constitution had made. If this bargain could not be made to work, then an answer must be found somewhere as to what constituted the essence of Southern nationalism upon which to focus men's patriotic energies. Patrick Henry, as Wirt had portrayed him, may have been indolent as a youth, but unlike Rip Van Winkle he did not sleep through the troubled times of the Revolution. It would seem that Southerners could not, as the 1850's progressed, understand why Henry had acted in behalf of an ideal of national union and independence. But they knew he had acted passionately and that independence and union were closely linked with this passionate action. Perhaps by duplicating all of the fire, the zeal, and the energy which Henry had displayed, they too might achieve the sense of unity which had inspired him.

13

In the decade preceding the Civil War, Southern conservatives constantly described the economic benefits the region derived from the Union. Secession would be inconsistent with the self-development of the South, Theodoric C. Lyon of Mississippi insisted. "The North gives her products; the South returns her staples. They are constituted by nature reciprocally dependent for perfect maintenance." [1] These men were loyal defenders of the South because they were seeking to perpetuate labor as the pursuit of personal gain. They called upon Southerners to continue to work as their forefathers had, but to reap the fruits of allurement would still require, as always, dependence upon outside sources. Hence Nathaniel Macon of Alabama insisted in 1860 that "it is the Union that gives to slavery perfect security, to slaves their present high value, and to slave labor its largest measure of success." Like most conservatives he was appalled by the demand of the fire-eaters for Congressional protection of slavery in the territories. If the advantages of allurement were allowed to operate, slavery would succeed wherever nature willed. It would fail elsewhere. A situation involving no Congressional power over slavery was safer than one in which power might some day be used for abolition. A unity of disunity seemed essential to the best interests of the South, and so Macon warned prophetically that "there are far more homogeneous elements to bind all the States together than will be found, after dissolution, to bind together the slave States." [2]

Conservatives feared that imprudent militancy would lead only to violence and disorder. In a speech before the Georgia legislature in opposition to secession, Alexander H. Stephens predicted that if the step were taken without sufficient cause, "instead of becoming gods, we will become demons, and at no distant day commence cutting one another's throats." [3] In contrast to the radicals, who believed in the constitutional right of secession, conservatives often spoke of revolution. What they had in mind was the effect of such an extreme measure if it were taken after all hope of a peaceful settlement was dead. Then all Southerners would be fully incensed and therefore united. Theodoric Lyon warned that a division of the states would produce "a dire conflict of fraternal hate, together with a war of races." Yet he also spoke of the last extremity when the South might be forced to "set up the red flag of revolution. . . . Then the arms which now hang down at the prospect of a disunion shall be made strong, and the South will advance a united front." [4] Although these men earnestly hoped that the need for revolution would never arise, it would be wrong to accuse them, as the fire-eaters often did, of being craven "submissionists" because they always held out for united Southern action. Their awareness of disunity in the South made them deeply conscious of the problems of effective action and willing, finally, to look to revolution as the only basis of unity.

At the Southern Commercial Convention in Montgomery in 1858 a conservative argued: "Give me a case of oppression and tyranny sufficient to justify a dissolution of the Union and give me a united South, and then I am willing to go out of the Union." Someone answered him: "If the gentleman waits for an undivided South, he never will go out of the Union." [5] This interchange took place during a discussion of the revival of the African slave trade, and the rejoinder more or less summed up the results of what had been intended by a few of the radicals as a means of making the South at last a land of industry. L. W. Spratt of South Carolina, a fervent proponent of this scheme, told the legislature of his state that if the price of slaves were cheap, then the price of subsistence could be made equally cheap. Thus "our enterprising tradesmen could compete with tradesmen in other sections of the world; instead of importing articles and implements for use, we could supply ourselves." [6] The plan was to provide a Negro for everyone and hence open the doors of economic opportunity to all whites. Edward A. Pollard thought it would revolutionize the agriculture of the region. The poor man "would be a proprietor himself; and in the great work of developing the riches of the soil of the South, from which he had hitherto been excluded, vistas of enterprise and wealth would open to him that would enliven his heart and transform him into another man." [7]

The desperation underlying this effort to energize and unify the South in terms of a system which was the product of individualism and disunity—or, in other words, laziness—was revealed in 1859 by Spratt at the Commercial Convention at Vicksburg. He confessed that "it is to be doubted whether, without the differences in social constitution which affect the sections North and South, there would be any sections North and South to wage a contest; and it is by no means certain that the cause of slavery would find its final triumph in an act of dissolution." Having admitted that slavery was intimately associated with Southern distinctiveness and that this distinctiveness constituted no basis of unity, Spratt must have felt he had no choice but to seek another level of conflict with the North. The contest was one, he maintained, between systems rather than sections, ideas rather than nations. The South must thus act only by protesting: "If slavery stand, as it must stand—for it is too abundant of blessings and too prodigal of promise to be given up—it must start from its repose; it must take the moral strength of an aggressive attitude." [8]

Many who rejected Spratt's conclusions about the South and the Union still agreed that the most hopeful course of action was to evoke self-interest to unite men behind a common defense of their economic opportunities. In 1860 J.D.B. De Bow issued his famous argument, *The Interest in Slavery of the Southern Non-Slaveholder*. While he made some attempt to show how slavery influenced the economy of the whole region, his main thesis was that "the non-slaveholder knows that as soon as his savings will admit he can become a slave-holder." If this does not prove true for him, "he will understand that by honesty and industry it may be realized to his children." [9] Nathaniel Macon was astounded by this whole effort to make of slavery something he felt it was not—that "while slavery is a matter of labor and profit alone, those interested in it should seek to connect it with politics, should thrust it into the foreground in every political controversy." The very profitability of staple-crop agriculture, made possible by slavery, had gone far, he thought, "in causing the people interested in it not only to cherish it as a special right, but to regard it as one of the pillars of the State." [10]

It was precisely because of their confidence in the allurements of slavery that the radicals could erect it into a pillar of the state. Like the conservatives, therefore, they built their system upon a definition of labor as the pursuit of personal gain, but they had to deal with many matters besides the opportunities each man would have to get rich. One is almost amazed by their sublime faith in the power of economic attractions. Nathaniel Beverley Tucker expressed his conviction that self-interest would unite the whole Confederacy when he spoke at the Southern Convention held to protest the Compromise of 1850. If Northern coercion did not drive the border states into joining the states of the lower South, "how long would those States be content to remain under the grinding misgovernment which taxes them for the benefit of their masters in the North while witnessing the prosperity of their Southern brethren living under a revenue tariff and enjoying the blessings of free trade?" [11] In 1858 William Lowndes Yancey argued that a Southern Confederacy would "have within itself a unity of climate, a unity of soil, a unity of production, and a unity of social relations—that unity which alone can be the basis of a successful and permanent government." [12] Like the early advocates of colonization, therefore, Yancey was looking to the land itself and by implication to the economic opportunities which it offered, opportunities which had resulted in staple crop agriculture (unity of production) and slavery (unity of social relations), to create a united nation.

For some men the Southern way would be changed simply as the result of the increased income that independence would automatically bring. In 1857 Edmund Ruffin predicted that the South's own revenues and resources, which would no longer be drained away by the North, "would thenceforward be retained and used to sustain and build up our own commerce and cities and general prosperity." Economic growth would be further stimulated by increased consumer demands and by immigration and foreign investment, brought about by the South's own advances and the economic decline of the North.[13] It would seem that Southerners had to do nothing but break away, and the revenues so long diverted into Northern pockets would flow in every direction to create a great nation. They could be assured of peaceful separation, Ruffin argued, because "war could not subserve or advance any interest of the North." [14] H. K. Berguin of North Carolina agreed and saw no reason why the two confederacies could not live side by side, "free from all commercial restrictions, permitting a close and friendly intercourse of citizens of each country and intimate business transactions just as at present." [15] If, however, the North were so foolish as to seek war, the South had many aces up its sleeve anyway. Ruffin argued that it would naturally prohibit all trade down the Mississippi, and so the Northwestern states "would soon secede from the Northeastern and Atlantic States and make a separate community and also would make a separate peace—if not seek to be reunited to the Southern States," which he had previously termed "their natural allies and best customers." [16] Yancey confidently stated that "England needs our cotton and must have it. Our treaties would protect our slaves where the power of the Constitution is in vain appealed to." [17]

The belief in the power of King Cotton was the keystone in the arch of the dream of allurement. The term itself had come from a Northerner, David Christy of Ohio, whose *Cotton Is King* (1855) was intended to show how extensively cotton had become interwoven with the business of the world in order to convince abolitionists of the folly of their program. Though he himself disliked slavery, he was sure that foreign nations would not support attempts to abolish it.[18] In place of Christy's cautious analysis, Southerners substituted grandiose dreams of the power of cotton to solve every international problem. It should also be pointed out that Christy only helped to give form to ideas long held in the South. In 1850 Albert Gallatin Brown of Mississippi had told the House of Representatives that Southerners knew that "fanaticism in the Old World, like fanaticism at home, assails our domestic relations, but we know how much British commerce and British labor depend for subsistence on our cotton, to feel at all startled by your threats of British power." [19] Louis T. Wigfall of Texas was saying virtually the same thing ten years later when he told the Senate "that cotton is king, and that he waves his sceptre not only over these thirty-three States but over the island of Great Britain and over continental Europe." [20] The appeal to King Cotton assumed that the South would remain an economically dependent, staple-producing area. Thus the functioning of allurement in foreign policy contradicted any expectation in reference to domestic affairs that somehow independence might bring changes to the South.

The dream of a confederacy whose every problem would be solved by the logic of allurement was the last and surely the most colossal of the dreams which had begun in England in the sixteenth century when men first cast their eyes on the attractions of the New World. Perhaps the hatred of Yankeeism was in large part a reflection of Southerners' uneasiness about how much they, in their own special way, depended upon self-interest. Proponents of the Southern dream of allurement did think essentially in terms of self-interest, even though it may not have been their own personal self-interest. When they spoke of slavery as the essence of the Southern way, which must be defended against the designs of the North, they admitted their preoccupation with vindicating the right to get rich through owning slaves. Hence their fanaticism was altogether different from that of the abolitionists. Whatever one may say of these Northern reformers, one cannot accuse them of propounding a philosophy ultimately based upon the individual's right to make his way in the world without limitations or restrictions. They cared about other people even if some of their procedures were ill advised and their motives not without stain. Southern militants did not care—at least as reflected in the social system they sought to vindicate. They did not want to change the North, but Northerners did want to meddle with their way of life. This meddlesome concern for others was perhaps the most perplexing and vexing aspect of the whole Northern stance. Southerners found it impossible to understand why the North should be ruled by any other than economic motives, and for this very reason they were constantly baffled by abolitionism. Somehow this ought not to have been. Economic self-interest should have made everything right. Yet, as the Augusta *Daily Constitutionalist* remarked in late December 1860, "we are told that interest will compel the North to do right, but have before demonstrated that it is religious zeal which impels them against interest." [21]

Proponents of Southern nationalism must have sensed that, while economic self-interest may have kept the plantation system operating, it would not inspire men to forsake the advantages of union and fight together if necessary. There had to be other ways of conceptualizing action. In this respect the dream of a confederacy based on allurement differed from the ideal of industry and patriotism men held during the Revolution. The earlier goal had contained its own basis for action and unity, while the dream of allurement assumed that everything would work out perfectly without any real effort on men's part.

The idea of an expansive destiny for the Southern Confederacy might conceivably have served as a call to action and a link with the dream of allurement. In 1857 Lawrence Keitt of South Carolina told the House of Representatives that the South had nothing to fear from the powers of the world because "the loss of the cotton crop would cover England with blood and anarchy and shake down the strongest thrones in Europe." He was convinced that "the institutions of the South must and will expand into the tropics, and you can no more repress her expansive energies than you can throw back the bursting seed into a state of 'torpor and undevelopment.' The South has her destiny to fulfill." [22] Two years later Robert Barnwell Rhett too spoke of a mission to cultivate the richest portions of the earth, but again the necessity simply to act seems to have been more important than the end toward which the action was aimed. "Pent up and confined within compulsory limits," he warned, "the labor of the two races may become valueless and the proportions between them possibly be so disturbed as to lead to insurrections, Northern intervention, and final emancipation." [23] Territorial expansion was thus considered necessary both as a means of preventing violence and as an avenue of energetic exertion virtually for its own sake. Lincoln's election eliminated this alternative as long as the South remained in the Union.

In the decade before the Civil War many men were preoccupied with action largely as a complete contrast to ease and inaction. In John Esten Cooke's *The Virginia Comedians* (1854), Champ Effingham's "languor is too perfect to be wholly affected." He is contrasted with Patrick Henry at the time of the Parson's Cause. Taken together, they are "the representatives of the Old World and the New, the past and the future, the court and the backwoods." [24] Unlike William Wirt's interpretation, Henry here represents a view of nature as wholly passionate action. He is a man of brooding vision, who destroys the hopes of young Charles Waters for conciliating the British; whereupon Waters cries out for revolution and is "carried away" by Henry's "fiery thoughts" and loses "all his calmness and self-control." [25] In the later *Henry St. John, Gentleman* (1859) Cooke spelled out even more clearly his conception of the Revolution as the violent destruction of a lazy past. "Upon one side of that gulf, now looking back, we discern the colonial regime of ease and tranquility—the slow rolling coach, the aristocratic dignity, the machinery of class, and courtly ceremony. On the other side, the mortal struggle of the new era, the leveling republicanism born of a common danger." [26] The story takes place just before the war with Waters now following in the footsteps of Henry. One day Waters and St. John have a long talk during a violent thunderstorm, and when it is over Waters compares it to the coming struggle. "The darkness and the gloom in which we are enveloped will be dissipated—the old things shall pass away, and behold all things shall become new!" [27]

The most compelling use of the storm as a metaphor for violent action was made by Yancey in a speech in July 1860. He gladly accepted the name of agitator because "agitation, incentives to exertion, inducements which impel inquiry are sources of knowledge and wisdom. The prophets of old were agitators." The wisdom he had in mind was the purgation wrought by sheer agitation as he referred to nature's disturbing the peace brooding over land and sea with the hurricane: "Languishing beneath a tropical sun, animated nature pantingly seeks shelter from its burning gaze. The green slime covers the still waters; the deadly miasma rises. Suddenly, the heavens are over-clouded, the blazing electric meteors shoot, the deep-toned thunders roll through the great vaults above, the torrents descend, the unrestrained winds career in madness, and, as suddenly, athwart this gloomy aspect, nature resumes a smiling face and a purified breath overspreads her dominion." [28] Possessing this element of fascination, agitation further seemed to Yancey the only means of stirring the South into action. In 1858 he had admitted that he "never expected a unity of action on the part of the South on any one issue. But one thing would influence one mind, another thing would influence still another mind, till at last all these influences would produce sufficient effect to enable the South to move forward from a Lexington to a Bunker Hill, and so go until the foe had been driven from the land." [29]

That the South should continue to submit to the assaults of her enemies, John Townsend cried in 1860, "merely because she was too cowardly and too indolent and too selfish to make the proper sacrifices to protect herself is to suppose an intensity of baseness on her part which would consign her to everlasting infamy." [30] As Southerners who had previously held back began to respond to such passionate appeals for action, Yancey's hopes seemed justified. George Fitzhugh wrote of the love of danger and war, noting that "foreign war begets social intestine peace and brotherhood. The rapacious greed of gain becomes less busy and exacting, rivalry and competition less active; economy takes the place of luxury, a hardy manliness of a degenerate effeminacy." [31] If the larger idea of the Confederacy as a dream of allurement enshrined the Southern way, this more personal emphasis upon vigorous action expressed the private fears Southerners had always had of ultimate meaninglessness.

By the latter half of 1860 conditions led William Gregg to stress again the importance of domestic industry, because "we have been forced to the conclusion that the time has come when the Southern people should begin in earnest to prepare for self-defense and self-reliance." Since he felt that separation had been agreed upon, he asked the question: "Are we prepared for separate nationality?" [32] His answer makes it clear that he viewed any changes in the direction of economic independence as abstract measures of policy; he offered no ideal of an independent land of industry. "Let every man whose custom is worth anything and let the ladies also," he cried, "show their patriotism by giving the preference to home manufactures." Many Southerners recalled that this was what people had done during the Revolution, but such activity never seemed anything more than appropriate. Moreover, it remained in conflict with the dreams of free trade harmony under the sceptre of King Cotton. Thus Gregg could only plead that "while we sell our cotton and buy from all nations, let us not forget that our power as a nation, or a people, an integral part of a nation, will depend on our economy and love for the protection of domestic industry." [33]

At the moment of crisis, therefore, any hopes for a changed South seemed to have little immediate meaning, and Southerners turned to more emotional interpretations of disunion. In November 1860 the Augusta *Daily Constitutionalist* announced that the ties of union were broken, and "the antagonism amounts not simply to aversion, but to bitter disgust and hatred." Two different nationalities are living nominally under the same government, *The New Orleans Bee* said the next month. "There is no longer a union of heart and feelings, of patriotism and nationality." [34] The emphasis upon passionate exertion was transformed into the notion of secession as a vigorous and conclusive response to Northern hatred and fanaticism. Mrs. Mary Boykin Chesnut linked these two themes in separate entries in her diary in early 1861. In February she wrote that "South Carolinians had exasperated and heated themselves into a fever that only blood-letting could ever cure. It was the inevitable remedy. So I was a seceder." The next month she noted: "We separated from the North because of incompatibility of temper. We are divorced, North from South, because we have hated each other so." [35]

Beyond the emotionalism, however, was an insistence that the reason for the divorce was the North's total failure to honor the Constitution as interpreted by Calhoun. "The one great evil from which all other evils have flowed is the overthrow of the Constitution of the United States," Rhett, in behalf of the people of South Carolina, told the rest of the South after secession. "The government of the United States is no longer the government of confederated republics, but of a consolidated democracy." [36] Evidently the South's economic utility had not prevented the North from altering the original terms of union. Southerners felt that their distinctiveness was threatened as it would not have been had these terms been honored, and throughout the conflict they remained convinced of the North's repudiation of a national union of mutual economic advantage. Near the end of the war Benjamin H. Hill of Georgia scorned the notion that Lincoln intended to restore the Constitution. It was "not that Constitution in which conflicting interests and opinions made mutual concessions for the general good, in which the South agreed to contribute to the commercial and manufacturing greatness of the North, and the North in consideration therefore agreed not to interfere with but to respect the industrial pursuits and domestic labor of the South." [37] Partly this concern for the Constitution represented an unwillingness to believe that the doctrine of allurement had failed with respect to the old Union. Partly too it indicated uncertainty and confusion about the new attempt to actualize the dream of allurement in a nation protected by the unlimited power of King Cotton.

Ultimately, therefore, constitutional theory and the dream of allurement intertwined, though one was a tribute to the past and the other to the future. Even if the past were gone and the future indistinct, still men could be assured, in the words of Alexander H. Stephens early in 1861, that "all the essentials of the old Constitution, which have endeared it to the hearts of the American people, have been preserved and perpetuated." At the same time he insisted that the foundations of the Confederacy "are laid, its cornerstone rests upon the great truth that the Negro is not equal to the white man." [38] With slavery as the cornerstone of the new edifice, "with such an area of territory, with such an amount of population, with a climate and soil unsurpassed by any on the face of the earth, with such resources already at our command, who can entertain any apprehensions as to our success, whether others [the border states] join us or not?" [39]

It does not explain the Civil War to describe the Southerners' conception of the Confederacy as an example of the old faith in the powers of allurement. Neither is it an explanation to say that for them secession was a means of acting to destroy the feelings of idleness or meaninglessness within themselves. Nevertheless, these elements in the situation do serve as a contrast to the vision of patriotic unity which inspired men in the South during the Revolution. Then they had fought in the hope that from their united efforts would eventually emerge a changed South. By contrast, men fought the Civil War to perpetuate the way of life which had developed from the first dreams of allurement nearly three centuries before. Socially speaking, the Revolution was an industrious undertaking, the Civil War a lazy one. The former was an attempt to implement a definition of labor which presupposed concern for the common interest. The latter was an effort to preserve an interpretation of work which implied only attention to one's own interest. Consequently, it is correct to say that the men who most strongly supported the cause of Southern nationalism had no concept of unity to impart to their followers. This was the crucial failing of the Confederacy—not that its members were divided as to the wisdom of separation. The citizens of the thirteen colonies were also divided, but their leaders had an ideal of unity, of patriotism, and of possibility.

Nowhere is this better illustrated than in the design of the Great Seal, which was approved in June 1782. On one side was the American Eagle with a scroll on which were the words, *E Pluribus Unum*. On the breast of the Eagle was a shield symbolizing "the several states in the union, all joined in one solid compact entire, supporting a chief which unites the whole and represents Congress." On the other side was a partially completed pyramid, symbolic of the infancy of the newly founded government. Above it was an eye over which were the words, *Annuit Coeptis*, "He sanctions our endeavors." Below was the date 1776 and under it the motto, *Novus Ordo Seclorum*. Of these the contemporary description ran: "The pyramid signifies strength and duration. The eye over it and the motto allude to the many signal interpositions of Providence in favor of the American cause. The date underneath is that of the Declaration of Independence, and the words under it signify the beginning of the new American Era, which commences from that date." [40] For Northerners, Lincoln was able to recapture this sentiment of unity and possibility. Early in 1861 he wrote that the Constitution and the Union were not the cause of the nation's prosperity. Rather "there is something back of these, entwining itself more closely about the human heart. That something is the principle of 'Liberty to all'—the principle that clears the path for all, gives hope to all, and by consequence enterprise and industry to all." [41] He did not see liberty and industry as private matters. They were intimately related to the question of national unity. When he later called for dedication "to the great task remaining before us" in order "that this nation, under God, shall have a new birth of freedom" and "not perish from the earth," he was not asking Northerners to fight for a dream of allurement.

In mid-February 1861 the *Daily Nashville Patriot* compared the journeys of the two different presidents to their respective seats of government. Lincoln was proceeding slowly and indirectly; "he eats his meals leisurely, sleeps comfortably, and goes as to a festival of ease and pleasure." By contrast Jefferson Davis went "with all the speed of steam" directly to his post "as to a scene of labor and of danger." [42] Arriving at Montgomery, Davis assured his fellow citizens that they were brothers, "not in name merely, but in fact— men of one flesh, one bone, one interest, one purpose, and of identity of domestic institutions." [43] In his inaugural address as provisional President he stressed the fact that "we have changed the constituent parts, but not the system of government. The Constitution framed by our fathers is that of these Confederate States." This preoccupation with the nature of the old Union was accompanied by a strong dedication to the Southern way and to the belief that it need undergo few if any changes. He described Southerners as "an agricultural people whose chief interest is the export of commodities required in every manufacturing country" and "whose true policy is peace and the freest trade which our necessities will permit." [44] They would fight if necessary, but they were honestly willing to live and let live.

Throughout the war Davis adhered to his faith in the Southern way and his obsession with the South's loyalty to the true principles of the old Constitution. In February 1862 he looked forward to independence and the time when "we are free to follow our interests and inclinations by cultivating foreign trade." Then the Southern states would "offer to manufacturing nations the most favorable markets which ever invited their commerce." [45] In his messages to Congress he reviewed the industrial accomplishments of the Confederacy, but he had no interest in them except as they were useful in winning the war. These same messages nearly always contained some such statement as: "They sought to infringe upon the rights we had, and we only instituted a new government on the basis of those rights." [46] In its last manifesto in June 1864 the Confederate Congress also insisted that "we were forced to dissolve our federal connection with our former associates by their aggressions on the fundamental principles of our compact of union with them. . . . The separate independence of the States as sovereign and co-equal members of the Federal Union had never been surrendered." [47] These expressions of past devotion to the doctrine of allurement and present loyalty to the principles of states' rights could only have the effect of undermining the cause of Southern unity.

The heated controversy between proponents of states' rights and personal liberty and supporters of the Confederate government only too clearly revealed the inability of the latter to find a convincing argument for united action. When Benjamin H. Hill tried to define what he meant by the South as a nation, he could only insist it had no territorial significance and then ask: "Are we not struggling for admission into the family of nations? Are we not claiming and demanding recognition by other nations? As what will we ask them to recognize us? By what name will we be called?" [48] L.Q.C. Lamar insisted in 1864 that "the best service anyone can render at this time to the cause of State Rights is to sustain and uphold the Government of these Confederate States. It was established to maintain State Rights and is based upon that principle." If the danger in the North was consolidation, in the South it was "inharmonious action and dismemberment." [49] When pleading did not solve the problem, some patriots finally advocated desperate measures. Edmund Ruffin longed for a dictator to give the South direction for one last effort.[50] Those who represented what was truly Southern, however, were the men who called for freedom, individual liberties, and states' rights. If the South had ever stood consistently for anything, it was freedom. Robert Toombs expressed this when he categorically refused to plant corn instead of cotton in 1862.[51] Alexander H. Stephens expressed this also when in defense of states' rights he said in 1864 that "liberty is the animating spirit, the soul of our system of government, and like the soul of man, when once lost it is lost forever." [52]

If the politicians who supported the cause of Southern nationalism failed to suggest a compelling ideal which could serve as a basis of national unity, the clergy failed also—and again not because of any lack of personal commitment.[53] A church periodical was convinced that "a sense of religion will animate our people and sustain them under any difficulties with which they may have to contend." [54] Indeed it was with a clear understanding of the demonstrated power of religion to inspire patriotism that the clergy sought to follow procedures which had worked well in the past. They rejoiced in the fact that the Confederate Constitution specifically acknowedged the existence and supremacy of God, and they allowed no occasion to pass without invoking the spirit of divine providence to aid their cause.[55] But the dogged repetition of a formula which was supposed to work because it had worked for others in the past only made these stereotyped incantations more hollow as the years went by. The ministers were also unable to get beyond a monotonous recapitulation of the principles of the American Constitution as Southerners understood them. Benjamin Palmer sought to give them universal significance by affirming that "in the organic law under which human governments were constituted by God, not consolidation but separation is recognized as the regulative and determining principle." [56] But this was only a different way of stating the same stale argument of the politicians.

In seeking to define the South as a nation the clergy too fell back on arguments of allurement. Palmer referred to "a broad land diversified by almost every variety of climate and soil and rich in all the products which man needs for sustenance, as well as in those great staples which must yet control the commerce of the world." Beyond this he hoped that sheer resistance would aid the South in becoming a united country. "Nations, like men," he argued, "are made compact and enduring through discipline," enforced by the sufferings of war.[57] But somehow the idea of resistance for its own sake, however effectively it might have provoked men to support secession, could not give them sufficient purpose to continue indefinitely, and there seemed nothing else to offer. Even at its best the message of the ministers fell short. In 1862 Stephen Elliott, Episcopal Bishop of Georgia, described the war as possibly "necessary for our purification." It would "quell faction, break up party spirit, bring out patriotism, valor, self-denial, heroism—which, although they be worldly virtues, are far better than selfishness and a narrow-minded avarice. It will stir up all the energies of the people, which were stagnating under the effects of indolence and isolation." It would bring men from the sea islands and the mountains and "mingle them with the great mass of the people, and out of the crucible will come a nation, with larger views, with nobler feelings, with energies high strung for all the purposes of national life." [58] Although he referred to the importance of developing natural resources, his whole argument is more a rehearsal of what ought to be expected than an example of the patriotism and sense of dedication necessary to make these predictions a reality. Even for Elliott, industry remained little more than activity to eliminate laziness.

Indeed religion during the war was most influential not in

promoting the cause, but in promoting revivals—which in effect offered a retreat from the whole struggle for independence. Benjamin Palmer took great consolation in 1863 in "the outpouring of God's spirit and the revival of true religion in the camps of our soldiery." Perhaps this was because at the same time he had to admit that "calculations based upon the most settled principles of political economy or founded upon the largest diplomatic experience have fallen to the ground." He was referring to the now discredited belief "that cotton would assert its vaunted supremacy and the embargo upon our ports would bring the world as suitors to our door." [59] The ignominious failure of King Cotton came as a bitter disappointment to a people who had always believed in the efficacy of allurement. After the mill workers of Manchester sent congratulations to Lincoln upon emancipation, J.D.B. De Bow could only note with incredulity that "the best of us have been deceived and must now admit that cotton is not king." [60]

When the exigencies of war caused Davis to contemplate the use of slaves as soldiers with the promise of emancipation, Rhett commented that slavery and independence must stand or fall together. He wanted no Confederate government without its institutions.[61] Time had thus proved that the requirements of unity and necessity could only serve to destroy what was truly Southern. When it was gone with the wind, the Confederacy might exist in men's memories as a Lost Cause. It would never exist in fact, for distinctiveness was no basis for separate nationality. As perhaps the most monumental version of the doctrine of allurement, the Southern Confederacy ended as all previous versions had ended—not in the creation of a united society, but in disintegration and isolation in which the pursuit of gain was the ultimate reality. The rapidity with which many former Confederates rushed to defend Northern financial interests in the South after the war only too amply demonstrated the truth of the observation by the *New York Commercial and Financial Chronicle* that "there can be no way so sure to make the late rebels of the

South loyal men and good citizens as to turn their energies to the pursuits of peace and the accumulation of wealth." [62] By the time Reconstruction ended, every Southern state was controlled by businessmen or friends of business.[63] The meaning and reality of the quest for a definition of Southern nationality and patriotic exertion were perhaps best summed up in a remark in 1862 by Yancey during a debate in the Confederate Congress over the question of curbing state authority. Someone spoke of defending the national life, and Yancey replied: "Sir, we have no 'National life.' " [64] He was right.

For lazy southerners,
by whom the south is largely populated

Epilogue

In 1886 Henry W. Grady, the spokesman of the New South, journeyed north to tell the assembled members of the New England Society of New York City that at last the South had repented of its indolent ways. "We have sowed towns and cities in the places of theories and put business above politics. . . . We have established thrift in city and country. We have fallen in love with work," he told the descendants of the saints. Later in his speech he noted that the New South was "a social system compact and closely knitted, less splendid on the surface but stronger at the core—a hundred farms for every plantation, fifty homes for every palace, and a diversified industry that meets the complex needs of this complex age." [1] If protestations of industry signified the effort to think of the region as resembling the North, protestations of leisure, reflected in the quantities of sentimental literature about the mythical Old South, indicated reservations and misgivings. As questions were being asked throughout the nation concerning the meaning of work in an environment of factories and huge corporations, it became increasingly possible to speak positively about leisure as a form of personal indulgence.

In 1902 Walter Hines Page criticized slavery, the politician, and the preacher for having prevented the development of

Southern rural society, which he described as "a state of life that keeps permanently the qualities of the frontier civilization long after the frontier has receded and been forgotten." Page would not be alone in using the idea of the South's remaining a frontier to describe the condition which earlier men had referred to as a state of idleness. While he could see great advantages in the development of industry in the South, he feared "that industrial activity may deal too rudely with the gentleness and dignity of the old-time life, and do violence to its genius for leisure and its imaginative quality." The problem which he set for the South, and indeed for America, was "how in the march of industrialism these qualities of hospitality and leisure may be retained in the habits of these people and how they may be transplanted to corresponding towns in other parts of the Union." [2]

Whether the South is truly a land of ease has always been less important than the need men have felt to insist upon it. When the twelve angry Southerners issued their protest against the New South, *I'll Take My Stand*, in 1930, they virtually admitted that most Southerners seemed unaware of the tradition of leisure, which, they insisted, was what made the South really Southern. Frank Lawrence Owsley insisted that in the past "the life of the South was leisurely and unhurried for the planter, the yeoman, or the landless tenant. It was a way of life, not a routine of planting and reaping merely for gain." [3] John Crowe Ransom even argued "that all were committed to a form of leisure, and that their labor itself was leisurely." [4] Perhaps the final ironic twist in the argument which had raged for centuries around the theme of industry and laziness lay in the fact that as modern urban and industrialized life came increasingly to be represented as destructive of a sense of community, Southern leisure was invoked as a communitarian concept. "There are a good many faults to be found with the old South," Ransom noted, "but hardly the fault of being intemperately addicted to work and to gross material prosperity." The arts of the South "were arts of living and not arts of escape; they were also community arts, in which every class of society could participate after its kind. The South took life easy, and is itself a tolerably comprehensive art." [5]

The tortured and critical analysis which W. J. Cash published a few years later in *The Mind of the South* stands as a modern jeremiad to the celebrations of the Twelve Southerners. "The South," he characteristically noted, "never developed any such compact and effective unit of government as the New England town." He used the analogy of the frontier to characterize the region's essential failure to develop into a meaningfully organized society. The antebellum "Southern world . . . was basically an extremely uncomplex, unvaried, and unchanging one. Here economic and political organization was reduced to its simplest elements." [6] To Cash the history of the South had been a series of failures to emerge from its frontier condition. While some gains had been made by the Civil War, the Yankee created a second frontier by Reconstruction, and the great push for Progress under the banner of the New South created yet a third frontier and revivified the old individualistic outlook. [7] Logically this should not have been, for "to bring in the factory and the town—and, let us not forget, to turn to the magnification of the school—would be, in other words, to set in motion almost incalculably great forces for the complication of the social scene." But the essence of the drive for Progress was identical with the essence of the frontier (and with the essence of all Southern busyness), "a world in which the hard, energetic, horse-trading type of man was remorselessly indicated for survival." The result, he went on to note, was that "all the elaborately built-up pattern of leisure and hedonistic drift; all the slow, cool, gracious and grateful gesturing of movement—which, if it had never been generally and fully established in sober reality, had nevertheless subsisted as an ideal and a tendency—was plainly marked out for abandonment as incompatible with success." [8]

Because the ideal of leisure had functioned, Cash felt, as a bulwark against the chaotic conditions of frontier individualism and the violence associated with it, he also related this ideal to the values which evolve with a highly organized and complex society, for both tend to control disorder. Indeed he thought that "restraint and complexity . . . are the very essence of the town." Moreover, "the processes of commerce are essentially orderly and deliberate." Thus he was justified in having already observed that "the degree of decline in mob violence of a given locality could be closely correlated to the degree of that locality's advance in Progress." The one exception was Virginia, which was not a leading industrial state, "but its case is perhaps sufficiently explained by the large number of the descendants of the old Southern gentry" and its comparatively small number of Negroes.[9] Since Cash associated the old Southern aristocracy and the virtues of leisure, decorum, and hospitality with what was really good and worth preserving of the Southern heritage, he conceded that the Twelve Southerners had done well "in recalling that the South must not be too much weaned away from its ancient leisureliness—the assumption that the first end of life is living itself—which, as they rightly contend, is surely one of its greatest virtues." [10]

The importance of curbing the chaos of economic competition was so great that Cash clung to these values in spite of their ambiguities. Once he referred to the pointless leisure of the poor white, and elsewhere he argued that in the South the idea of social responsibility "remained always a narrow and purely personal one." This was owing in part to the aristocratic example of Virginia, for "the Virginians themselves, if they had long since become truly aristocratic, had nevertheless never got beyond that brutal individualism . . . which was the heritage of the frontier: that individualism which, while willing enough to ameliorate the specific instance, relentlessly laid down as its basic social postulate the doctrine that every man was completely and wholly responsible for himself." [11] In praising the ideals of aristocracy and leisure, Cash was in fact giving support to the very individualism whose extremes he deplored, just as Beverley and Byrd had done in glorifying busyness.

The basic difference in the approaches of men of colonial times and of the present lies in the contemporary doubts about urbanized economic life. When such doubts are few, it is possible for a Southerner like Hodding Carter in his *Southern Legacy* (1950) to call for reformation in largely traditional terms. "The Southern society remains frontier in many aspects," he notes, particularly in its violence and celebration of self-reliance. The region's "development was not urban. Its social organization was built loosely around the farm, the plantation, and the small town; and behind the white-pillared façade of the mansion, as in the poor white's cabin, lived people who were in actuality frontiersmen." [12] He sees the South as having been "almost entirely bypassed during the period of the great European emigration to America, and so its disbelief in the dignity of all useful labor has never been sufficiently challenged since the beginning of its peculiar agricultural economy and the establishment of a mutually debilitating occupational relationship between white men and Negroes." Therefore, in accordance with the tradition of the jeremiad Carter laments the way Southerners have betrayed "a region surpassingly endowed and as wastefully negligent of its endowment." [13]

When skepticism about change increases, the passion for leisure also increases, as in James McBride Dabbs's *The Southern Heritage* (1958). He speaks "both for canny Scotchmen, by whom the South is partly populated, and for lazy Southerners, by whom the South is largely populated." Yet he insists that "in this land there exists a society where leisure, however it may fail in fact, is still sought as ideal." [14] This quality of leisure functions as the mean between "on the one side, indolence; on the other, violence. The South at its best is relaxed; at its worst it is either asleep or frenzied." [15] He insists that "Southern violence is also frontier violence. The South has been and still is a frontier." And he argues that to deal with the violence which slavery implied the South "cultivated good manners, human relationships. As the years passed, the manners became more suave, and it became increasingly impertinent to ask what lay beneath the smooth surface." Regardless of the real basis of the tradition of leisure and decorum, Dabbs has already asserted that "the emphasis upon manners, upon custom, upon an accepted way of doing things is an emphasis upon community." [16]

A weakness in the positions of Southerners like Cash and Dabbs lies in the conceptualization of the life of leisure as a basis of social unity or as a means of defining a society. Leisure is not a concept which in America has come to imply social responsibility or cohesion.[17] Quite the contrary, it is assumed to refer essentially to one's private sphere of activity —to what one has for oneself outside the realm of social responsibility. This is what leisure as an ideal has essentially always meant in the South—taking life easy. And this is why before the Civil War it was so intimately linked in men's minds with other aspects of the Southern way. Whether it was considered an element in a general pattern of laziness or as something good depended upon whether one's point of view was social or personal. When Southerners glorify leisure as a basis for characterizing the South as a society, they are attempting to make a private activity grounds for uniting a society in the same way that attractionists once sought to make the personal pursuit of gain an argument for social unity.

What has traditionally been associated with the ideal of leisure and is often taken as evidence of a sense of community —courtesy, hospitality, graciousness—is simply a series of devices for minimizing friction at the most intimate and personal level. David M. Potter, nevertheless, sees the characteristically Southern emphasis upon personalism as part of an authentic folk culture, which "survived in the South long after it succumbed to the onslaught of urban-industrial culture elsewhere." Thus he asks if the nostalgia for the Southern past "persists was it because even t   inequality and wrong were parts of a life that still had a   tedness and meaning which our more bountiful life in the   ss culture seems to lack?" [18] Doubtless at times in the past o 1 certain limited areas of the South people's lives did attain re. tedness and meaning. But for the region as a whole the persistently disorienting effects of economic conditions, outside criticism, and geographical and even social mobility have been too common to permit personal relationships to impart the kind of stability which one usually associates with folk cultures.

It may in fact be argued that the way in which the stress upon the personal has operated in the South has in many respects militated against a real sense of belonging. Among strangers the social graces function only to create the appearance of intimacy or affection, and the element of formality often governs even the closest personal relations. Contacts between the races are highly formalized, and whites tend to view Negroes mainly in terms of stereotypes. Thus emphasis upon personal relationships seems essentially to focus on appearances rather than on human emotions. At best, many Southerners must have been left unsatisfied by this tendency to ignore how people really feel. At worst, in the area of race relations, it has meant misunderstanding and insult. Viewing contemporary Mississippi society, Walker Percy deplores the absence of any really private and public spheres of life—the result of the fact that everyone is forced to live as if he were a member of one great family. "It is this hypertrophy of pleasant familial space at the expense of a truly public sector which accounts for the extraordinary apposition in Mississippi of kindliness and unspeakable violence," Percy notes.[19] This society, one feels, differs from the rest of the South past and present only in the unrelieved intensity with which the personal emphasis operates to undercut both social values and individual rights.

The persistent metaphor of the frontier seems especially appropriate, for it suggests a people living in a state of nature without ever really having formulated a social compact among themselves. Yet from the arguments of allurement to the celebrations of leisure and personal relationships, Southerners have been searching for a definition of how a society is united, how men are bound together to fulfill through labor the purposes of organized social life. In sociological terms, they have been seeking their own definition of social integration. In his study *The Integration of American Society*, Robert Cooley Angell argues that if American society were very small, it might be integrated on the basis of intimate personal relationships because "affection and friendship are the chief cementing forces in small groups." But no society can cohere on these terms. It must be integrated, if at all, by ties which do not necessitate intimacy of acquaintance. Over long periods of time "societies are chiefly knit together by a common attachment of their members to systems of value like those of a religion or of democracy, systems that define the character of the collective life." [20] Angell further notes that "an integrated society . . . is in some respects a moral community. Its members have at least a few ultimate values in common." [21] While his study is aimed at testing the degree to which modern American society is successfully integrated, it is possible to apply his definitions specifically to the society of the South considered separately and historically. Neither the celebrations of allurement nor those of leisure and its associated characteristics are values which define collective life—however descriptive they may be of certain widely held assumptions.

The geographical conditions of the South permitted a form of society consisting of nearly isolated individuals, who depended almost exclusively upon traders, merchants, and financiers from the outside to perform many essential social services for them. But geography did not create the South. As Richard Shryock has pointed out, Pennsylvania, with a soil as well adapted to tobacco as that of Virginia and Maryland and an excellent river system for ready marketing, could just as easily have become a staple-producing area as its neighbors.[22] The difference lay not in the land but in the people, and that difference was ultimately due to the different attitudes and assumptions which they brought with them and their descendants perpetuated. Both the Quakers and to an even greater degree the Puritans in New England founded societies based on communities of consent and common goals. Imbued with a sense of community and social purposefulness, these people were truly able to build cities in the wilderness.

The doctrine of allurement can be viewed as a very early expression of the idea of *laissez-faire*, a point which is further supported by the views of George Fitzhugh. In England the social implications of this philosophy were limited by the fact that it was, after all, preached in an old and fully elaborated society. Only in the South (and the sugar islands) were attempts made to form whole societies in accordance with this notion. And these attempts worked—after a fashion. Only the jeremiads remained to testify to disappointed expectations. Always in the background lay the example first of New England and later of the North in general. Southerners were urged to repent and become like those whose way of life best seemed to approximate what men expected. In fact Northern society only imperfectly exemplified a sense of community, for the American experience as a whole has involved the weakening of institutions and the ascendency of the individual. The South represents the logical extreme of this tendency. To the degree that America has meant economic opportunity without social obligations or limitations, Southerners are Americans and Americans Southerners. Yet America has also been a nation of men professing a common allegiance and social values which have operated to check unlimited self-aggrandizement and its effects. In this sense the jeremiads were not really mistaken in noting differences North and South.

When the formation of a united nation made the issue of national cohesion explicit, the question of the distinctiveness of the South became important in a way it had not been earlier. What the jeremiads have always implied and what the Civil War proved is that Southern distinctiveness has never meant a cohesive and separate identity. It is not really accurate to equate the persistent feeling of distinctiveness with Southerners' sense of sectionalism. The latter is of relatively recent origin and is ironically the creation of outside forces—first the anti-slavery agitation, then the Civil War, and finally Reconstruction—which have not changed the essential pattern of distinctiveness. Recently C. Vann Woodward has defined the unique quality of the Southern experience in terms of a tradition of poverty, failure, and guilt—in a nation which values abundance, success, and innocence. Also Southerners are aware of the weight of the past as Northerners are not.[23] One can, however, argue that the South as a whole does not exhibit a style of politics or social behavior which in any way reflects these elements of difference. Quite the contrary, poverty and failure have never discouraged Southerners from pursuing opportunity and success, and protestations of purity are more common than affirmations of guilt. Uniqueness, as Woodward employs it, serves essentially as a frame of reference by means of which Americans and Southerners in particular can understand and gain a perspective upon the national experience and contemporary society. This makes the South not a social reality, but rather a concept existing only in the realm of values.

The sense of distinctiveness has never defined a real society, and yet it persists. If it keeps alive the old interest in a changed South, it also encourages a special loyalty to what makes the South Southern. And so when Southerners begin to celebrate their own distinctiveness too loudly, a Jeremiah usually appears to remind them that they know better.

Notes

.~.~.~.

PROLOGUE

1. *More's Utopia and a Dialogue of Comfort,* introd. John Warrington (London and New York: Everyman's Library, 1951), pp. 23, 27.
2. Ibid. p. 123.
3. Ibid. pp. 75–6, 64.
4. Ibid. p. 92.
5. Ibid. pp. 66, 69.
6. Ibid. p. 94.
7. J. H. Hexter, *More's Utopia: The Biography of an Idea* (Princeton, 1952), p. 84.
8. Ernst Troeltsch, *The Social Teaching of the Christian Churches,* trans. Olive Wyon (New York, 1931), I, 321, 292–5.
9. Ibid. I, 317.
10. Max Weber, *The Protestant Ethic and the Spirit of Capitalism,* trans. Talcott Parsons (New York and London, 1930), p. 159.
11. This phrase is taken from John Redford, *Wit and Science,* written some time between 1531 and 1547, reprinted (Oxford, 1951), p. 14.
12. *Tudor Economic Documents,* eds. R. H. Tawney and Eileen Power (London, 1924), III, 19.
13. Thomas Starkey, *A Dialogue between Reginald Pole and Thomas Lupset,* ed. Kathleen M. Burton (London, 1948), p. 147.
14. Sir Thomas Elyot, *The Boke Named the Governour* (London: Everyman's Library, [1907]), p. 145.
15. Hexter, *More's Utopia,* pp. 59–60.
16. R. H. Tawney, *Religion and the Rise of Capitalism* (New York, 1952), ch. III; *Harrison's Description of England in Shakspere's Youth. The Second and Third Books. Edited from the First Two Editions of Holinshed's Chronicle,* A. D. *1577, 1587,* ed. Frederick J. Furnivall (London: The New Shakspere Society, 1877–81), pt. 1,

pp. 213, 214n; *England under Elizabeth (1558–1603), Illustrated from Contemporary Sources*, eds. R. B. Wernham and J. C. Walker (London, New York, and Toronto, 1932), pp. 196–7; *Tudor Economic Documents*, III, 425, 442.

17. "A Treatise of the Vocations, or, Callings of Men," in *The Works of William Perkins, newly corrected according to his owne copies* (Cambridge, 1605), p. 909.

18. See, for example, Richard Hooker, *The Laws of Ecclesiastical Polity*, Bk. V, ch. lxx, 4.

19. Perkins, *Works*, p. 913.

20. See Charles H. George and Katherine George, *The Protestant Mind of the English Reformation, 1570–1640* (Princeton, 1961), p. 136.

21. Perkins, *Works*, p. 903.

22. "A Supplycacion to our moste Soveraigne Lorde Kynge Henry the Eyght" (1544), in *A Supplicacyon for the Beggers*, ed. J. Meadows Cowper (London, 1871), p. 25.

23. Perry Miller, *The New England Mind: The Seventeenth Century* (New York, 1939), p. 399.

24. Perkins, *Works*, p. 909.

25. William Holbrook, *A Sermon Preached before the Antient Company of Black-smiths in S. Marie Magdalens Church in London* (London, 1612), p. 17.

26. Miller, *New England Mind*, pp. 476, 480–81.

27. Weber, *Protestant Ethic*, p. 157.

28. *The Sermons of Edwin Sandys, D. D.*, ed. John Ayre (Cambridge, England, 1841), p. 145.

29. Ibid. p. 61.

30. *A Discourse of the Common Weal of This Realm of England, First printed in 1581 and commonly attributed to W. S.*, ed. Elizabeth Lamond (Cambridge, England, 1893), pp. 57–8.

31. Robert Hitchcok, *A Pollitique Platt for the honour of the Prince* . . . (London, 1580), sigs. a1ʳ–a1ᵛ.

32. Tawney, *Religion and the Rise of Capitalism*, pp. 175f.

33. Sandys, *Sermons*, p. 337.

34. See, for example, Starkey, *Dialogue*, p. 80.

35. Relevant to the question of exploration are A. L. Rowse, *The Elizabethans and America* (New York, 1959) and Louis B. Wright, *Religion and Empire: The Alliance Between Piety and Commerce in English Expansion, 1558–1625* (Chapel Hill, 1943); for early reactions see Richard Hakluyt, *Divers Voyages Touching the Discovery of America and the Islands Adjacent* (1582), ed. John Winter Jones (London: The Hakluyt Society, 1850), pp. 58, 101, and *The Interlude of the Four Elements: An Early Moral Play*, ed. James Orchard Halliwell (London, 1848), esp. pp. 29–30.

36. Hakluyt, *Divers Voyages*, pp. 27, 31.

37. Ibid. pp. 32, 33-4.

38. *The Voyages and Colonising Enterprises of Sir Humphrey Gilbert*,

ed. David Beers Quinn (London: The Hakluyt Society, 1940), II, 470–71.

39. *The Original Writings and Correspondence of the Two Richard Hakluyts,* ed. E. G. R. Taylor (London: The Hakluyt Society, 1935), II, 282.

40. See, for example, John Brereton, *A Briefe and true Relation of the Discoverie of the North part of Virginia* (London, 1602), p. 17.

41. *Humphrey Gilbert,* II, 462.

42. *Hakluyts,* II, 234, 217, 319.

43. *The Roanoke Voyages, 1584–1590,* ed. David Beers Quinn (London: The Hakluyt Society, 1955), I, 219.

44. *The Works of Michael Drayton,* ed. J. William Hebel (Oxford, 1932), II, 363.

45. Erwin Panofsky, *Meaning in the Visual Arts* (Garden City, N. Y., 1957), pp. 302–3.

46. *Roanoke Voyages,* I, 108.

47. Sandys, *Sermons,* p. 337.

CHAPTER I

1. "Nova Britannia: Offering Most Excellent fruites by Planting in Virginia" (London, 1609), in *Tracts and Other Papers, Relating Principally to the Origin, Settlement, and Progress of the Colonies in North America,* comp. Peter Force (Washington, D. C., 1836–47), reprinted in facsimile (New York, 1947), I, No. 6, pp. 11, 12.

2. "A True Declaration of the estate of the Colonie in Virginia" (London, 1610), in Force, *Tracts,* III, No. 1, p. 13.

3. For a discussion of the development of society in Virginia see Sigmund Diamond, "From Organization to Society: Virginia in the Seventeenth Century," *American Journal of Sociology,* LXIII (1957–58), 457–75. The interpretation in this chapter differs somewhat from Diamond's in emphasizing this general social expectation as an element in the policy of the Virginia Company.

4. "Nova Britannia," p. 19.

5. Ibid. p. 8.

6. *Narratives of Early Virginia, 1606–1625,* ed. Lyon Gardiner Tyler (New York, 1907), pp. 9–10, 21.

7. "A True Declaration," p. 14.

8. *The Genesis of the United States,* ed. Alexander Brown (Boston and New York, 1891), I, 411.

9. Alexander Whitaker, *Good Newes from Virginia* (London, 1613), p. 11.

10. W. Crashaw, *A Sermon Preached in London before the right honorable the Lord Lawarre* (London, 1610), sig. B3^v.

11. Ibid. sigs. E4^v–F1^r.

12. Ibid. sig. K1^v.

13. Ibid. sig. F2^r.

14. Robert Gray, *A Good Speed to Virginia* (London, 1609), ed.

Wesley F. Craven (New York: Scholars' Facsimiles & Reprints, 1937), sig. D1^r.

15. Ibid. sig. D3^v.
16. Brown, *Genesis*, I, 70.
17. John Smith, "A True Relation of such occurrences and accidents of noate as hath hapned in Virginia" (London, 1608), in *Narratives of Early Virginia*, pp. 36, 37.
18. Captaine [John] Smith, "A Map of Virginia with a Description of the Countrey . . . Whereunto is annexed the proceedings of those Colonies . . ." (Oxford, 1612), in *Narratives of Early Virginia*, p. 180.
19. George Percy, "A Trewe Relacyon," in *Tyler's Quarterly Historical and Genealogical Magazine*, III (1922), 264.
20. "A Discourse of virginia per: Ed: Ma: Wingfield," in Capt. John Smith, *Works, 1608–1631*, ed. Edward Arber (Birmingham, England, 1884), p. lxxxiv.
21. Brown, *Genesis*, I, 344.
22. "A True Declaration," pp. 19–20.
23. Wesley Frank Craven, *The Southern Colonies in the Seventeenth Century, 1607–1689* ([Baton Rouge], 1949), pp. 104–6.
24. "For the Colony of Virginea Britannia. Lawes Divine, Morall and Martiall, &c." (London, 1612), in Force, *Tracts*, III, No. 2, pp. 6–7.
25. Brown, *Genesis*, II, 797.
26. Ibid. I, 355.
27. *The Records of the Virginia Company of London*, ed. Susan Myra Kingsbury (Washington, D.C. 1906–35), III (1933), 259.
28. *Narratives of Early Virginia*, p. 128.
29. Sigmund Diamond has argued ("From Organization to Society," pp. 467f.) that Virginia under Dale's Laws was not really a society because each person had only one role defined in terms of his military rank. However, Wesley Craven (*Southern Colonies*, pp. 105–6) has pointed out that the code sought to distinguish between civil and military spheres of life, and thus it is not accurate to think of Virginians as living strictly under martial law.
30. Kingsbury, *Va. Co.*, III, 469, 474.
31. Lewis Cecil Gray, *History of Agriculture in the Southern United States to 1860* (Washington, D. C., 1933), I, 260; Thomas J. Wertenbaker, *The Planters of Colonial Virginia* (Princeton, 1922), pp. 25, 27.
32. *Narratives of Early Virginia*, p. 434.
33. Kingsbury, *Va. Co.*, III, 278.
34. John Bonoeil, *His Majesties Gracious Letter to the Earle of Southhampton* (London, 1622), p. 61.
35. Kingsbury, *Va. Co.*, III, 613, 669.
36. Ibid. III, 670; for the reaction of Virginians see IV, 12–13, 65–6.
37. Wesley Frank Craven, *Dissolution of the Virginia Company: The Failure of a Colonial Experiment* (New York, 1932), pp. 42, 47–9.
38. Kingsbury, *Va. Co.*, III, 493.
39. Ibid. II (1906), 350.

40. Craven, *Dissolution*, p. 274.
41. Kingsbury, *Va. Co.*, II, 347.
42. Ibid. IV, 146.
43. "The New Life of Virginea" (London, 1612), in Force, *Tracts*, I, No. 7, pp. 13, 17.
44. Captaine John Smith, "The Generall Historie of Virginia, New-England, and the Summer Isles" (London, 1624), *Works*, p. 726.
45. Captaine John Smith, "Advertisements for the unexperienced Planters of New-England, or any where" (London, 1631), *Works*, pp. 964–5.
46. Samuel Purchas, "Virginias Verger," in *Hakluytus Posthumus, or Purchas His Pilgrimes* (Glasgow, 1906), XIX, 236.
47. Richard Eburne, *A Plaine Path-Way to Plantations* (London, 1624), p. 11.
48. Ibid. p. 14.
49. Ibid. p. 16.
50. Richard Whitbourne, *A Discourse and Discovery of New-Found-Land* (London, 1620), sig. B3ʳ.
51. Max Weber, *The Protestant Ethic and the Spirit of Capitalism*, trans. Talcott Parsons (New York and London, 1930), p. 60.
52. Eburne, *Plaine Path-Way*, sig. B2ᵛ.
53. Ibid. pp. 59, 62.
54. Kingsbury, *Va. Co.*, IV, 232.
55. Ibid. IV, 59.

CHAPTER 2

1. *Narratives of Early Virginia, 1606–1625*, ed. Lyon Gardiner Tyler (New York, 1907), pp. 284–5.
2. *The Records of the Virginia Company of London*, ed. Susan Myra Kingsbury (Washington, D. C., 1906–35), III (1933), 589.
3. *Narratives of Early Virginia*, pp. 81–2.
4. *The Genesis of the United States*, ed. Alexander Brown (Boston and New York, 1891), II, 640.
5. Ralph Hamor, *A True Discourse of the Present State of Virginia* (London, 1615), introd. A. L. Rowse, reprinted in facsimile (Virginia State Library Publications, 1957), p. 22.
6. Ibid. p. 17.
7. Ibid. p. 27.
8. Ibid. p. 50.
9. Ibid. p. 24.
10. "John Rolf's Relation of the State of Virginia," *The Virginia Historical Register, and Literary Advertiser*, I, No. 3 (1848), 105.
11. Ibid. pp. 110–11.
12. Ibid. p. 113.
13. William Symonds, *Virginia: A Sermon Preached at White-Chapel, in the presence of many, Honourable and Worshipfull, the Adventurers and Planters for Virginia* (London, 1609), pp. 23, 24.
14. Ibid. p. 26.

15. [John White], "The Planters Plea. Or The Grounds of Plantations Examined, And usuall Objections answered" (London, 1630), in *Tracts and Other Papers*, comp. Peter Force (Washington, D. C., 1836–47), II, No. 3, pp. 1–2.
16. Ibid. p. 18.
17. Ibid. pp. 10, 11.
18. Ibid. p. 20.
19. Ibid. pp. 24, 26.
20. Quoted in William Bradford, *Of Plymouth Plantation, 1620–1647*, ed. Samuel Eliot Morison (New York, 1952), p. 33.
21. Quoted, ibid. p. 76.
22. "Winthrop's Conclusions for the Plantation in New England," *Old South Leaflets* (Boston, n. d.), II, No. 50, p. 8.
23. Sumner Chilton Powell, *Puritan Village: The Formation of a New England Town* (Middletown, Conn., 1963), p. 142; see also chs. 1–4.
24. Daniel Denton, *A Brief Description of New York* (London, 1670), printed in facsimile with a note by Victor Hugo Paltsits (New York, 1937), p. 16.
25. *American History told by Contemporaries*, Vol. I: *Era of Colonization, 1492–1689*, ed. Albert Bushnell Hart (New York, 1897), p. 566.
26. Perry Miller, *Errand into the Wilderness* (Cambridge, Mass., 1956), pp. 139, 138.
27. Edwin B. Bronner, *William Penn's "Holy Experiment," The Founding of Pennsylvania* (New York and London, 1962), p. 8.
28. Ibid. p. 59.
29. [William Penn], *The Frame of the Government of the Province of Pennsylvania in America* (London, 1682), sig. A2^v.
30. William Penn, "A Further Account of the Province of Pennsylvania and Its Improvements" (London, 1685), in *Narratives of Early Pennsylvania, West New Jersey and Delaware, 1630–1707*, ed. Albert Cook Myers (New York, 1912), p. 263.
31. Bronner, *Penn's "Holy Experiment,"* pp. 91–2, 110.
32. Ibid. p. 207.
33. Quoted, ibid. p. 259.
34. Thomas Morton, "New English Canaan" (London, 1632), in Force, *Tracts*, II, No. 5, p. 74.
35. Richard Whitbourne, *A Discourse and Discovery of New-Found-Land* (London, 1620), pp. 64–5.
36. Wesley Frank Craven, *The Southern Colonies in the Seventeenth Century, 1607–1689* ([Baton Rouge], 1949), pp. 148–9.
37. *The Virginia Magazine of History and Biography*, VIII (1900), 42.
38. "Extracts from a Manuscript Collection of Annals relative to Virginia," in Force, *Tracts*, II, No. 6, pp. 4, 5.

CHAPTER 3

1. Charles M. Andrews, *The Colonial Period of American History* (New Haven, 1937–38), II, 203.

2. *Narratives of Early Maryland, 1633–1684,* ed. Clayton Colman Hall (New York, 1910), pp. 21–2, 20.
3. Lewis Cecil Gray, *History of Agriculture in the Southern United States to 1860* (Washington, D. C., 1933), I, 35.
4. Wesley Frank Craven, *The Southern Colonies in the Seventeenth Century, 1607–1689* ([Baton Rouge], 1949), pp. 221–2.
5. *The Virginia Magazine of History and Biography,* II (1895), 394.
6. Ibid. II, 287.
7. Ibid. III (1895), 16.
8. Ibid. XIV (1907), 364.
9. Philip Alexander Bruce, *Economic History of Virginia in the Seventeenth Century* (New York and London, 1896), I, 408.
10. *William Fitzhugh and His Chesapeake World, 1676–1701,* ed. Richard Beale Davis (Chapel Hill, 1963), pp. 82–3, n. 2.
11. Francis Makemie, *A Plain and Friendly Perswasive* (London, 1705), pp. 5, 7.
12. Ibid. pp. 10, 11.
13. "A Perfect Description of Virginia" (London, 1649), in *Tracts and Other Papers,* comp. Peter Force (Washington, D.C., 1836–47), II, No. 8, p. 6.
14. "Anthony Langston on Towns, and Corporations; and on the Manufacture of Iron," *William and Mary College Quarterly,* 2nd ser., I (1921), 101–2.
15. William Bullock, *Virginia Impartially examined, and left to publick view* (London, 1649), sig. +3^r.
16. Ibid. sigs. C3^r, C3^v.
17. Ibid. sig. K1^r.
18. Ibid. sigs. D2^v, E3^r.
19. *Va. Mag.,* LXV (1957), 462.
20. Bruce, *Economic History,* I, 300–301, 459.
21. Quoted in Gray, *Southern Agriculture,* I, 231.
22. *Va. Mag.,* XXIV (1916), 359.
23. Ibid. XXV (1917), 132.
24. Ibid. XXV, 144, 147.
25. "A Letter from Mr. John Clayton," in Force, *Tracts,* III, No. 12, p. 11; for a summary of the efforts to promote towns in Virginia in the seventeenth century see Bruce, *Economic History,* II, 522–65.
26. Craven, *Southern Colonies,* pp. 324, 342.
27. *Collections of the South Carolina Historical Society,* Vol. V: *The Shaftesbury Papers and Other Records Relating to Carolina,* ed. Langdon Cheves (Charleston, 1897), p. 315.
28. Ibid. p. 126.
29. *Records in the British Public Record Office Relating to South Carolina, 1663–1684,* indexed by A. S. Salley, Jr. (Atlanta, 1928), p. 55.
30. "Carolina, or a Description of the Present State of that Country" (London, 1682), in *Narratives of Early Carolina, 1650–1708,* ed. Alexander S. Salley, Jr. (New York, 1911), p. 147.

31. Ibid. p. 157.
32. Craven, *Southern Colonies*, pp. 355, 348–9.
33. *Shaftesbury Papers*, pp. 296, 302.
34. *Records in the British Public Record Office Relating to South Carolina, 1663–1684*, pp. 83–4.
35. Ibid. p. 293.
36. *Records in the British Public Record Office Relating to South Carolina, 1691–1697* (Atlanta, 1931), pp. 139, 141.
37. Gray, *Southern Agriculture*, I, 278, 57.
38. In William J. Rivers, *A Chapter in the Early History of South Carolina* (Charleston, 1874), p. 100.
39. Quoted in C. Robert Haywood, "Mercantilism and South Carolina Agriculture, 1700–1763," *The South Carolina Historical and Genealogical Magazine*, LX (1959), 16, 17.
40. *The Journal of William Stephens*, ed. E. Merton Coulter (Athens, Ga., 1958–59), I, 194.
41. Gray, *Southern Agriculture*, I, 288.
42. Robert L. Meriwether, *The Expansion of South Carolina, 1729–1765* (Kingsport, Tenn., 1940), p. 20; Gray, *Southern Agriculture*, I, 379.
43. David Duncan Wallace, *South Carolina, A Short History, 1520–1948* (Chapel Hill, 1951), p. 156.
44. Andrews, *Colonial Period*, III, 248–9.
45. Gray, *Southern Agriculture*, I, 44.
46. Hugh Talmage Lefler and Albert Ray Newsome, *The History of a Southern State: North Carolina* (Chapel Hill, 1954), pp. 50, 65.
47. *The Colonial Records of North Carolina*, ed. William L. Saunders (Raleigh, 1886–90), I, 764.
48. Ibid. III, 338.
49. Ibid. IV, 424.
50. Ibid. IV, 919.
51. See, for instance, Vincent T. Harlow, *A History of Barbados, 1625–1685* (Oxford, 1926), pp. 6–7, 13, 21; *Colonising Expeditions to the West Indies and Guiana, 1623–1667*, ed. V. T. Harlow (London: The Hakluyt Society, 1925), pp. 67, 69; *The Narrative of General Venables with an Appendix of Papers Relating to the Expedition to the West Indies and the Conquest of Jamaica, 1654–1655*, ed. C. H. Firth (London, 1900), p. 146; C. S. S. Higham, *The Development of the Leeward Islands under the Restoration, 1660–1688* (Cambridge, England, 1921), p. 178; *The Groans of Plantations: Or a True Account of their Grievous and Extreme Sufferings By the Heavy Impositions upon Sugar, and other Hardships* (London, 1689), p. 21. The virtual extinction of the small planter class in the West Indies constitutes an important difference from the southern colonies; on this topic see Harlow, *History of Barbados*, pp. 41–3 and Frank Wesley Pitman, *The Development of the British West Indies, 1700–1763* (New Haven and London, 1917), pp. 91, 98–9.

CHAPTER 4

1. John Hammond, "Leah and Rachel, or, the Two Fruitfull Sisters, Virginia, and Mary-land" (London, 1656), in *Narratives of Early Maryland, 1633–1684,* ed. Clayton Colman Hall (New York, 1910), p. 284.
2. Ibid. pp. 285–6.
3. Ibid. pp. 292, 295.
4. Ibid. pp. 290, 294.
5. [George Milligan-Johnston], "A Short Description of the Province of South Carolina, written in the Year 1763" (London, 1770), in *Colonial South Carolina: Two Contemporary Descriptions,* ed. Chapman J. Milling (Columbia, 1951), pp. 6–7 (of the original).
6. William Gerard De Brahm, "Philosophico-Historico-Hydro-geography of South Carolina, Georgia, and East Florida," in *Documents Connected with the History of South Carolina,* ed. Plowden Charles Jennett Weston (London, 1856), pp. 195, 196. De Brahm was Surveyor for the Southern District of North America and had lived in the colonies for some twenty years.
7. "A Letter from Doctor More with Passages out of Several Letters from Persons of Good Credit" (London, 1687), in *Narratives of Early Pennsylvania, West New Jersey and Delaware, 1630–1707,* ed. Albert Cook Myers (New York, 1912), pp. 284, 285.
8. William Penn, "A Further Account of the Province of Pennsylvania and Its Improvements" (London, 1685), in ibid. p. 264.
9. Captaine [John] Smith, "A Map of Virginia" (Oxford, 1612), in *Narratives of Early Virginia, 1606–1625,* ed. Lyon Gardiner Tyler (New York, 1907), p. 201.
10. Alexander Whitaker, *Good Newes from Virginia* (London, 1613), pp. 33–4.
11. *Narratives of Early Maryland,* p. 283.
12. Robert Beverley, *The History and Present State of Virginia,* ed. Louis B. Wright (Chapel Hill, 1947), p. 319.
13. Ibid. p. 298.
14. *The Prose Works of William Byrd of Westover: Narratives of a Colonial Virginian,* ed. Louis B. Wright (Cambridge, Mass., 1966), pp. 159, 160.
15. Ibid. p. 312.
16. Ibid. p. 205.
17. Ibid. p. 195.
18. *The State Records of North Carolina,* Vol. XXIII: *Laws, 1715–1776,* ed. Walter Clark (Goldsboro, 1904), p. 3.
19. *The Colonial Records of North Carolina,* ed. William L. Saunders (Raleigh, 1886–90), V, 571.
20. Ibid. V, 497.
21. *The Genesis of the United States,* ed. Alexander Brown (Boston and New York, 1891), I, 84, 107.

22. "A True Declaration of the estate of the Colonie in Virginia" (London, 1610), in *Tracts and Other Papers*, comp. Peter Force (Washington, D. C., 1836-47), III, No. 1, p. 15.

23. Captaine John Smith, "New Englands Trials" (London, 1620), in Capt. John Smith, *Works, 1608-1631*, ed. Edward Arber (Birmingham, England, 1884), pp. 243-4.

24. Beverley, *History*, p. 311.

25. *William Byrd's Natural History of Virginia, or, The Newly Discovered Eden* (1737), eds. Richmond Croom Beatty and William J. Mulloy (Richmond, 1940), p. 54.

26. Beverley, *History*, p. 30.

27. Ibid. p. 55.

28. Ibid. pp. 319, 57-8.

29. *Another Secret Diary of William Byrd of Westover, 1739-1741, With Letters & Literary Exercises, 1696-1727*, ed. Maude H. Woodfin, trans. Marion Tinling (Richmond, 1942), p. 55, n. 1.

30. Hugh Jones, *The Present State of Virginia, From Whence Is Inferred a Short View of Maryland and North Carolina* (London, 1724), ed. Richard L. Morton (Chapel Hill, 1956), p. 73.

31. *The Virginia Magazine of History and Biography*, XXXVI (1928), 40.

32. Byrd, *Prose Works*, p. 192.

33. Carl Bridenbaugh, *Myths and Realities: Societies of the Colonial South* (Baton Rouge, 1952), p. 58.

34. John Lawson, *History of North Carolina* (London, 1714), ed. Frances Latham Harriss, 2nd ed. (Richmond, 1952), p. 75.

35. Byrd, *Prose Works*, 192.

36. Beverley, *History*, p. 295.

37. *A Huguenot Exile in Virginia* (1687), ed. Gilbert Chinard (New York, 1934), pp. 112, 111.

38. Jones, *Virginia*, p. 77.

39. *Narratives of Early Carolina, 1650-1708*, ed. Alexander S. Salley, Jr. (New York, 1911), p. 217.

40. Henry Hartwell, James Blair, and Edward Chilton, *The Present State of Virginia and the College*, ed. Hunter Dickinson Farish (Williamsburg, 1940), p. 9.

41. Lewis Cecil Gray, *History of Agriculture in the Southern United States to 1860* (Washington, D. C., 1933), I, 460.

42. John Brickell, *The Natural History of North-Carolina* (Dublin, 1737), reprinted (Raleigh, 1911), p. 269.

43. *Col. Rec. of N. C.*, IV, 18-19.

44. Byrd, *Prose Works*, p. 215.

45. *George Whitefield's Journals* (Guildford and London, 1960), p. 156.

46. *Col. Rec. of N. C.*, IV, 1312.

47. *Journal and Letters of Eliza Lucas* (Wormsloe, Ga., 1850), p. 17.

48. Byrd, *Prose Works*, pp. 143, 311-12. Comparison is facilitated by using *William Byrd's Histories of the Dividing Line Betwixt Virginia and North Carolina*, ed. William K. Boyd (Raleigh, 1929),

because corresponding parts of the two histories are printed on facing pages—in this instance, pp. 304-5.

49. Ibid. pp. 54, 175 (Boyd ed., pp. 40–41).
50. Perry Miller, *The New England Mind: From Colony to Province* (Cambridge, Mass., 1953), p. 28.
51. Byrd, *Prose Works*, pp. 192, 204; Lawson, *History*, p. 85.
52. Beverley, *History*, p. 272.
53. Ibid. p. 308.
54. *Va. Mag.*, IX (1902), 227.
55. Byrd, *Prose Works*, p. 290.
56. Ibid. p. 184.
57. Beverley, *History*, p. 319.
58. *The Secret Diary of William Byrd of Westover, 1709–1712*, eds. Louis B. Wright and Marion Tinling (Richmond, 1941), pp. 27, 113.
59. *Another Secret Diary of William Byrd*, p. 277.

CHAPTER 5

1. *The Prose Works of William Byrd of Westover: Narratives of a Colonial Virginian*, ed. Louis B. Wright (Cambridge, Mass., 1966), p. 162.
2. Quoted in Frank Wesley Pitman, *The Development of the British West Indies, 1700–1763* (New Haven and London, 1917), pp. 42–3.
3. Quoted, ibid. p. 20.
4. *The Colonial Records of North Carolina*, ed. William L. Saunders (Raleigh, 1886–90), II, 420.
5. Sir William Keath, "A Discourse on the Present State of the British Plantations in America" (1728), in *A Collection of Papers and Other Tracts* (London, 1749), VI, 172.
6. *Col. Rec. of N. C.*, III, 148–9.
7. Ibid. III, 196.
8. Charles M. Andrews, *The Colonial Period of Amercan History* (New Haven, 1937–38), IV, 326, 343.
9. Written in the late seventeenth century, quoted ibid. p. 379.
10. [Edmund Burke], *An Account of the European Settlements in America*, new ed. (London, 1766), II, 158, 159.
11. Ibid. II, 181.
12. [Benjamin Martyn], *Reasons for Establishing the Colony of Georgia* (London, 1733), p. 3.
13. Ibid. p. 23.
14. The first phrase is Martyn's; the second is from Thomas Rundle, *A Sermon Preached at S. George's Church* (London, 1734), p. 15.
15. William Berriman, *A Sermon Preach'd before the Honourable Trustees for Establishing the Colony of Georgia in America* (London, 1739), p. 8.
16. Martyn, *Reasons*, p. 29.
17. Lewis Cecil Gray, *History of Agriculture in the Southern United States to 1860* (Washington, D. C., 1933), I, 97.
18. Martyn, *Reasons*, p. 28.

19. Ibid. p. 15.
20. Ibid. p. 30.
21. Ibid. pp. 17–18.
22. [James Oglethorpe], "A New and Accurate Account of the Provinces of South Carolina and Georgia" (London, 1733), in *Collections of the Georgia Historical Society* (Savannah, 1840–), I, 57.
23. Francis Moore, "A Voyage to Georgia, Begun in the Year 1735" (London, 1744), in ibid. I, 84.
24. William Best, *The Merit and Reward of a good Intention. A Sermon Preached before the Honourable Trustees for Establishing the Colony of Georgia in America* (London, 1742), p. 23.
25. [Benjamin Martyn], "An Impartial Inquiry into the State and Utility of the Province of Georgia" (London, 1741), in *Coll. of the Ga. Hist. Soc.*, I, 155.
26. Ibid. I, 177.
27. "An Account, Shewing the Progress of the Colony of Georgia in America, From Its First Establishment" (London and Annapolis, 1741–42), in *Tracts and Other Papers*, comp. Peter Force (Washington, D.C., 1836–47), I, No. 5, p. 18.
28. Martyn, "Inquiry," p. 200.
29. Ibid. p. 159.
30. Ibid. p. 155.
31. *The Journal of William Stephens*, ed. E. Merton Coulter (Athens, Ga., 1958–59), I, 58–9.
32. "An Account," pp. 8, 10.
33. *A True Historical Narrative of the Colony of Georgia*, By Pat. Tailfer and Others with Comments by the Earl of Egmont, ed. Clarence L. Ver Steeg (Athens, Ga., 1960), p. 11.
34. Ibid. pp. 89–90.
35. Ibid. p. 153.
36. Best, *Sermon*, p. 17.
37. Tailfer, *Narrative*, pp. 17, 21; see also pp. 89, 91.
38. [Thomas Stephens], "A Brief Account of the Causes that Have Retarded The Progress of the Colony of Georgia in America" (London, 1743), in *Coll. of the Ga. Hist. Soc.*, II (1842), 90.
39. Tailfer, *Narrative*, p. 51.
40. Thomas Stephens, *The Hard Case of the Distressed People of Georgia* (London, 1742), p. 2.
41. Ibid.
42. *The Virginia Magazine of History and Biography*, XXXVI (1928), 220.

CHAPTER 6

1. *The Records of the Virginia Company of London*, ed. Susan Myra Kingsbury (Washington, D.C., 1906–35), III (1933), 226.
2. Ibid. III, 489.

3. Thomas J. Wertenbaker, *The Planters of Colonial Virginia* (Princeton, 1922), pp. 44, 59.
4. Ibid. pp. 125, 126, 131, 132, 152.
5. The argument for the gradual fixation of Negro slavery has been recently advanced by Oscar Handlin, *Race and Nationality in American Life* (Boston and Toronto, 1957), pp. 3–28. For an opposing view in answer to Handlin see Winthrop D. Jordan, "The Influence of the West Indies on the Origins of New England Slavery," *William and Mary Quarterly*, 3rd ser., XVIII (1961), esp. pp. 248–50; and Jordan, "Modern Tensions and the Origins of American Slavery," *Journal of Southern History*, XXVIII (1962), 18–30.
6. Quoted in Ann Maury, *Memoirs of a Huguenot Family* (New York, 1872), p. 352.
7. *Narratives of the Insurrections, 1675–1690,* ed. Charles M. Andrews (New York, 1915), pp. 49, 52.
8. Wilcomb E. Washburn, *The Governor and the Rebel: A History of Bacon's Rebellion in Virginia* (Chapel Hill, 1957), pp. 37–8, 45.
9. *The Virginia Magazine of History and Biography*, XIV (1907), 274.
10. Written by Governor Gooch in 1746 and quoted in Richard L. Morton, *Colonial Virginia*, Vol. II: *Westward Expansion and Prelude to Revolution, 1710–1763* (Chapel Hill, 1960), p. 527.
11. *Va. Mag.*, XXXVII (1929), 29.
12. Richard Maxwell Brown, *The South Carolina Regulators* (Cambridge, Mass., 1963), p. 28.
13. *The Carolina Backcountry on the Eve of the Revolution: The Journal and other Writings of Charles Woodmason, Anglican Itinerant,* ed. Richard J. Hooker (Chapel Hill, 1953), p. 246.
14. Brown, *Regulators,* p. 50.
15. Charles Chauncy, *The Idle-Poor secluded from the Bread of Charity by the Christian Law. A Sermon Preached in Boston, before the Society for encouraging Industry, and employing the Poor* (Boston, 1752), pp. 11, 12.
16. Ibid. p. 24.
17. [Alexander Hewit], "An Historical Account of the Rise and Progress of the Colonies of South Carolina and Georgia" (London, 1779), in *Historical Collections of South Carolina,* ed. R. B. Carroll (New York, 1836), I, 358.
18. [Benjamin Martyn], "An Impartial Inquiry into the State and Utility of the Province of Georgia" (London, 1741), in *Collections of the Georgia Historical Society* (Savannah, 1840–   ), I, 169.
19. Hewit, "Historical Account," pp. 351–2.
20. Quoted in Frank J. Klingberg, *An Appraisal of the Negro in Colonial South Carolina* (Washington, D.C., 1941), pp. 6, 7; see also p. 56.
21. Quoted in Lewis Cecil Gray, *History of Agriculture in the*

Southern United States to 1860 (Washington, D.C., 1933), I, 327.
22. *George Whitefield's Journals* (Guildford and London, 1960), p. 385; see also *The Carolina Chronicle of Dr. Francis Le Jau, 1706–1717*, ed. Frank J. Klingberg (Berkeley and Los Angeles, 1956), p. 108.
23. Quoted in Maury, *Memoirs of a Huguenot Family*, p. 364.
24. *Va. Mag.*, XXXVI (1928), 220.
25. *The Secret Diary of William Byrd of Westover, 1709–1712*, eds. Louis B. Wright and Marion Tinling (Richmond, 1941), pp. 412, 514; see also p. 533 and Kenneth S. Lynn, *Mark Twain and Southwestern Humor* (Boston and Toronto, 1959), esp. pp. 3–6, 19–20.
26. *Secret Diary*, p. 540.
27. *Historical Collections Relating to the Amercian Colonial Church*, Vol. I: *Virginia*, ed. William Stevens Perry (Hartford, 1870), pp. 202, 230.
28. Ibid. p. 101; see also p. 125.
29. Ibid. p. 83.
30. James Blair, *Our Saviour's Divine Sermon on the Mount*, 2nd ed. (London, 1740), I, 256.
31. Ibid. I, 60, 62–3.
32. Ibid. I, 176.
33. Ibid. I, 131.
34. Ibid. I, 144, 149.
35. Ibid. III, 321–2, 373.
36. Samuel Davies, *Religion and Patriotism, the Constituents of a Good Soldier. A Sermon* (Philadelphia, 1755), p. 7.
37. Samuel Quincy, *Twenty Sermons on the following Subjects . . . Preach'd in the Parish of St. Philip, Charles-Town, South Carolina* (Boston, 1750), p. 88.

CHAPTER 7

1. Arthur P. Scott, *Criminal Law in Colonial Virginia* (Chicago, 1930), pp. 273–4; *The Colonial Records of the State of Georgia*, comp. Allen D. Candler (Atlanta, 1904–16), XVIII, 588.
2. *The South Carolina Historical and Genealogical Magazine*, XXXII (1931), 5.
3. Ibid. XXXII, 22.
4. Ibid. XXXII, 98.
5. *The Carolina Chronicle of Dr. Francis Le Jau, 1706–1717*, ed. Frank J. Klingberg (Berkeley and Los Angeles, 1956), pp. 18, 38.
6. Ibid. p. 30.
7. Ibid. pp. 69, 94.
8. Ibid. p. 12.
9. *Carolina Chronicle: The Papers of Commissary Gideon Johnston, 1707–1716*, ed. Frank J. Klingberg (Berkeley and Los Angeles, 1946), pp. 110, 78.

10. Ibid. p. 122.
11. [William Borden], "An Address to the Inhabitants of North-Carolina" (Williamsburg, 1746), in *Some Eighteenth Century Tracts Concerning North Carolina,* ed. William K. Boyd (Raleigh, 1927), pp. 75–7.
12. George Micklejohn, "On the important Duty of Subjection to the Civil Powers. A Sermon" (Newbern, 1768), in ibid. p. 403.
13. [Herman Husband], "A Fan for Fanning, and Touch-Stone to Tryon" (Boston, 1771), in ibid. p. 353.
14. [Herman Husband], "An Impartial Relation of the First Rise and Cause of the Recent Differences, in Publick Affairs, in the Province of North-Carolina" (n. p., 1770), in ibid., p. 312.
15. Husband, "Fan," p. 373.
16. For similar complaints against the proprietary government of Maryland in 1689 see *Archives of Maryland,* ed. William Hand Browne (Baltimore, 1883–   ), VIII (1890), 103; and against that of South Carolina in 1719 see William J. Rivers, *A Chapter in the Early History of South Carolina* (Charleston, 1874), pp. 45, 47.
17. *The Virginia Magazine of History and Biography,* I (1893), 59.
18. Wilcomb E. Washburn, *The Governor and the Rebel: A History of Bacon's Rebellion in Virginia* (Chapel Hill, 1957), p. 84.
19. *Narratives of the Insurrections, 1675–1690,* ed. Charles M. Andrews (New York, 1915), pp. 137–8, 139.
20. Robert L. Meriwether, *The Expansion of South Carolina, 1729–1765* (Kingsport, Tenn., 1940), p. 181.
21. Quoted in Richard Maxwell Brown, *The South Carolina Regulators* (Cambridge, Mass., 1963), p. 12.
22. *The Carolina Backcountry on the Eve of the Revolution: The Journal and other Writings of Charles Woodmason, Anglican Itinerant,* ed. Richard J. Hooker (Chapel Hill, 1953), p. 226.
23. Ibid. p. 231.
24. Ibid. pp. 27–8.
25. Ibid. p. 284.
26. Brown, *Regulators,* pp. 83–95.
27. *Carolina Backcountry,* p. 249.
28. Isaac Chanler, *New Converts Exhorted to Cleave to the Lord. A Sermon* (Boston, 1740), p. 19.
29. Samuel Davies, *Sermons on the Most useful and Important Subjects, Adapted to the Family and Closet,* 2nd ed. (London, 1767), II, 176, 177
30. Josiah Smith, *The Church of Ephesus arraign'd. The Substance of five short Sermons, Contracted into one. Delivered 1760, at Charles-Town, South-Carolina* (Charles-Town, 1768), p. 7.
31. Josiah Smith, *The Character, Preaching, &c. of the Reverend Mr. George Whitefield* (Boston, 1740), p. 12.
32. Davies, *Sermons,* II, 178.
33. Quoted in William Sumner Jenkins, *Pro-Slavery Thought in the Old South* (Chapel Hill, 1935), p. 42.

34. Samuel Davies, *Virginia's Danger and Remedy* (Williamsburg, 1756), p. 6.
35. Samuel Davies, *The Duty of Christians to propagate their Religion among Heathens, Earnestly recommended to the Masters of Negroe Slaves in Virginia* (London, 1758), pp. 36, 27.
36. Ibid. p. 35.
37. Davies, *Sermons*, III, 250.
38. I am indebted to Alan Heimert for my whole approach to the Great Awakening and its secular implications. This debt carries over into the next three chapters, specifically with reference to the discussion of the role of the ministers. See his recent study, *Religion and the American Mind: From the Great Awakening to the Revolution* (Cambridge, Mass., 1966).
39. Samuel Davies, *The Crisis: or, The uncertain Doom of Kingdoms at particular Times* (London, 1757), pp. 19, 12.
40. Samuel Davies, *The Curse of Cowardice* (London, 1758), pp. 12–13.
41. Samuel Davies, *Religion and Patriotism, The Constituents of a Good Soldier* (Philadelphia, 1755), pp. 18–19.
42. John Evans, *National Ingratitude lamented* (Charles-Town, 1745), p. 6.
43. Davies, *Religion and Patriotism*, pp. 12, 14.

CHAPTER 8

1. Derek Hudson and Kenneth W. Luckhurst, *The Royal Society of Arts: 1754–1954* (London, 1954), pp. 4, 155–6.
2. Sir Henry Trueman Wood, *A History of the Royal Society of Arts* (London, 1913), p. 101.
3. Hudson and Luckhurst, *Royal Society*, p. 153.
4. *The Papers of Benjamin Franklin*, ed. Leonard W. Labaree (New Haven, 1959–   ), IV, 228–9.
5. Ibid. IX, 73, 85.
6. [Daniel Dulany], *Considerations on the Propriety of Imposing Taxes in the British Colonies, for the Purpose of raising a Revenue, by Act of Parliament* ([Annapolis], 1765), p. 27.
7. Ibid. p. 34.
8. Richard Bland, *An Inquiry into the Rights of the British Colonies* (Williamsburg, 1766), pp. 30, 20.
9. *The Writings of George Washington from the Original Manuscript Sources, 1745–1799*, ed. John C. Fitzpatrick (Washington, D. C., 1931–44), II, 426; see also Dulany, *Considerations*, pp. 45, 46.
10. *The Revolutionary Records of the State of Georgia*, comp. Allen D. Candler (Atlanta, 1908), I, 9.
11. *Centennial Offering: Republication of The Principles and Acts of the Revolution in America*, ed. Hezekiah Niles (New York, Chicago, and New Orleans, 1876), pp. 272–3.
12. *Rev. Records of Ga.*, I, 45.
13. Niles, *Principles*, p. 110.

14. Ibid. pp. 210, 209.
15. Richard Walsh, *Charleston's Sons of Liberty: A Study of the Artisans, 1763–1789* (Columbia, 1959), esp. pp. 19, 46, 51.
16. Hugh Alison, *Spiritual Liberty: A Sermon* (Charlestown, 1769), p. 22.
17. *The Papers of James Madison*, eds. William T. Hutchinson and William M. E. Rachal (Chicago, 1962–   ), I, 112.
18. *American Archives: Fourth Series. Containing a Documentary History of the English Colonies in North America, from the King's Message to Parliament, of March 7, 1774 to the Declaration of Independence by the United States*, eds. M. St. Clair Clark and Peter Force (Washington, D. C., 1837–46), I, 383, 384.
19. *Reminiscences of an American Loyalist, 1738–1789, Being the Autobiography of the Reverend Jonathan Boucher*, ed. Jonathan Boucher (Boston and New York, 1925), pp. 132, 134.
20. *Documentary History of the American Revolution: Consisting of Letters and Papers Relating to the Contest for Liberty, Chiefly in South Carolina . . . 1764–1776*, ed. R. W. Gibbes (New York, 1855), pp. 233, 234–5.
21. "Writings of the Reverend William Tennent, 1740–1777," ed. Newton B. Jones, *The South Carolina Historical Magazine*, LXI (1960), 190, 204.
22. John Hurt, *The Love of our Country. A Sermon, Preached Before the Virginia Troops in New-Jersey* (Philadelphia, 1777), pp. 10–11.
23. Ibid. p. 19.
24. William M. Dabney and Marion Dargan, *William Henry Drayton and the American Revolution* (Albuquerque, 1962), pp. 27, 48, 57, 70.
25. Gibbes, *Doc. Hist.*, p. 280.
26. Ibid. p. 287.
27. Niles, *Principles*, p. 351.
28. Ibid. p. 363.
29. David Ramsay, *An Oration on the Advantages of American Independence* (Charles-Town, 1778), p. 2.
30. Ibid. p. 11.
31. Ibid. p. 14.
32. *Rudiments of Law and Government, Deduced from the Law of Nature* (Charlestown, 1783), p. 44.

CHAPTER 9

1. Hugh Talmage Lefler and Albert Ray Newsome, *The History of a Southern State: North Carolina* (Chapel Hill, 1954), p. 252; Kenneth Coleman, *The American Revolution in Georgia, 1763–1789* (Athens, Ga., 1958), p. 213; John Harold Wolfe, *Jeffersonian Democracy in South Carolina*, The James Sprunt Studies in History and Political Science, Vol. XXIV, No. 1 (Chapel Hill, 1940), pp. 8, 11; *Travels in the Confederation, 1783–1784, from the German of*

Johann David Schoepf, trans. and ed. Alfred J. Morrison (Philadelphia, 1911), II, 40, 90; *Journal of a Tour to North Carolina by William Attmore, 1787*, The James Sprunt Historical Publications, Vol. XVII, No. 2 (Chapel Hill, 1922), p. 39.

2. W. A. Low, "Merchant and Planter Relations in Post-Revolutionary Virginia, 1783–1789," *The Virginia Magazine of History and Biography*, LXI (1953), 309, 311; Ulrich B. Phillips, "The South Carolina Federalists, with Accompanying Documents," *American Historical Review*, XIV (1908–9), 541.

3. David Ramsay, *The History of the Revolution of South Carolina, from a British Province to an Independent State* (Trenton, 1785), I, 6–8.

4. Ibid. I, 83, 160–61.

5. Ibid. II, 385.

6. *The Writings of James Madison*, ed. Gaillard Hunt (New York and London, 1900–1910), II, 28, 57; see also pp. 147-8.

7. Ibid. II, 218, 228–9.

8. In Phillips, "South Carolina Federalists," pp. 537–8.

9. *Centennial Offering: Republication of The Principles and Acts of the Revolution in America*, ed. Hezekiah Niles (New York, Chicago, and New Orleans, 1876), p. 386.

10. *Documents Illustrative of the Formation of the Union of the United States*, ed. Charles C. Tansill (Washington, D.C., 1927), p. 38.

11. Madison, *Writings*, II, 159.

12. John Richard Alden, *The South in the Revolution, 1763–1789* ([Baton Rouge], 1957), pp. 2–3; see also Alden, *The First South* (Baton Rouge, 1961), p. 23.

13. Charles Pinckney, *Observations on the Plan of Government Submitted to the Federal Convention, in Philadelphia* (New York, [1787]), p. 17.

14. *The Debates in the Several State Conventions, on the Adoption of the Federal Constitution, as Recommended by the General Convention at Philadelphia, in 1787*, ed. Jonathan Elliott, 2nd ed. (Washington, D. C., 1836), III, 231.

15. Ibid. III, 295.

16. Major William Pierce, *An Oration, Delivered at Christ Church, Savannah* (Savannah, 1788), p. 9.

17. Ibid. p. 17.

18. *The Massachusetts Magazine: Or, Monthly Museum of Knowledge and Rational Entertainment*, I (1789), 163, 176.

19. Madison, *Writings*, II, 306.

20. Elliott, *Debates*, III, 78.

21. Ibid. IV, 284.

22. [David Ramsay], *An Address to the Freemen of South-Carolina, on the Subject of the Foederal Constitution* (Charleston, [1788]), pp. 10, 12.

23. Alexander Hamilton, James Madison, and John Jay, *The Federalist*,

ed. Benjamin Fletcher Wright (Cambridge, Mass., 1961), pp. 153–4.
24. *The Papers of James Madison*, eds. William T. Hutchinson and William M. E. Rachal (Chicago, 1962–   ), III, 72.
25. Madison, *Writings*, II, 368.
26. Elliott, *Debates*, IV, 261.
27. Ibid. IV, 323, 324.
28. Ibid. IV, 326–7, 331–2.
29. Ibid. IV, 321, 322.
30. *The Federalist*, p. 124.
31. Ibid. p. 139.
32. Philip A. Crowl, *Maryland During and After the Revolution: A Political and Economic Study* (Baltimore, 1943), pp. 123–4, 160; Richard Walsh, *Charleston's Sons of Liberty: A Study of the Artisans, 1763–1789* (Columbia, 1959), pp. 127, 18.
33. *The Writings of George Washington from the Original Manuscript Sources, 1745–1799*, ed. John C. Fitzpatrick (Washington, D. C., 1931–44), XXVI, 488.
34. Ibid. XXVIII, 108.
35. Ibid. XXIX, 298; Washington's writings on agriculture are conveniently collected in *The Agricultural Papers of George Washington*, ed. Walter Edwin Brooke (Boston, 1919).
36. *Writings*, XXIX, 310.
37. Ibid. XXXVII, 460.
38. Ibid. XXXVII, 471, 472.
39. In William Wirt Henry, *Patrick Henry, Life, Correspondence and Speeches* (New York, 1891), I, 114, 115.
40. Ibid. I, 222.
41. In Richard H. Lee, *Memoir of the Life of Richard Henry Lee* (Philadelphia, 1825), I, 18.
42. *The Letters of Richard Henry Lee*, ed. James Curtis Ballagh (New York, 1911–14), I, 301.
43. In *Henry*, II, 193, 194.
44. Ibid. II, 196.
45. Lee, *Letters*, II, 155.
46. Ibid. II, 200.
47. Ibid. II, 389.
48. *Empire and Nation: Letters from a Farmer in Pennsylvania*, John Dickinson/*Letters from the Federal Farmer*, Richard Henry Lee, introd. Forrest McDonald (Englewood Cliffs, N.J., 1962), p. 106.
49. Ibid. p. 147.
50. Lee, *Letters*, II, 471.
51. In *Henry*, III, 481.
52. Ibid. III, 520.
53. Ibid. III, 576.
54. In Kate Mason Rowland, *The Life of George Mason, 1725–1792* (New York and London, 1892), II, 161.

55. Elliott, *Debates*, III, 269–70.
56. *Essays on the Constitution of the United States, Published during Its Discussion by the People, 1787–1788,* ed. Paul Leicester Ford (Brooklyn, 1892), p. 164.
57. Elliott, *Debates*, III, 635.
58. Ibid. III, 345, 365.
59. Ibid. IV, 184–6.
60. Ford, *Essays*, p. 91.
61. Cecilia M. Kenyon, "Men of Little Faith: The Anti-Federalists on the Nature of Representative Government," *William and Mary Quarterly*, 3rd ser., XII (1955), 9.
62. Ford, *Essays*, p. 83.
63. In *Henry*, II, 559.

CHAPTER 10

1. David Rice, *Slavery Inconsistent with Justice and Good Policy, proved at a Speech Delivered in the Convention, Held at Danville, Kentucky* (Philadelphia, 1792), pp. 36, 16.
2. Ibid. pp. 35–6.
3. St. George Tucker, *A Dissertation on Slavery with a Proposal for the Gradual Abolition of it, in the State of Virginia* (Philadelphia, 1796), pp. 102–4.
4. *The Writings of Thomas Jefferson*, ed. Paul Leicester Ford (New York and London, 1892–99), III, 266, 267.
5. Ibid. III, 214, 213.
6. Ibid. III, 268, 269.
7. *The Papers of Thomas Jefferson*, ed. Julian P. Boyd (Princeton, 1950–   ), VIII, 426.
8. *Writings*, III, 271, 273.
9. *Papers*, XI, 250, 349.
10. Ibid. XI, 633.
11. Ibid. VIII, 633.
12. *Writings*, VI, 4, 5.
13. Ibid. VI, 480, 482.
14. Ibid. VIII, 123; see also pp. 186–7.
15. Ibid. IX, 223.
16. Oliver Hart, *America's Remembrancer, with Respect to Her Blessedness and Duty. A Sermon, Delivered in Hopewell, New Jersey, on Thanksgiving Day, November 26, 1789* (Philadelphia, 1791), pp. 8, 10.
17. Ibid. pp. 12, 13.
18. Ibid. pp. 22–3.
19. David Duncan Wallace, *South Carolina, A Short History, 1520–1948* (Chapel Hill, 1951), p. 213; see also note 16.
20. George Buist, *An Oration Delivered at the Orphan-House of Charleston* (Charleston, [1795]), p. 10.

21. Richard Furman, *An Oration Delivered at the Charleston Orphan-House* (Charleston, 1796), pp. 4, 10.
22. Ibid. p. 23.
23. John Taylor, *Arator, Being a Series of Agricultural Essays, Practical and Political*, 5th ed. (Petersburg, 1818), pp. 41, 42.
24. Ibid. p. 45.
25. Ibid. p. 218.
26. Ibid. p. 152.
27. Ibid. pp. 185, 193.
28. Henry William Desaussure, *An Oration, Prepared, to be Delivered in St. Phillip's Church* (Charleston, 1798), p. 16.
29. [Henry William Desaussure], *Address to the Citizens of South-Carolina, on the Approaching Election of President and Vice-President of the United States* (Charleston, 1800), p. 5.
30. Charles Pinckney, *Three Letters, Addressed to the People of the United States* (Charleston, 1799), p. 44.
31. John Drayton, *A View of South-Carolina, as Respects Her Natural and Civil Concerns* (Charleston, 1802), pp. 110, 113.
32. Ibid. pp. 149, 149–50.
33. Ibid. p. 146.
34. Ibid. p. 221.
35. David Ramsay, *The History of South-Carolina, from its First Settlement in 1670, to the Year 1808* (Charleston, 1809), I, 121.
36. David Ramsay, *An Oration Delivered in St. Michael's Church* (Charleston, [1794]), pp. 12, 17, 18.
37. Ramsay, *History*, II, 258.
38. Ibid. II, 401.
39. Ibid. II, 410–11.
40. Ibid. II, 414, 415.
41. Ibid. II, 448–9.

CHAPTER II

1. [William Wirt], *The Letters of the British Spy*, 4th ed. (Baltimore, 1811), pp. 111, 125.
2. [William Wirt], *The Old Bachelor* (Richmond, 1814), p. 37.
3. Ibid. p. 172.
4. *Spy*, pp. 45–6, 58.
5. *Bachelor*, p. 196.
6. William Wirt, *Sketches of the Life and Character of Patrick Henry*, 2nd ed. (Philadelphia, 1818), pp. 4, 6.
7. Ibid. p. 426.
8. William R. Taylor, *Cavalier and Yankee: The Old South and American National Character* (New York, 1961), pp. 81–3.
9. Wirt, *Henry*, p. 7.
10. Taylor, *Cavalier and Yankee*, esp. Ch. 11.
11. Washington Irving, *The Sketchbook of Geoffrey Crayon, Gent.* (New York, 1857), pp. 45, 46, 48.

12. Lewis Cecil Gray, *History of Agriculture in the Southern United States to 1860* (Washington, D. C., 1933), I, 496.

13. [George Tucker], *The Valley of Shenandoah; or, Memoirs of the Graysons* (New York, 1824), II, 195.

14. Ibid. I, 21, 20.

15. Ibid. I, 112–13.

16. Ibid. I, 70.

17. [George Tucker], *Essays on Various Subjects of Taste, Morals, and National Policy* (Georgetown, D. C., 1822), p. 83.

18. *Valley*, II, 52, 106.

19. Ibid. II, 105; see also Taylor, *Cavalier and Yankee*, pp. 37–65.

20. John Pendleton Kennedy, *Swallow Barn, or A Sojourn in the Old Dominion*, 2nd ed. (1851), ed. Jay B. Hubbell (New York, 1929), p. 3. It seems most pertinent to the present argument to use the edition of this work which Kennedy issued in the turbulent period preceding the Civil War.

21. Ibid. pp. 26, 29.

22. Ibid. p. 133.

23. Ibid. p. 58.

24. Ibid. p. 261.

25. Ibid. p. 382.

26. Taylor, *Cavalier and Yankee*, pp. 190–91.

27. *Swallow Barn*, p. 415.

28. James Hungerford, *The Old Plantation, and What I Gathered There in an Autumn Month* (New York, 1859), pp. 84, 105, 337.

29. [William Alexander Caruthers], *The Kentuckian in New York. Or, the Adventures of Three Southerns* (New York, 1834), I, 181, 154, 163, 164–5.

30. Ibid. I, 76, 77.

31. Ibid. II, 194.

32. Taylor, *Cavalier and Yankee*, pp. 210, 216.

33. [Nathaniel Beverley Tucker], *George Balcombe* (New York, 1836), I, 224.

34. [Nathaniel Beverley Tucker], *The Partisan Leader: A Tale of the Future* (Washington, [1836]), reprinted (New York, 1861), pp. 53–4.

35. Ibid. pp. 319, 327.

36. W. Gilmore Simms, *The Forayers, or the Raid of the Dog-Days* (1855), collected ed. (New York, 1882), p. 162.

37. W. Gilmore Simms, *Woodcraft, or, Hawks about the Dovecote* (1852), collected ed. (New York, 1882), pp. 355, 290–91.

38. Taylor, *Cavalier and Yankee*, p. 317.

39. Henry A. Wise, "The Wealth, Resources, and Hopes of Virginia," *De Bow's Review*, XXIII (1857), 60.

40. Ibid. p. 61.

41. Ibid. p. 62.

42. Ibid. p. 68.

43. Edmund Ruffin, "Southern Agricultural Exhaustion and Its Remedy," *De Bow's Review*, XIV (1853), 43.

44. Edmund Ruffin, *Report of the Commencement and Progress of the Agricultural Survey of South Carolina, for 1843* (Columbia, 1843), p. 73.
45. Edmund Ruffin, "The Influence of Slavery, or of its Absence, on Manners, Morals, and Intellect" (1852), included as an appendix to *The Political Economy of Slavery* (n. p., [*c.* 1858]), p. 26.

CHAPTER 12

1. *Speech of the Hon. Robert Y. Hayne, (of South Carolina,) on the Reduction of the Tariff. Delivered Jan. 9, 1832, in the Senate of the United States* (Washington, D. C., 1832), p. 18.
2. Ibid. pp. 27, 28.
3. Herbert Wender, *Southern Commercial Conventions, 1837–1859* (Baltimore, 1930), pp. 10–11, 18.
4. *The Industrial Resources, etc., of the Southern and Western States,* ed. J.D.B. De Bow (New Orleans, 1853), III, 106, 107; for Hayne's views see esp. pp. 93, 95.
5. James H. Hammond, *An Address Delivered before the South Carolina Institute, at its First Annual Fair* (Charleston, 1849), pp. 8, 11.
6. Ibid. pp. 15–16.
7. Ibid. pp. 36, 37.
8. Ibid. p. 16.
9. *De Bow's Review,* VIII (1850), 134–5.
10. Ibid. XII (1852), 497.
11. Ibid. XII, 420.
12. Philip G. Davidson, "Industrialism in the Antebellum South," *The South Atlantic Quarterly,* XXVII (1928), 413f.; Ottis Clark Skipper, *J.D.B. De Bow, Magazinist of the Old South* (Athens, Ga., 1958), pp. 24, 52.
13. *De Bow's Review,* XVIII (1855), 357.
14. Charles S. Sydnor, *The Development of Southern Sectionalism, 1819–1848* ([Baton Rouge], 1948), p. 274.
15. Hammond, *Address,* p. 24.
16. [Daniel R. Goodloe], *Inquiry into the Causes which Have Retarded the Accumulation of Wealth and Increase of Population in the Southern States* (Washington, D. C., 1846), p. 13.
17. In Joseph Clarke Robert, *The Road from Monticello: A Study of the Virginia Slavery Debate of 1832,* Historical Papers of the Trinity College Historical Society (Durham, N. C., 1941), p. 79.
18. Hinton Rowan Helper, *The Impending Crisis of the South: How To Meet It* (New York, 1857), p. 357.
19. Ibid. pp. 327–8; see also Henry Ruffner, *Address to the People of West Virginia* (Louisville, Ky., 1847), p. 31.
20. In Robert, *Road,* p. 61.
21. Ibid. p. 77.
22. *The Pro-Slavery Argument; as Maintained by . . . Chancellor*

269

Harper, Governor Hammond, Dr. Simms, and Professor Dew (Philadelphia, 1853), pp. 260, 261.

23. [William Grayson], *The Hireling and the Slave* (Charleston, 1854), pp. 77, vii.

24. *Cotton Is King, and Pro-Slavery Arguments: Comprising the Writings of Hammond, Harper, Christy, Stringfellow, Hodge, Bledsoe, and Cartwright, on This Important Subject*, ed. E. N. Elliott (Augusta, Ga., 1860), pp. 715, 717.

25. Ibid. pp. 551, 552.

26. Ibid. p. 564.

27. Edmund Ruffin, *The Political Economy of Slavery* (n. p., [c. 1858]), p. 22.

28. *Pro-Slavery Argument*, pp. 314–15.

29. [Edward Brown], *Notes on the Origin and Necessity of Slavery* (Charleston, 1826), pp. 24, 30.

30. *Pro-Slavery Argument*, p. 461.

31. [William Grayson], "Slavery in the Southern States," *Southern Quarterly Review*, VIII (1845), 354.

32. *Cotton Is King*, p. 615.

33. Ralph E. Morrow, "The Proslavery Argument Revisited," *Mississippi Valley Historical Review*, XLVIII (1961–62), 88.

34. Henry Hughes, *Treatise on Sociology, Theoretical and Practical* (Philadelphia, 1854), pp. 95–6, 165.

35. *The Papers of John C. Calhoun*, ed. Robert L. Meriwether (Columbia, 1959–), 355, 348.

36. Ibid. I, 317–18, 325.

37. *The Works of John C. Calhoun*, ed. Richard K. Crallé (New York, 1851–70), VI, 83, 77.

38. Ibid. I, 1–2, 3, 4.

39. Ibid. I, 52, 56.

40. Ibid. I, 59.

41. Ibid. I, 38.

42. Ibid. I, 122.

43. Ibid. III, 196.

44. J. H. Hammond, *An Oration on the Life, Character and Services of John Caldwell Calhoun* (Charleston, 1850), p. 35.

45. Calhoun, *Works*, IV, 557.

46. Quoted in F. R. Cossitt, *The Life and Times of Rev. Finis Ewing* (Louisville, 1853), p. 217.

47. Ibid. p. 206.

48. Charles A. Johnson, *The Frontier Camp Meeting: Religion's Harvest Time* (Dallas, 1955), pp. 180–81.

49. Theodore Clapp, *Slavery: A Sermon* (New Orleans, 1838), p. 26.

50. J. H. Thornwell, *Report on the Subject of Slavery, Presented to the Synod of South Carolina* (Columbia, 1852), p. 5.

51. Cossitt, *Ewing*, pp. 16–17, 17.

52. Calhoun, *Works*, III, 180.

53. Ibid. I, 395.

54. See, for instance, Beverley Tucker, *A Discourse on the Genius of the Federative System of the United States* (Richmond, 1839) and William Gilmore Simms, *The Social Principle . . . An Oration* (Tuscaloosa, Ala., 1843).
55. Simms, *Social Principle*, p. 23.
56. Thomas R. R. Cobb, *An Historical Sketch of Slavery, from the Earliest Periods* (Philadelphia and Savannah, 1858), p. ccxv.
57. George Fitzhugh, *Sociology for the South: or the Failure of Free Society* (Richmond, 1854), p. 11.
58. Ibid. pp. 14–15, 16.
59. Ibid. p. 27.
60. George Fitzhugh, *Cannibals All! Or Slaves Without Masters* (1857), ed. C. Vann Woodward (Cambridge, Mass., 1960), p. 72.
61. Ibid. pp. 28–9.
62. Ibid. p. 63.
63. *De Bow's Review*, XXV (1858), 663, 664.
64. *Cannibals*, pp. xxx–xxxi.
65. *Sociology*, p. 31.
66. [Charles Fenton Mercer], *An Exposition of the Weakness and Inefficiency of the Government of the United States of North America* (n. p., 1845), pp. 86, 303.
67. Ibid. p. 235.
68. Ibid. pp. 141, 167, 183.
69. Ibid. pp. 357, 373.
70. "The Prospects and Policy of the South, As They Appear to the Eyes of a Planter," *Southern Quarterly Review*, XXVI (1854), 432.
71. Ibid. pp. 434, 445.
72. Ibid. p. 448.

CHAPTER 13

1. Theodoric C. Lyon, *Do the Times Demand a Southern Confederacy?* (n. p., n. d.), p. 6.
2. *The Destruction of the Union is Emancipation. Letters of Nathaniel Macon to Charles O'Conor* (Philadelphia, 1862), pp. 20, 10.
3. In Henry Cleveland, *Alexander H. Stephens, in Public and Private. With Letters and Speeches, Before, During, and Since the War* (Philadelphia, [1867]), p. 704.
4. Lyon, *Southern Confederacy*, pp. 5, 7; see also *Annual Report of the American Historical Association for the Year 1911*, Vol. II: *The Correspondence of Robert Toombs, Alexander H. Stephens, and Howell Cobb*, ed. Ulrich B. Phillips (Washington, D. C., 1913), pp. 251–8.
5. *De Bow's Review*, XXIV (1858), 583.
6. L. W. Spratt, *Speech upon the Foreign Slave Trade, Before the Legislature of South Carolina* (Columbia, 1858), p. 6.
7. Edward A. Pollard, *Black Diamonds Gathered in the Darkey Homes of the South* (New York, 1859), p. 54.

8. *De Bow's Review*, XXVII (1859), 208, 213.
9. [J.D.B. De Bow], *The Interest in Slavery of the Southern Non-Slaveholder* (Charleston, 1860), pp. 9, 10.
10. *Letters of Nathaniel Macon*, pp. 21, 23.
11. *Southern Convention. Remarks of the Hon. Beverley Tucker of Virginia. 1850* ([Richmond, c. 1850]), p. 10.
12. Quoted in John Witherspoon DuBose, *The Life and Times of William Lowndes Yancey* (Birmingham, Ala., 1892), p. 359.
13. *De Bow's Review*, XXIII (1857), 604, 605.
14. Ibid. XXII (1857), 591.
15. [H. K. Berguin], *Considerations Relative to a Southern Confederacy* (Raleigh, 1860), pp. 12, 11.
16. *De Bow's Review*, XXIII (1857), 603.
17. Quoted in DuBose, *Yancey*, p. 533.
18. David Christy, *Cotton Is King* (Cincinnati, 1855), pp. 38–9, 185.
19. *Speeches, Messages, and Other Writings of the Hon. Albert G. Brown, a Senator in Congress from the State of Mississippi*, ed. M. W. Cluskey (Philadelphia, 1859), p. 168.
20. *Speech of Hon. Louis T. Wigfall, of Texas, in Reply to Mr. Douglas, and on Mr. Powell's Resolution. Delivered in the Senate of the United States, December 11th and 12th, 1860* (Washington, D. C., 1860), p. 12.
21. *Southern Editorials on Secession*, ed. Dwight Lowell Dumond (New York and London, 1931), p. 383.
22. *Speech of Hon. Lawrence M. Keitt, of South Carolina, on Slavery, and the Resources of the South; Delivered in the House of Representatives, Jan. 15, 1857* (Washington, D. C., 1857), p. 13.
23. Daniel Wallace, *The Political Life and Services of the Hon. R. Barnwell Rhett, of South Carolina . . . and also, His Speech at Grahamville, S. C., July 4th, 1859* (n. p., [1859]), p. 40.
24. [John Esten Cooke], *The Virginia Comedians: Or, Old Days in the Old Dominion* (New York, 1854), I, 18, 136.
25. Ibid. I, 190.
26. John Esten Cooke, *Henry St. John, Gentleman* (New York, 1859), pp. x–xi.
27. Ibid. p. 158; see also W. Gilmore Simms, *The Forayers, or the Raid of the Dog-Days* (1855), collected ed. (New York, 1882), p. 530.
28. Quoted in DuBose, *Yancey*, p. 440.
29. *De Bow's Review*, XXIV (1858), 600.
30. [John Townsend], *The Doom of Slavery in the Union: Its Safety out of It* (Charleston, 1860), p. 30.
31. *De Bow's Review*, XXVIII (1860), 303–4.
32. Ibid. XXIX (1860), 77, 78.
33. Ibid. XXIX, 496, 500.
34. Dumond, *Editorials*, pp. 243–4, 316.
35. Mary Boykin Chesnut, *A Diary from Dixie*, ed. Ben Ames Williams (Boston, 1950), pp. 3, 20.
36. *De Bow's Review*, XXX (1861), 352.

37. In Benjamin H. Hill, Jr., *Senator Benjamin H. Hill of Georgia: His Life, Speeches and Writings* (Atlanta, 1893), p. 275.
38. In Cleveland, *Stephens*, pp. 718, 721.
39. Ibid. p. 724.
40. Quoted in Gaillard Hunt, *The History of the Seal of the United States* (Washington, D. C., 1909), p. 42.
41. *The Collected Works of Abraham Lincoln*, ed. Roy P. Basler (New Brunswick, N. J., 1953–55), IV, 169.
42. Dumond, *Editorials*, p. 463.
43. *Jefferson Davis, Constitutionalist: His Letters, Papers and Speeches*, ed. Dunbar Rowland (Jackson, Miss., 1923), V, 48.
44. Ibid. V, 53, 51.
45. Ibid. V, 202.
46. Ibid. VI, 357.
47. *Echoes from the South. Comprising the Most Important Speeches, Proclamations, and Public Acts Emanating from the South during the Late War*, [ed. Edward A. Pollard] (New York, 1866), p. 200.
48. In Hill, *Senator Benjamin H. Hill*, p. 268.
49. *Speech of Hon. L.Q.C. Lamar, of Miss., on the State of the Country* (Atlanta, 1864), p. 23.
50. Avery Craven, *Edmund Ruffin, Southerner: A Study in Secession* (New York and London, 1932), p. 255.
51. Phillips, *Correspondence of Toombs, Stephens, and Cobb*, p. 595.
52. In Cleveland, *Stephens*, p. 785.
53. E. Merton Coulter, *The Confederate States of America, 1861–1865* ([Baton Rouge], 1950), p. 532.
54. Quoted in James W. Silver, *Confederate Morale and Church Propaganda*, Confederate Centennial Studies, No. 3 (Tuscaloosa, Ala., 1957), p. 15.
55. See, for instance, B. M. Palmer, *The Rainbow Round the Throne* (Milledgeville, Ga., 1863), p. 25; Clergy of the Confederate States of America, *Address to Christians throughout the World* (London, 1863), p. 6.
56. Palmer, *Rainbow*, p. 31.
57. Ibid. pp. 32, 40.
58. Stephen Elliott, *"New Wine Not To Be Put into Old Bottles." A Sermon Preached in Christ Church, Savannah* (Savannah, 1862), pp. 17–18.
59. Palmer, *Rainbow*, pp. 36, 35.
60. Quoted in Ottis Clark Skipper, *J.D.B. De Bow, Magazinist of the Old South* (Athens, Ga., 1958), p. 146.
61. Laura A. White, *Robert Barnwell Rhett: Father of Secession* (New York and London, 1931), pp. 238–9.
62. Quoted in Grady McWhitney, "Reconstruction: Index of Americanism," in *The Southerner as American*, ed. Charles Grier Sellers, Jr. (Chapel Hill, 1960), p. 99.
63. Ibid. p. 101.
64. Quoted in DuBose, *Yancey*, p. 682.

1. Raymond B. Nixon, *Henry W. Grady: Spokesman of the New South* (New York, 1943), pp. 238, 345, 348.
2. Walter Hines Page, "The Rebuilding of Old Commonwealths," *Atlantic Monthly*, LXXXIX (1902), 654, 658, 652.
3. Twelve Southerners, *I'll Take My Stand: The South and the Agrarian Tradition* (New York and London, 1930), p. 71.
4. Ibid. p. 14.
5. Ibid. p. 12.
6. W. J. Cash, *The Mind of the South* (New York, 1941), pp. 33-4, 95-6.
7. Ibid. pp. 103, 196, 215.
8. Ibid. pp. 180, 149-50.
9. Ibid. pp. 307, 308, 306.
10. Ibid. p. 384.
11. Ibid. pp. 50, 77.
12. Hodding Carter, *Southern Legacy* (Baton Rouge, 1950), pp. 59, 60.
13. Ibid. pp. 116, 180.
14. James McBride Dabbs, *The Southern Heritage* (New York, 1958), pp. 25, 27.
15. Ibid. p. 35.
16. Ibid. pp. 147, 123.
17. Leisure does not have to be considered in these terms. It has been argued by Bennett M. Berger that an important task of a sociology of leisure is to define its social function (see "The Sociology of Leisure: Some Suggestions," in *Work and Leisure: A Contemporary Social Problem*, ed. Erwin O. Smigel [New Haven, 1963], pp. 21-40). Until this has been done, however, there would seem to be ample warrant for assuming that leisure really means in the South, as in the rest of the country, a private and therefore essentially socially meaningless activity.
18. David M. Potter, "The Enigma of the South," *Yale Review* (Autumn 1961), 150, 151.
19. Walker Percy, "Mississippi: The Fallen Paradise," *Harper's Magazine* (April 1965), 171.
20. Robert Cooley Angell, *The Integration of American Society: A Study of Groups and Institutions* (New York and London, 1941), pp. 14-15.
21. Ibid. p. 19.
22. Richard H. Shryock, "British versus German Traditions in Colonial Agriculture," *Mississippi Valley Historical Review*, XXVI (1939-40), 39-54.
23. C. Vann Woodward, *The Burden of Southern History* (Baton Rouge, [1960]), Chs. 1, 2, 8.

Index

Davies, the Rev. Samuel, cautions troops against violence, 113–14; urges religious industry, 124, 125; on treatment of slaves, 125; on the social duty of Christians, 126; his patriotic sermons, 126–7

Davis, Jefferson, 229–30, 233

De Bow, J. D. B., on improvement, 196; activities, 196–7; *The Interest in Slavery of the Southern Non-Slaveholder*, 219; on King Cotton, 233

De La Warr, Lord, governor of Va., 25

Denton, Daniel, 43

Desaussure, Henry William, 171

Dew, Prof. Thomas Roderic, 200, 201

Diamond, Sigmund, 249, n. 3, 250, n. 29

Discourse of the Common Weal, 10

Distinctiveness, Revolution as a means of ending, 137–8; Drayton on, 140–41; accepted by Southern Federalists, 149–50; Pinckney on, 151–2; and Antifederalism, 157, 160; Wise on in Va., 190; Calhoun's desires to preserve, 206; Spratt on, 218; no basis for a united nation, 233; not equated with sectionalism, 245

Dobbs, Gov. Arthur, 69–70

Drayton, John, *A View of S.C.*, 171–2

Drayton, Michael, "To the Virginian Voyage," 14

Drayton, William Henry, 138, 140–41

Duels, 114, 172, 206

Dulany, Daniel, 133

E

Ease, as defined by Blair, 111–12; *see also* Leisure

Eastern states, defined, 146; *see also* New England

Eburne, Richard, *A Plain Pathway to Plantations*, 32–3

Egmont, Earl of, 94

Elliott, the Rev. Stephen, 232

Elyot, Sir Thomas, 6

England, problem of idleness in 16th century, 3, 5–6; Puritans in, 6–9; attractionists in, 9–11; home benefits of colonization, 13; social policies regarding idleness compared with colonial policies, 106

Evans, the Rev. John, 127

Ewing, the Rev. Finis, 208

F

Faulkner, Charles J., 198

Federalists, Southern: as heirs of the jeremiad, 147; compared with Northern counterparts, 148, 152–3; general views, 148–52; post-war celebrations, 170–71

Feudal analogies, in antebellum literature, 177, 184, 185, 186, 209

Fire-eaters, *see* Radicals

Fitzhugh, George, *A Sociology for the South*, 210–11; *Cannibals All!*, 211–13; on war, 225

Fontaine, the Rev. Peter, 104, 109

Franklin, Benjamin, contrasted with Byrd, 76, 83; on the imperial system, 132

Free Trade, 193, 195, 211, 219, 229–30

Frontier, South as a, 238; used by Cash, 239–40; by Carter, 241; by Dabbs, 241–2; and social integration, 243–4

Frugality, *see* Industry

Furman, the Rev. Richard, 168–9

G

Gates, Sir Thomas, 25, 71

Georgia, Whitefield on Swiss there, 77; under the Trustees, 88–96; compared with Va., 88, 95; pro-

Georgia (*continued*)
hibition on slavery, 108; policy toward vagrants, 116
Golden Age, influence on early colonists, 14; and emphasis upon leisure, 65
Goodloe, Daniel R., 197
Grady, Henry W., 237
Gray, Lewis Cecil, 75
Gray, the Rev. Robert, 22–3
Grayson, William, answer to Madison, 160
Grayson, William, on Negroes, 199, 201
Great Awakening, 124–6
Great Seal, 228–9
Gregg, William, criticism of S.C., 195; calls for home manufactures, 225–6
Grenville, Sir Richard, 14

H

Hakluyt, Richard, the younger: propaganda for colonization, 12–13; omits reference to effortless abundance, 14
Hamilton, Alexander, 152–3
Hammond, James H., on S.C. society and cotton manufacturing, 194–5; encourages busyness, 197; on Calhoun, 207
Hammond, John, *Leah and Rachel*, 63–5; vindicates Va., 67
Hamor, Ralph, 36–7
Handlin, Oscar, 259, n. 5
Harper, Chancellor William, 199–200, 201–2
Hart, the Rev. Oliver, 167–8
Heimert, Alan, 262, n. 38
Helper, Hinton R., *The Impending Crisis of the South*, 198
Henry, Patrick, early views on towns and toleration, 154–5; on Virginia's post-war prospects, 155; **Anti**federalist views, 157–8; support of Washington, 161–2; described by Wirt, 178–9; Calhoun's answer to,

206; in *The Virginia Comedians*, 223–4
Hewit, Alexander, 108
Hexter, J. H., 6
Hill, Benjamin H., 227, 230
Hitchcock, Robert, 10
Holbrook, the Rev. William, 8
Hospitality, 65
Hughes, Henry, 202–3
Hungerford, James, *The Old Plantation*, 186
Hurt, the Rev. John, 139–40

I

Idleness, and More's *Utopia*, 3–4; in eighteenth-century England, 5–6; and Puritanism, 8, 9; attractionists' solution for, 10; colonization as a cure for, 13; moral cures for in early Va., 21; authoritarian responses to in Va., 21–6; royal admonition to suppress in Va., 48; problems in early S.C., 55–6; early manifestations discussed, 69; analyzed and explained, 70–72; appearance of discussed, 75–7; efforts of Ga. Trustees to prevent, 88–9; and violence, 102, 104–6; in Mass., 106–7; and slavery, 108–9; in Blair's thought, 113, 114–15; coercive cures for, 116–24; and the S.C. Regulators, 122–3; Davies on, 125; and patriotism, 126–7; Revolution to lead people away from, 137; Washington's concern for, 154; and slavery in Rice, 163; Jefferson's concern for, 165–6; Ramsay's concern for among the lower classes, 174; and Wirt on Va. and Henry, 177, 178; and Rip Van Winkle, 180; and aristocratic analogies, 183–4; Faulkner and Helper on, 198; in proslavery theory, 199; Fitzhugh refutes charges of, 212; and the Civil War, 228
Indigo, 57
Indolence, Beverley attacks, 67;

Tucker on, 181-2; *see also* Idleness, Laziness

Industrialization, campaign for, 193-7

Industry, Dobbs on, 70; beavers as symbols of, 72; confusion in definitions of, 82; religious and secular definitions of in Great Awakening, 126-7; and opposition to Great Britain, 134-5; and patriotism, 136-7; merging of definitions of, 139-40; redefinition of after war, 143-9; Patrick Henry on, 157-8; ministers' vision of, 168; John Taylor on, 170; encouragement for in Ramsay, 174; in early N.E. as explained by Ruffin, 200; and interdependence, 201; quest for definitions of in antebellum South, 212-13; and resembling the North, 237

Integration, social, 244

Iredell, James, 160

Irving, Washington, 180

J

Jefferson, Thomas, *Notes on the State of Va.*, 164-5; on idleness, 165-6; growing nationalism, 166-7

Jeremiad, as a tool of social reform for Puritans, 8; and for attractionists, 9; works of Beverley and Byrd as examples of, 67-8; these compared to jeremiads of N.E. preachers, 79-80; a conservative device, 119; and Southern Federalists, 147; and expectations about the new government, 150-51; and Ramsay's history, 172-4; and antebellum literature of change, 195; results of, 197; and Helper, 198; and proslavery theory, 202; used by Fitzhugh, 211; and Cash, 239; and Carter, 241; and Southern-ness, 245

Johnson, Alderman Robert, 19, 20, 30-31

Johnston, Gov. Gabriel, 58

Johnston, Commissary Gideon, 117-18

Jones, the Rev. Hugh, 73, 75

Jordan, Winthrop, D., 259, n. 5

K

Keith, Sir William, 86

Keitt, Lawrence, 223

Kennedy, John Pendleton, *Swallow Barn*, 184-6

King Cotton, assumptions of men's faith in, 220-21; and industrialization, 226; failure of, 233

L

Labor, *see* Work

Lamar, L. Q. C., 230-31

Lamar, Gen. M. B., 197

Langston, Anthony, 50-51

Lawson, John, 74, 80

Laziness, reference to by Va. Co., 24; Byrd's concern about, 68; term preferred by Beverley, 72; judgment of further explained, 72-9; and the lush land, 80; and busyness, 82-4; coercive cures for, 116-17, 118-19; possible victory over, 124; and distinctiveness, 160-61; John Taylor's cures for, 169-70; Ramsay's laments over, 173; and Kennedy's approach, 184; and his unionism, 186; and Southern militancy in Beverley Tucker, 188; in Dabbs, 241

Lee, Richard Henry, 155, 156-7

Leisure, early hints, 65; and the jeremiad, 81; and laziness in Tucker, 182-4; inability to find a satisfactory definition of, 190; ideal of in Wise, 190; and anti-northern sentiment, 237; in Page and the Twelve Southerners, 238-9; as ideal in Cash, 239-40; in Dabbs, 241; critique of definitions in Cash and Dabbs, 242; social meaning of, 274, n. 17

Le Jau, the Rev. Francis, 117
Lincoln, Abraham, 229
Lubberland, 68–9
Lucas, Eliza, 78
Lyon Theodoric, 216, 217

M

Macon, Nathaniel, 216–17, 219
Madison, James, contrasts Va. and Pa., 136; on conditions in post-war Va., 144–5; on Monroe's objections to northern power, 146; on factions and a unity of disunity, 150–51; on interest as a bond of union, 160
Makemie, the Rev. Francis, 49–50
Malcontents, 92–6
Manufactures, absence of in early S.C., 56; dependence of southern colonies on Great Britain because of absence of, 86; N.C. threatens to turn to, 87; promotion of in resistance to Great Britain, 134–5; Tennent on, 139; post-war efforts, 143; Henry's hopes for, 155, 157; Jefferson on, 166–7; Hammond's program for cotton manufacturing, 194–5; Calhoun's early praise of, 203; Fitzhugh on, 211
Marshall, John, 146–7
Martyn, Benjamin, in behalf of the Ga. Trustees' policies, 89, 90, 91, 92; on slavery, 108
Maryland, early development of, 47–8; Hammond's description of, 63–5
Mason, George, 159
Massachusetts, compared with southern colonies in resistance to Great Britain, 135; Lee's admiration for, 156; see also New England
Mayflower Compact, 41
McDuffie, George, 193–4
Meaninglessness, and fascination with violence, 114–15; in the lives of fictional characters, 182–4; war as response to, 225

Mercantile theory, altered views of colonies, 85–7; and assumptions of Ga. Trustees, 89–90, 95; and the Royal Society of Arts, 131
Mercer, Charles Fenton, 213
Micklejohn, the Rev. George, 120
Miller, Perry, 8, 9, 43
Monroe, James, 146
Moore, Francis, 90–91
More, Sir Thomas, *Utopia*, 3–4, 5, 6, 11
Morrow, Ralph E., 202
Morton, Thomas, 45

N

Navigation Laws, *see* Mercantile theory
Negroes, *see* Slavery
New England, as an example for Va., 49; a model for Carolina proprietors, 53; compared with southern colonies, 80; values questioned by mercantile theorists, 85–6; praised by Burke, 88; Boucher rejects union with, 138; as a symbol of Yankee values, 180; Ruffin on, 200
North Carolina, development, 57–8; Byrd on Lubberland, 68–9; Bishop Spangenburg on its inhabitants, 77; Albemarle residents' threats, 87; land use, 87; Regulator movement, 120–21
Nullification crisis, 193

O

Oglethorpe, Gen. James, 90
Owsley, Frank Lawrence, 238

P

Page, Walter Hines, 237–8
Palmer, the Rev. Benjamin, 231–2, 233
Peckham, Sir George, 12, 13
Pendleton, Edmund, 147

Pendleton, Judge Henry, 145
Penn, William, 43-4, 66
Pennsylvania, compared with Va. and Mass., 43-4; vindication of in comparison with Va., 66; compared with southern colonies, 80; praised by Burke, 88; compared with southern colonies on manufactures, 135; religious tolerance praised by Madison, 136; possibility of tobacco there, 244
Percy, George, 20, 24
Percy, Walker, 243
Perkins, William, 7, 8
Personalism, as a basis of social unity, 65; in the antebellum period, 209-10, 211-12; David Potter on, 242-3
Pierce, Major William, 147-8
Pinckney, Charles, on economic regulation, 146; on Southern distinctiveness and national union, 151-2; compared with Federalists in the late 1790's, 171
Pinckney, Charles Cotesworth, 149
Plantation legend, 180-90
Pollard, Edward A., 218
Pory, John, 35
Potter, David M., 242
Powell, Sumner Chilton, 43
Purchas, Samuel, 31
Puritans, compared with coercionists on work and idleness, 6-9; practices in Mass., 39-41; effect of ideas in N.Y. and N.J., 43-4; no City upon a Hill in southern colonies, 79-80

Q

Quincy, the Rev. Samuel, 114

R

Radicals, pre-Civil War position, 219-25; compared with abolitionists, 221-2

Raleigh, Sir Walter, 19
Ramsay, Dr. David, 4th of July oration, 1778, 141-2; *History of the Revolution of S.C.*, 143-4; on the importation of slaves, 149-50; 4th of July oration, 1794, 173; *History of S.C.*, 172, 173-4
Randolph, Gov. Beverley, 149
Ransom, John Crowe, 238-9
Regulators, N.C., 120-21; S.C., 105-6, 122-4
Revolution, American: 132-42; ideal of patriotism and unity in southern colonies, 137-8
Rhett, Robert Barnwell, indifference to manufacturing, 196; on the expansion of the South, 223; on the Constitution, 226; on freeing the slaves, 233
Rice, in S.C., 56-7
Rice, David, 163
Rolf, John, 37-8
Romanticism, in William Wirt, 177-8; and the plantation legend, 179, 180-90
Royal Society of Arts, 131
Ruffin, Edmund, on agricultural affairs, 191; on slavery, 192, 200, 202; on economic effects of secession, 220; wants a dictator for the South, 231

S

Sandys, Edwin, Archbishop of York: on God's allurements, 9; on the ambiguities of rest, 11, 15
Sandys, Sir Edwin, on recruiting poor London children, 26; policies for the Va. Co., 29; faction compared with Smith faction, 30
Shryock, Richard, 244
Simms, William Gilmore, Revolutionary War novels, 188-9; on slavery, 199; contrasts South and England, 210
Slavery, Beverley on, 81; in Georgia, 92-6; Byrd on, 97; origins of, 102-

Slavery (*continued*)
4; and the doctrine of allurement, 108; evangelical clergy on, 125; R.H. Lee on slave trade, 155; Henry on, 158; Mason on, 159; Rice and Tucker on emancipation, 163–4; Jefferson on, 164; John Taylor on, 170; Drayton on, 172; in *The Valley of Shenandoah*, 181; in *Swallow Barn*, 185; Gov. Wise on, 190; Ruffin on, 191; criticisms of, 197–8; defense of, 199–203; and the Southern clergy, 208; Fitzhugh on, 212; Mercer on, 213; Macon on, 216; revival of African slave trade, 217–18; as a pillar of the state, 219; as the cornerstone of the Confederacy, 227; Davis and emancipation, 233

Sloth, *see* Idleness, Laziness

Smith, Capt. John, authoritarian policy in Va., 23–4; on planters for N.E., 31; celebration of the land, 35–6; on authority, 71–2; described by Kennedy, 185

Smith, Josiah, 124

Smith, Sir Thomas, 29–30, 45

South, contrasting images of, 101, 115; usage of capitalization, 146; *see also* Distinctiveness, Southern colonies, Southern nationalism, Southern states, Southern way

South Carolina, early development, 53–7; celebrations of, 65–6; Eliza Lucas on poor of, 78; Ga. as a frontier defense for, 89–90; Regulator movement, 105–6, 122–4; in the Revolution, 138–9; prospects as seen after the war, 142; Ramsay on colonial period and the war, 143–4; on present situation of, 173–4; Pendleton on post-war conditions in, 145; Hammond's criticisms of, 194–5; Gregg's criticisms of, 195

Southern colonies, and mercantile theory, 86–7; slavery a sign of distinctiveness of, 104; indigenous

opposition in to status quo, 116–24; and the imperial system, 133–5; ideal of a changed society in, 137–8

Southern nationalism, and manufacturing, 196; Mercer on, 213; Macon on, 216–17; radical views of, 219–25; explanations of secession, 226–7; and dream of allurement, 227–7; contrasted with Revolution, 228–9; and Davis, 229–30; and states' rights, 230–31; and the clergy, 231–2; collapse of, 233–4

Southern states, development of a Southern interest during the Revolution, 140–41; as exploited victims of outside interests, 169

Southern way, first discussed, 162; and leisure, 190–91; and Hammond, 195; and the diversifiers, 196; vindication of, 213–14

Spratt, L.W., 218

Stephens, Alexander H., on secession, 217; on slavery and the Confederacy, 227; in defense of states' rights, 231

Stephens, Thomas, in defense of liberty in Ga., 94–5; on the Malcontents' position, 96

Stephens, William, 92

Stewart, John, 116–17

Strachey, William, 25

Sydnor, Charles, 197

Symonds, the Rev. William, 38–9

T

Tailfer, Patrick, 93–4

Tawney, R.H., 11

Taylor, John, of Caroline, *Arator*, 169–70

Taylor, William R., 179, 189

Tennent, the Rev. William, 138–9

Thorne, Robert, 12

Thornwell, the Rev. J.H., 208

Tobacco, early criticism of, 27–8; early celebrations of, 35, 37; efforts to limit in Va., 48–9, 50;

awareness of disadvantages of but unwillingness to abandon, 52–3; lack of interest in S.C., 54; Byrd's concern about, 73–4; Beverley on, 82; redeemed, 86; Jefferson's criticisms of, 165; and Pa., 244

Toombs, Robert, 231

Towns and cities, failure of in early Va., 28–9; meaning of in N.E., 42; later promotional efforts in Va., 48–9; proposals for in Va., 49–51; efforts to promote in S.C., 53, 55, 56, 57; in N.C., 58; Byrd's and Beverley's desires for, 73; Bacon on, 122; Henry on absence of in Va., 154–5; Faulkner on absence of, 198; Cash on, 239; Carter on, 241

Townsend, John, 225

Troeltsch, Ernst, 4–5

Trustees of Ga., aims defined, 88–9; and mercantile theory, 89–90; increasing stress on work, 90–91; and foreign Protestants, 92; on slavery, 92–3; controversy with Malcontents, 92–6

Tucker, Nathaniel Beverley, *George Balcombe* and *The Partisan Leader*, 188; on a Southern confederacy, 219

Tucker, George, *The Valley of Shenandoah*, 181–3

Tucker, St. George, 163–4

Twelve Southerners, *I'll Take My Stand*, 238–9

U

Utopia, see More, Sir Thomas

V

Vagrants, Va. moves against, 105; policy in Va. and Ga. regarding, 116

Violence, and idleness, 102, 104–6; and slavery in S.C. and Ga., 108; and Byrd, 110; and Blair, 111–12,

113; and Bacon's Rebellion and the S.C. Regulators, 121–4; and the duel, 172; and Calhoun, 206; conservative fears of, 217; in response to the North, 224; and the frontier for Cash, 239–40; for Carter, 241; for Dabbs, 241–2; for Percy, 243

Virginia, early history, 19–34; early celebrants of, 35–8; compared with N.E., 38–42; compared with Pa., 44; after the dissolution of the Va. Co., 45–6, 48–53; Hammond's description of, 63–5; discussed by Byrd and Beverley, 67–8; compared with N.E., 85; praised by Martyn, 89; planters and slavery, 102–4; Bacon's Rebellion, 104–5, 121–2; impressing vagrants, 105; as seen by Blair and Davies, 110–14; policy toward vagrants, 116; postwar conditions in, 144–5; Henry's view of prospects of, 155; Jefferson on, 164–5; Wise's view of, 190–91

Virginia Company, initial social expectations of, 19–20; consolidation of authoritarian policy of, 25; goal of a commonwealth, 26–7; and tobacco production, 27–8; and towns, 28–9; under Sandys, 29; dissolution controversy, 29–30; retrospective views of, 45; intention to prevent idleness, 71

W

Washburn, Wilcomb, 105

Washington, George, on importations, 134; on national unity and Southern ways, 153–4; on idleness, 154

Weber, Max, 8–9, 32, 76–7

Wertenbaker, Thomas J., 103

West Indies, 58, 85, 86, 245

Whitaker, the Rev. Alexander, 21, 67

Whitbourne, Richard, 32, 45

283